LOVE *real* FOOD

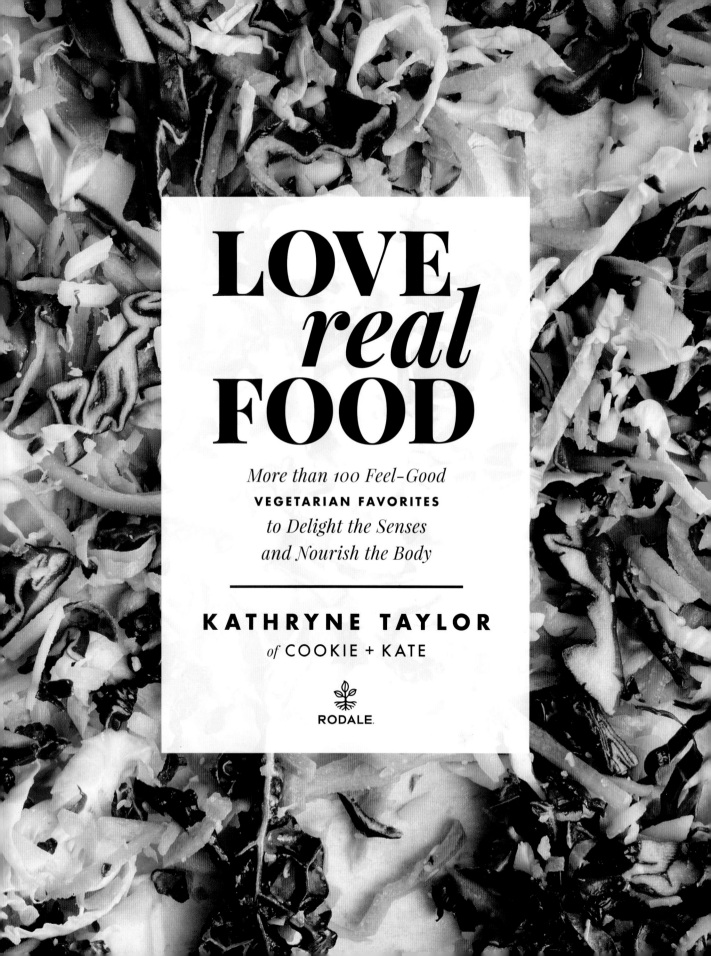

LOVE
real
FOOD

More than 100 Feel-Good
VEGETARIAN FAVORITES
*to Delight the Senses
and Nourish the Body*

KATHRYNE TAYLOR

of COOKIE + KATE

RODALE.

RODALE *wellness*

Live happy. Be healthy. Get inspired.

Sign up today to get exclusive access to our authors, exclusive bonuses,
and the most authoritative, useful, and cutting-edge information on health,
wellness, fitness, and living your life to the fullest.

Visit us online at RodaleWellness.com
Join us at RodaleWellness.com/Join

Rodale books may be purchased for business or promotional use or for special sales.
For information, please write to:
Special Markets Department, Rodale Inc., 733 Third Avenue, New York, NY 10017.

Printed in China

Rodale Inc. makes every effort to use acid-free ♾, recycled paper ♻.

Book design by Rae Ann Spitzenberger

Photographs pages v, viii, xii, xvi–xvii, xx, xxi, xxiii, 34, 61, 71, 108–109, 114,
136, 156, 226, 228, 244 © Sarah Sweeney

All other photographs © Kathryne Taylor

Library of Congress Cataloging-in-Publication Data is on file with the publisher.

ISBN-13: 978-1-62336-741-1 hardcover

Distributed to the trade by Macmillan

17   hardcover

RODALE.

Follow us @RodaleBooks on

We inspire health, healing, happiness, and love in the world.
Starting with you.

TO THE READERS OF COOKIE AND KATE:
This book is all for you.

TO COOKIE:
I'm so lucky I got you.

CONTENTS

*Colorful Weeknight
Burrito Bowls*
(page 142)

Introduction:
**COOKIE AND KATE
LOVE REAL FOOD**   *ix*

1 Good Morning
1

2 Salads
47

3 Soups
79

4 Happy Hour
97

5 Let's Feast
141

6 Sweet Treats
193

7 Extras
215

COOKING CHEAT SHEET   *224*
**MENUS AND HELPFUL
RECIPE LISTS**   *229*
ACKNOWLEDGMENTS   *232*
INDEX   *234*

Cookie and Kate
LOVE *real* FOOD

My dog, Cookie, is the most effective alarm clock I've ever met. You can't push snooze on Cookie–once she's decided it's breakfast time, she morphs into a squirmy, insistent, enthusiastic little alarm bell who will shove the pillow right out from under my head. She's lucky she's so cute.

Every morning, Cookie herds me into our Kansas City kitchen. I feed her first (she wouldn't have it any other way), and then I start shuffling around to make my own breakfast. I always eat breakfast, in part because I know I'll feel lousy later in the day if I don't, but also because I adore breakfast. Cookie and I both *love* food.

I might reach for a bag of granola in the freezer, and some yogurt to go with it. I know exactly what's in that granola because I made it myself: old-fashioned oats sweetened with maple syrup and made crispy with the help of some coconut oil, plus spices, nuts, and dried fruit. Learning to make my own granola was a revelation. It's super easy and tastes so much better than the store-bought kind.

Later in the day, lunch might consist of a giant, colorful bean salad (left over from last night's dinner) with fresh greens and crumbled goat cheese. Dinner could be a spicy, vegetable-packed stir-fry. Whatever I throw together, you can bet it will be a well-balanced meal that lights up my taste buds and keeps me energized for hours.

I haven't always eaten so well, and I haven't always felt so good. I was a picky kid who tried to get away with eating pancakes with maple syrup for breakfast, but my body wouldn't allow it, even when my parents would. Those pancakes would turn me into a shaky, miserable, sweaty mess. My doctor called my extreme reaction to simple carbohydrates hypoglycemia. Trust me, if eating pancakes for breakfast turned you into a mumbling zombie, you wouldn't touch them no matter how good they tasted.

The funny thing about metabolism is that I'm just an exaggerated example of how every human body functions in response to processed foods and unbalanced meals. I simply have a more immediate reaction to the foods that are contributing to our country's growing obesity epidemic, and the chronic diseases that come with it.

You might think, then, that eating well came easily for me. It didn't. When I left for college, I thought that cardboard-flavored 100-calorie snack packs were healthy options, and that fat was best avoided. I tallied up calories in my head and repented for them on the elliptical machine. When I felt overwhelmed or sad, I turned to food for comfort, oftentimes to an unhealthy extreme. I struggled with binge eating, and I am all too familiar with the self-loathing and despair that go along with it. Basically, I asked far more of food than food could provide, and rode a miserable roller coaster of sugar highs and food-related guilt for years. My story is all too common, and I would do anything to spare you from these struggles. We all have to eat, after all. It doesn't have to be so hard.

Fortunately, my conscience is no longer at war with my taste buds. After a lot of self-reflection, I've learned to deal with stress and anxiety in ways that make me feel better, not worse–like reaching out to friends, going to a yoga class, and taking walks with Cookie. Perhaps most valuably, I've learned to listen to my appetite and eat accordingly. Now, I open the refrigerator and greet the contents like trusted friends, and my body thanks me for it.

Learning more about nutrition was tremendously helpful in shifting my habits and helping me cut through the marketing noise. Once I started reading, I was shocked to hear that the food pyramid wasn't quite the pinnacle of nutrition I had once believed, and that protein comes in all different kinds of foods, not just meat. The more I read, the more I naturally gravitated toward the whole foods philosophy set forth by food writers and researchers like Michael Pollan and Marion Nestle. Their recommendations made sense to me on multiple levels. Of course I should be eating foods that my grandmothers would recognize, not artificially sweetened, processed foods with a "healthy" sticker on the front. The truth is always in the ingredients list.

HOW TO READ A NUTRITION LABEL

1. **FOCUS ON THE INGREDIENTS.** Roughly how many ingredients are there? Five to ten ingredients is a good sign. Do you recognize them as ingredients you cook with at home? Ingredients are listed by weight, so the first few are the most telling. If you see a long list that sounds more like chemical compounds than food, move on to a better option. You have probably disqualified all heavily processed foods at this point, but be sure to avoid ingredients such as high-fructose corn syrup, food dyes, hydrogenated oils, and preservatives like sodium nitrate.

2. **GLANCE AT THE SUGAR CONTENT UNDER THE NUTRITION FACTS.** For reference, 4 grams of sugar equals 1 teaspoon of sugar. Flavored 16-ounce lattes often contain 30 to 50 grams of sugar–that's a lot! Naturally occurring sugars in whole foods (like fruit) aren't of concern, but processed foods with lots of added sugars (like high-fructose corn syrup) are not good for you.

3. **CHECK THE SODIUM PERCENT DAILY VALUE, TOO.** If one serving contains a significant portion of the sodium you need for the day (say, 40 percent or more), the manufacturer is probably trying to make up for a lack in flavor or freshness by adding tons of salt. Excess sodium can cause health problems, too.

When you're eating real, wholesome food in accordance with your appetite, you don't need to worry much about the rest.

Moroccan Roasted Carrot, Arugula, and Wild Rice Salad (page 62)

WHAT ARE WHOLE FOODS, ANYWAY?

Whole foods are foods that come directly from nature, with very little processing (if any) on their way to the table. In other words, they have not been stripped of their inherent goodness. Think fresh vegetables and ripe fruits, leafy greens, whole grains, beans, nuts, and seeds. Unrefined oils count, like quality olive oil and coconut oil. Wine and dark chocolate do, too (not that I would ever give them up)! So do minimally processed dairy and meat from healthy animals, in moderation.

WHOLE FOODS ARE THE NATURAL SOLUTION

My hero, Michael Pollan, summed it up well when he declared, "Eat food. Not too much. Mostly plants." Or as Dr. David Katz, the founding director of Yale University's Prevention Research Center, says, "If you focus on real food, nutrients tend to take care of themselves." As if it could get any better, this way of eating benefits the environment as well. "Consistent evidence indicates that, in general, a dietary pattern that is higher in plant-based foods, such as vegetables, fruits, whole grains, legumes, nuts, and seeds, and lower in animal-based foods is more health promoting and is associated with lesser environmental impact (GHG emissions and energy, land, and water use) than is the current average US diet," according to Scientific Report of the 2015 Dietary Guidelines Advisory Committee.

We live in a crazy, wonderful, modern world of abundant calories. Did you know that there are over 40,000 products in the average American grocery store? Our eating choices aren't working very well for us. According to the 2015–2020 Dietary Guidelines for Americans, "today, about half of all American adults—117 million people—have one or more preventable, chronic diseases, many of which are related to poor quality eating patterns and physical inactivity. Rates of these chronic, diet-related diseases continue to rise, and they come not only with increased health risks, but also at high cost."

We're in trouble and, naturally, overwhelmed by the conflicting health claims and weight-loss advice out there. "Butter is bad! Eat margarine instead!" was followed years later by, "Put down the margarine! *It will kill you!*" As a society, we've been programmed to think of foods as "good" or "bad," which bums me out. This polar mentality is entirely unhelpful. It's why our best intentions are often derailed after just one french fry. We've been eating for fuel since the dawn of humanity, but we only started counting calories when Wilbur Olin Atwater invented the calorimeter about 125 years ago. If counting calories is the solution, wouldn't we all be thinner by now? Why are we making it so complicated, when it doesn't need to be?

I know I already said that I *love* food, but I should clarify my previous statement: I love *real* food. Highly processed food is not really food. I know it's not real food because of how I feel afterward. My stomach is unhappy, I feel jittery, and is it lunchtime yet? I'm hungry already. Real food, when prepared well, can both delight the senses and nourish the body. Food can be delicious, nutritious, approachable, and affordable all at once, and I spread the word with each of my recipes. That's why my blog's motto is, "Celebrating whole foods!"

Whole Foods Guidelines

Real foods have been around for ages, and nutrition is a new, complex science. We're learning more about the benefits of whole foods every day, and I suspect that we'll someday look back at nutrition labels as primitive indicators of their contents. Regardless, research is showing that food really can be the best preventive medicine, and the beauty in following a whole foods approach is that you don't need to keep up with the latest research to know that you're eating well. Here are my basic suggested guidelines for following a whole foods–focused diet, which are rooted in science and backed up by my personal experiences.

▸ While it's true that some whole foods might offer more nutritional bang for the buck, **let the seasons and your appetite guide your decisions.** By filling up on a variety of whole foods, you'll likely meet your nutritional needs with minimal effort.

▸ **Choose organic,** when possible, to avoid modern chemicals that don't belong in our bodies (fertilizers, pesticides, antibiotics, hormones, waxes, and other bad guys).

▸ **Choose local when you can, too.** Generally, the fresher the product, the more vitamins and minerals it has to offer. Buying local is also a great way to support your local community and minimize your environmental footprint.

▸ These days, even basics like bread are often composed of a long list of unrecognizable ingredients. While you're at the grocery store, **take a quick glance at ingredients lists.** For example, basic bread products should have around 5 familiar ingredients, not 25.

▸ I hate to chime in with the choir, but **moderation really is key.** Eat what you want! Within reason. If you really want some ice cream, go ahead–have some. If you feel compelled to eat an entire carton of ice cream, though, maybe now is the time to address the source of your stress. Trust me, I've been there, and I never found an answer to my problems at the bottom of the carton.

▸ Above all, **pay attention to how different foods make you feel.** Great meals should leave you feeling great afterward. If you feel like you've been run over by a bus after you eat, you might find that option slightly less tempting the next time it comes around. Maybe you fully embrace the "everything in moderation" approach, or you find good reason to omit a certain food(s). Either way, you have my full support.

As your taste buds get acquainted with more nutritious foods, your cravings will likely become better indicators of the nutrients your body needs. That has been my experience and that is why I only share recipes that make me feel good *and* taste amazing. You'll find over 100 of them in this book!

DOGS AND FOOD

Cookie adores carrot and sweet potato peels, bites of bananas and apples, and pretty much everything else. Her "treat" when she comes inside from the backyard is often a leftover slivered almond or chopped pecan.

Not all people-foods are safe for dogs, so be careful about what you feed your dog. Moderation is important for dogs, too, and they can be allergic to different foods just like people can. Be cautious, and don't give your dog too much of any one thing (dairy, nuts, oils, and salt can cause problems in sufficient quantities). Don't feed them any food that has gone bad, either! If you suspect poisoning, call your vet immediately. You can also call the Animal Poison Hotline at 888-232-8870 or the ASPCA Animal Poison Control Center at 888-426-4435.

FOODS THAT ARE TOXIC TO DOGS

Alcohol	Coffee and tea	Raw potatoes	Xylitol, a sugar substitute found in gum, candies, baked goods, and more
Alliums: onions, garlic, chives, and leeks, including onion powder and garlic powder	Grapes, raisins, and currants	Rhubarb	
	Macadamia nuts	Seeds from apples and pears	Yeast dough, which can expand in their stomachs
Chocolate	Pits from apricots, cherries, peaches, and plums	Star fruit	

Don't give dogs whole fruits or vegetables that could become choking hazards, such as avocados, corn on the cob, or persimmons.

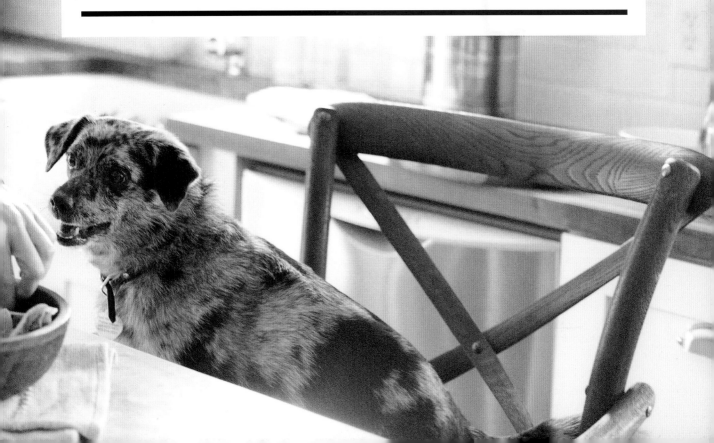

"Eat food. Not too much. Mostly plants."

—MICHAEL POLLAN

ON VEGETARIANISM

I became a vegetarian shortly after graduating from college, after reading Michael Pollan's chapters about the meat industry. It was an easy decision for me, one that began as a New Year's resolution in 2009. I don't see myself ever going back.

Why did I give up meat? First of all, I had always been very picky about meat, and I don't think I was ever truly comfortable with the concept of eating animals. For as many chicken fingers as I used to eat, I never could eat from the bone. Once I learned about the sustainability issues, widespread antibiotic treatment, and the oftentimes poor treatment of animals in mass meat production, I decided I didn't want to support the industry. Granted, higher-quality, lower-impact meat from local and organic farms is becoming more widely available, but I would just rather go without.

When I stopped eating meat, I naturally gravitated toward more plant-based protein, in the form of <u>beans and whole grains</u>. I also found myself making more creative meals featuring a wider variety of vegetables, greens, and fruits. It

has been fun to share these meal concepts with my family, and to find more meatless options on our table during the holidays. Vegetarianism works well for me, and I rest easy knowing that I am doing the environment, my body, and my wallet a favor.

In my book, less meat is simply better than more meat, and my only goal is to inspire readers to cook more wholesome, produce-driven meals. I won't stop you from adding grilled chicken to my salads, but you might find that you're satisfied without it.

Most of my blog readers are not vegetarians, but they appreciate my fresh cooking style. I always want to jump up and down when I hear that my recipes have changed someone's life for the better. I love it when people tell me that I've changed their minds about kale and quinoa, or that their kids are eating more vegetables. I've also heard from individuals and couples who have discovered that cooking can be really fun. I often hear from visitors who have recently received a scary health diagnosis, and they're relieved to find recipes that work for their new diets but don't feel anything like a prescription. My job is so rewarding, and I wouldn't trade it for anything.

In this cookbook, you'll find a carefully crafted selection of over 100 recipes to suit a variety of cravings and situations. Like the recipes on my blog, these recipes are made with whole foods—no fake stuff here! I'm a stickler for using whole-grain products, rather than refined grains and flours. I love developing wholesome, naturally sweetened baked goods and desserts that are healthier than conventional recipes. I hope this cookbook offers a collection of new favorite recipes that you can dog-ear on the couch and splatter with tomato sauce in the kitchen.

This cookbook is divided into seven chapters: Good Morning (everyday breakfasts and fun brunch options), Salads (from side salads to dinner portions), Soups (perfect for cold days), Happy Hour (fun appetizers, snacks, and cocktails), Let's Feast (hearty, hot main dishes), Sweet Treats (all pretty healthy, as far as desserts go), and Extras (sauces to help you improvise, and more).

HOW TO READ THIS BOOK

I've tried to make this book the best resource it can possibly be by offering fun variations on the recipes (look for the "Change It Up" label) and simple substitutions for common dietary restrictions whenever possible.

Make sure to skim through each recipe's headnote and ingredients list before you begin cooking, so you have a good idea of what's to come. I've tried to minimize or eliminate any steps that require advance preparation (although if you don't own a powerful blender, there are a few recipes that require the soaking of cashews). You'll also find lots of recipe tips that might come in handy.

You might notice that my method of cooking quinoa or draining tofu is a little different, but that's because it works better. I don't add salt, sweetener, fat, or dairy willy-nilly. When you see them in a recipe, it's because they offer a substantial improvement in flavor or texture, so please trust me. If you're concerned about any of those ingredients, check the dietary notes for potential substitutions.

Likewise, trust your senses. I've provided sensory cues to help guide you successfully through the recipes. For example, if your oven runs a little cool, your muffins might not be finished baking within my suggested time range, but you can stick them back in the oven "until the muffins are golden on top and a toothpick inserted into a muffin comes out clean." You also know your preferences better than I do—if you're sensitive to spicy food, you might omit the red pepper flakes from a recipe, and use the lowest suggested amounts of spicy ingredients such as Sriracha or adobo sauce.

If you have food allergies or sensitivities, use your best judgment and double-check your ingredients to make sure they're safe for you.

Serving sizes are approximate. If the recipe says that it yields 4 to 6 servings, that means that it yields 4 larger or 6 smaller servings. If you're going to count a salad or soup as a meal, make it a big one!

*Colorful Kale, Apple, and
Fennel Slaw with Tart
Cherries (page 68)*

MEASUREMENTS NOTES

A **pinch** is $1/8$ teaspoon.

A **handful** is around $1/4$ cup. Use more or less as you see fit.

Scant means just shy of the given measurement.

Heaping means just over the given measurement.

Divided means that you won't use the quantity listed all at once. It's divided among two or more steps, and I've explained how much to use in each step.

Liquid ingredients, like honey and milk, are measured in liquid measuring cups.

Semi-liquid ingredients, such as peanut butter, Greek yogurt, and mashed bananas, are challenging to level off in liquid measuring cups, so measure them in dry measuring cups instead.

Dry ingredients, like flour, are measured in dry measuring cups using the "spoon and swoop" method (see below).

"Spoon and swoop" measuring method: Spoon flour into a dry measuring cup until it's slightly overflowing (don't scoop flour into the cup because you could end up with 50 percent more flour). Then, level the top with a knife to get rid of the excess.

Produce size is always assumed to be medium, unless otherwise specified.

OVEN NOTES

Always bake on the middle rack, unless otherwise specified.

Always place your pan or baking dish in the center of the rack.

INGREDIENTS EXAMPLES

1 cup chopped dried tart cherries, dried blueberries, or chopped dried apricots
Any of those options will work well, but I've listed my favorite first, followed by my second, and so on.

2 cloves garlic, pressed or minced
Assume that the cloves are medium-sized. If you have 1 large clove and 1 small clove, they average out to 2 medium cloves. That works! You can press the garlic through a garlic press (the easier option) or mince it by hand with a sharp chef's knife.

1 block (12 to 15 ounces) organic extra-firm tofu
The various brands of tofu come in different size packages, so I've offered a range of suitable volumes. Any organic extra-firm tofu that falls somewhere between 12 and 15 ounces will work.

2 cups thinly sliced red cabbage (about $1/2$ pound)
The recipe will use 2 cups sliced cabbage. The weight given in parentheses is just an approximation to help you pick out a suitable size of cabbage at the grocery store.

1 cup mashed bananas ($2^1/2$ medium or 2 large bananas)
The recipe will use 1 cup mashed bananas. The number of bananas in parentheses is meant to give you a sense of how many you need to buy at the grocery story. Mash the bananas, spoon into a dry measuring cup, and level with a knife (because it's a semi-liquid ingredient; see Measurements Notes).

$1/2$ cup crumbled goat cheese (about $2^1/2$ ounces)
The volume of cheese varies quite a bit depending on whether it's crumbled, grated, or shredded. You can go by the volumes listed in the recipes (just measure the cheese in a dry measuring cup). The weight given in parentheses will help you decide how much to buy.

COOKING TIPS AND FLAVOR BOOSTERS

I've tested the heck out of each recipe in this book to make sure it turns out great for you. However, it's important to understand some cooking fundamentals in order to get amazing results, every time. Some of them are especially important when it comes to working with whole foods such as fresh produce, which inevitably varies in size and flavor. Here are some tips that will help you become a better cook.

USE HIGH-QUALITY INGREDIENTS AND STORE THEM PROPERLY. I'm not just talking about fresh produce! Cooking oils and any product that contains naturally occurring oils (whole grains and whole-grain flours, nuts and nut butters, seeds, and spices) can go rancid. Once they have gone rancid, they will introduce off flavors or aromas to your food. Another downside is that rancid ingredients lose some of their nutritional merits.

Oxygen, light, heat, and time are the four culprits that make good oils go bad. So, proper storage is key to preserving the quality of your ingredients (or investments, as I like to think of them). Store oil-containing foods in the appropriate sizes of airtight containers, in a dark, cool place (like a cupboard, or the refrigerator, if you have room). Sniff your ingredients to make sure they don't smell funny before you add them to a recipe, because they can ruin the whole thing. Have you ever tasted a bitter whole wheat baked good? That's because the flour was rancid!

TOAST THOSE NUTS AND SEEDS.
Sometimes, toasted nuts or seeds are the savory element that sends a recipe over the top. I recommend buying raw nuts and seeds, and toasting them as needed. Raw nuts keep longer, and freshly toasted nuts taste so much better.

I've included instructions for toasting nuts and seeds in every recipe that calls for it. Basically, you just warm them in a skillet on the stove, or in the oven, until they are golden on the edges and plenty fragrant. Don't stop too soon. Keep a watchful eye on them and stir frequently to reduce the risk of burning. If you are the forgetful/distracted type (that's me), set a timer so you don't let them burn.

The skillet method works especially well for nuts and seeds that are mostly flat and thin, like pepitas (hulled pumpkin seeds) or sliced almonds, but the oven brings out more flavor from thick nuts, like walnuts. That said, you can chop those thicker nuts and toast them in a skillet if it's more convenient.

CARAMELIZE THOSE VEGGIES.
Caramelization is what happens when natural sugars concentrate along the edges of sautéed and roasted vegetables, turning them golden brown and extra delicious. It makes vegetables taste magically more intense and complex. Caramelized roasted vegetables are one of my favorite recipe components. They can make a vegetarian entree seem extra hearty and satisfying, so you'll find a lot of them in the Let's Feast chapter.

For maximum caramelization, slice your vegetables into even pieces with lots of flat surfaces, so they can bake directly against the hot pan. Toss them in enough oil to lightly coat them on all sides. The oil helps distribute heat evenly over their surfaces. Tossing the vegetables halfway through roasting helps, too.

Don't overcrowd the vegetables or they'll steam each other instead of crisping up. If necessary, use two pans: one on the middle rack and one in the upper third, swapping them halfway.

Most importantly, don't take your vegetables out of the oven too soon, or they won't reach their full caramelized potential. Go for deeply golden edges and tender insides. When in doubt, refer to my recipe photos.

USE FRESH HERBS LIBERALLY. Fresh herbs, such as cilantro, parsley, basil, and mint, offer loads of fresh flavor and some extra vitamins, too. I've tried to use mostly inexpensive fresh herbs throughout the book, so you can use them liberally at minimal expense. To improvise with fresh herbs, just try a bite of your completed recipe with a small piece of torn fresh herb on top. If it's good, add more!

My Favorite Granola (page 5)

Tip: If you'd like to grow your own herb garden, try growing mint, basil, oregano, and/or rosemary. I've had the best luck with those.

Tip: To easily prolong the life of a store-bought bunch of fresh herbs, remove the rubber band at the base, which is where the leaves start going bad. Then, wrap the bunch loosely in a half-sheet of paper towel before placing it back into the bag (or better yet, in a sealed plastic storage bag). Store the bags on top of all the other veggies in your vegetable drawer so they don't get squished.

DON'T BE AFRAID OF SALT. Most of the sodium consumed in the standard American diet comes from processed foods. When you're starting off with raw, unprocessed ingredients, you're in control of their sodium content, and you're probably going to need more salt than just a few dashes. Unless your doctor has told you otherwise, you probably don't need to worry about it. You're highly unlikely to add as much salt as you would find in a frozen dinner or a restaurant meal.

When used properly, salt reduces the bitterness in a dish, and makes all of the other flavors taste more like themselves. Dishes don't actually taste "salty" until you've added too much. I am perpetually amazed at the difference that adding just a pinch or ¼ teaspoon of salt can make. Please, experiment at home and see for yourself! Try adding a little salt in stages to homemade salad dressings, soups, or whole grains, and taste them at every addition.

If you prepare a recipe and it doesn't have enough "oomph" to taste totally awesome, try adding a little more salt. That just might do the trick. Add just a little at a time, because it's easy to add more, but difficult to subtract. To help you get it right, I've provided a range of final salt measurements when appropriate. You could also consider adding a little more of a complementary salty ingredient, such as Parmesan, feta, tamari, hot sauce, or pickled ingredients.

TINKER WITH FINAL SEASONINGS AS NECESSARY. You and I don't share the same taste buds, and we are working with different ingredients in different kitchens. On top of that, natural ingredients can vary significantly in flavor. A juicy, red, ripe summer tomato will yield far more intense tomato flavor than a pale winter tomato. Lemons vary in sourness from one to another. My medium Granny Smith apple might be a little bigger and sweeter than the medium Granny Smith you pick up. As a recipe writer who is always striving to create the "perfect" recipe, this is absolutely maddening!

So, for recipes to truly sing, you might need to tinker with them a bit at the end. If you have been conservative with the salt, add a little more, as described above. If the dish still tastes dull, it might need more acidity–add another dash of vinegar, lemon juice, or lime juice to bring it to life. If it's too sour, balance it with a sweeter ingredient–add more fruit, honey, maple syrup, or sugar. If fresh flavor is missing, you could add more of the fresh herbs called for in the recipe. You'll know when you hit it right, because it will make your taste buds dance for joy.

Okay, let's start cooking! If any of these details seem complicated, don't worry–they will make sense as you cook through the recipes. I've provided troubleshooting tips for any snag you might encounter, so you will feel confident through every step of the process.

MY FAVORITE INGREDIENTS

Meet a few of my favorite ingredients! Here are a few that might be new to you, as well as details on some common ingredients that I want to share before you start cooking.

CANNED TOMATOES can fill a dish with rich, comforting tomato flavor when fresh tomatoes are out of season. Be sure to buy tomato products in BPA-free cans or glass jars because the acidity of the tomatoes draws out BPA from the can's lining. My favorite brand of delicious, organic, BPA-free tomatoes is Muir Glen, which is widely available now.

CHIPOTLE PEPPERS IN ADOBO SAUCE are smoked and dried jalapeños that have been rehydrated and canned in an irresistible blend of tomato, vinegar, garlic, and spices. They're smoky, spicy, and tangy, and I've used the adobo sauce component in several recipes in this book.

Where to find it: The International/Hispanic aisle of your grocery store.

Tip: You can freeze leftover chipotle peppers in adobo sauce. Just transfer the extra to a small freezer bag and press the air out before sealing the bag and freezing it flat. Later, you can just pull off as much as you want and thaw it.

COCONUT MILK is a rich and luxurious, plant-based alternative to heavy cream. I always use unsweetened, canned coconut milk. I opt for *regular (full-fat) coconut milk* when I want super creamy ice creams and rich sauces. *Light (reduced-fat) coconut milk* has simply been diluted with water (see page 225 to learn how to turn regular coconut milk into light). I recommend Native Forest and Trader Joe's brands of coconut milk because they come in BPA-free cans.

Where to find it: The International/Asian aisle of your grocery store.

COCONUT OIL is a great non-dairy alternative to butter in baked goods. I also like to cook with it when its subtle coconut flavor complements the other ingredients. I only use virgin (unrefined) coconut oil, which starts smoking at 350°F (for reference, refined coconut oil starts smoking around 400°F).

COCONUT SUGAR (also called coconut palm sugar) is new to me but growing quickly in popularity. While coconut sugar contains as many calories as regular sugar, it's minimally processed and contains far less fructose, which is hard on the liver. It also offers a high vitamin and mineral content. Coconut sugar tastes similar to brown sugar and I often use it in place of brown sugar, with varying degrees of success.

Where to find it: Health food stores, or in the baking aisle or health food section of your grocery store.

EXTRA-VIRGIN OLIVE OIL is my go-to oil. I use it for salad dressings, sautéing, and roasting vegetables. That's right, I cook with it! Quality extra-virgin olive oils can actually tolerate temperatures between 400° to 425°F before they start smoking, which is plenty hot for roasting and sautéing. Extra-virgin olive oil offers greater anti-inflammatory benefits and more antioxidants than later pressings, and those antioxidants actually help prevent the oil from breaking down at higher temperatures. My favorite brand is California Olive Ranch.

FARRO has been around for a long time—Italians have been cooking it for centuries, and the Egyptian kings enjoyed it before them. It's an ancient strain of wheat with a delicious, mildly nutty flavor, and an addictive chewy texture that's great in salads and soups. Bonus? Cooked farro freezes well for later use.

Where to find it: Near the rice or pasta in your grocery store, in the bulk bins, or in the health food section.

FINE SEA SALT is my default salt. It has a cleaner flavor than regular iodized table salt and a few trace minerals. Table salt is even more fine than fine-grain sea salt, so if you are using regular table salt in recipes that call for fine-grain sea salt, you may need to scale back a little on your measurements.

Where to find it: The baking aisle at the grocery store.

MEDJOOL DATES taste similar to chewy caramel candies, but they grow on trees. Medjool dates are the sweetest and the most common variety. Dates are sold fresh, but they dry out with age. Fresh dates are nice and plump; older dates are wrinkled and need a brief soak in hot water to rehydrate. Dates are very sweet, but they're so high in fiber that they don't spike blood sugar levels like other sweeteners.

Where to find them: In the chilled produce section in the grocery store or health food store.

QUINOA (pronounced KEEN-wah) is a seed that grows in South America. It's ready in about 20 minutes, so it's a great option when you're in a pinch for time. I like to add quinoa to chopped salads, where it contributes a unique texture and additional protein, amino acids, and fiber.

Where to find it: Near the rice in your grocery store.

MAPLE SYRUP is nature's caramel sauce. Technically, it's the concentrated sap of maple trees. Don't try to substitute artificial maple syrup for the real kind–it's made almost entirely of high fructose corn syrup and won't behave properly in my recipes. I know maple syrup can be pricy (and hard to find outside of the U.S.), so I've offered alternatives whenever I can.

PARMESAN is a hard cow's milk cheese. It's salty, slightly sweet, rich in savory umami flavor, and tastes best when freshly grated or sliced. Like many other hard cheeses, most Parmesan is made with the help of animal rennet, which is not vegetarian. Whole Foods 365 and BelGioioso Cheese brands offer vegetarian Parmesan, if you'd like to seek them out.

PEPITAS (green pumpkin seeds) are a tasty snack, a delicious addition to Mexican recipes, and an affordable alternative to pine nuts in pesto. Freshly toasted pepitas offer a distinctive nutty flavor and a delightful little crunch. Pepitas are an excellent source of protein, fiber, iron, zinc, manganese, and magnesium.

Where to find them: The health food section in your grocery store, the bulk bins, or in health food stores.

REDUCED-SODIUM TAMARI is my soy sauce of choice. It's a Japanese soy sauce with a smoother, rich flavor than the super salty kind offered at Chinese buffets. Unlike regular soy sauce, it's usually wheat-free (and therefore gluten-free), but check the label to be sure if that's a factor for you. My favorite brand is San-J.

Where to find it: The International/Asian aisle of your grocery store.

TAHINI is made from ground sesame seeds, like peanut butter is made from ground peanuts. It's creamy and nutty, with a tang that keeps me coming back for more. Tahini is a staple ingredient in Middle Eastern cuisine, but I love to use it in creamy, non-dairy dressings and sauces, too. Be sure to stir tahini well before using since the oil tends to separate from the rest. My favorite brand is Whole Foods 365.

Where to find it: Near the peanut butter, olives, or in the International aisle in well-stocked grocery stores (or in a health food store).

WHITE WHOLE WHEAT FLOUR is 100-percent whole wheat flour ground from white wheat berries, rather than standard red wheat berries. It has a lighter color and less "wheaty" flavor than regular whole wheat flour. Feel free to swap white whole wheat flour for whole wheat flour in any recipe. My favorite brands are Bob's Red Mill (they call it "ivory" wheat) and King Arthur Flour.

Where to find it: At health food stores, or in the baking aisle or health food section of your grocery store.

1 *Good Morning*

BREAKFAST IS MY FAVORITE. No, wait–breakfast is my favorite *morning* meal, while lunch is my favorite afternoon meal, and dinner is my favorite evening meal. Frankly, they're *all* my favorite, and I can't skip any one of them.

Breakfast really is the most important meal of the day. A good breakfast can wake up your taste buds and boost your metabolism and energy levels for the rest of the day. Good choices include some combination of oats or other whole grains, nuts, eggs, yogurt, veggies, and/or fruit. Complex carbohydrates, protein, fiber, and healthy fats offer steady energy that will keep you going until lunch.

Choose the wrong breakfast, and it can send your blood sugar levels on a roller coaster that begins with a jittery sugar high and ends with a nap. I'm looking at you, cute iced doughnut with sprinkles on top. The sugar content in that doughnut isn't the only issue. Refined carbohydrates, such as the white flour used to make doughnuts, are quickly processed by the body as sugar, too. You're essentially knocking yourself down with a one-two punch.

In this chapter, you will find plenty of quick weekday options, which are both delicious and well balanced. You will also find some brunch-worthy recipes and breakfast treats, including my favorite fluffy, whole-grain pancakes, waffles, and scones. It concludes with fresh, egg-based dishes, which are also great for lunch or dinner.

Mango Lassi Smoothie Bowl with Toasted Coconut Muesli

MUESLI

4 cups old-fashioned rolled oats

1½ cups unsweetened shredded coconut

¾ cup raw pepitas (hulled pumpkin seeds)

¾ cup sliced almonds

¾ teaspoon fine sea salt

½ teaspoon ground cinnamon

½ teaspoon ground ginger

3 tablespoons maple syrup or honey

2 tablespoons melted coconut oil

2 teaspoons vanilla extract

½ cup chia seeds

MANGO YOGURT

Heaping 2 cups frozen mango chunks

2 cups plain Greek yogurt

Optional sweeteners: pitted Medjool dates, honey, or maple syrup

---

These sunny smoothie bowls are a riff on traditional Indian mango lassis, which are refreshing blended mango and yogurt drinks. The smoothie component is just equal parts fruit (fresh or frozen) blended with thick, protein-rich Greek yogurt. If you're always in a hurry on weekday mornings (who isn't?!), you could easily prepare enough fruity yogurt on Sunday night to last you through the week.

MAKES 7½ CUPS MUESLI AND FOUR 1-CUP SERVINGS OF MANGO YOGURT

---

1. *To make the muesli:* Preheat the oven to 350°F. Line a large rimmed baking sheet with parchment paper for easy cleanup.

2. In a large bowl, combine the oats, coconut, pepitas, almonds, salt, cinnamon, and ginger. Stir to combine. Pour in the maple syrup, coconut oil, and vanilla. (The chia seeds are added after baking.) Stir until the mixture is well blended.

3. Pour the mixture onto the prepared baking sheet and smooth it into an even layer. Bake until the oats and coconut are lightly golden and fragrant, about 15 minutes, tossing halfway. Set aside to cool.

4. Once the muesli has cooled to room temperature, stir in the chia seeds. Store the muesli in a freezer bag with the air squeezed out. It keeps best in the freezer (no thawing time required), for up to 3 months.

5. *To make the mango yogurt:* In a blender, combine the mango and yogurt and blend until smooth. (If the frozen mango is too hard for your blender to handle, let it thaw at room temperature for 5 to 10 minutes before trying again.) Taste and, if necessary, add a sweetener and blend again.

6. To assemble the smoothie bowls, spoon the mango yogurt into as many bowls as you plan on serving and top with as much muesli as you'd like. Serve immediately. Cover and refrigerate any remaining yogurt for up to 5 days.

GLUTEN FREE: *Use certified gluten-free oats.* • **DAIRY FREE/VEGAN:** *Use maple syrup instead of honey and substitute nondairy coconut yogurt for the Greek yogurt.* • **EGG FREE** • **NUT FREE:** *Replace the sliced almonds with additional pepitas.* • **SOY FREE**

CHANGE IT UP

You can blend any variety of frozen fruit into yogurt to make your own low-sugar, fruity yogurts. You can also top these bowls with fresh fruit (sliced bananas are great).

TIP: *Muesli is usually made from raw oats and other add-ins, which are soaked in liquid overnight. I toast my muesli with a touch of maple syrup and coconut oil for extra flavor and treat it like a lightened-up granola or homemade cereal. This muesli features toasted coconut, pumpkin seeds, almonds, and spices, plus omega-3-rich chia seeds—all of which play nicely with mango. The beauty of muesli is that you can make a batch and store it in the freezer for several months. It's ready to go when you are.*

My Favorite Granola

Meet my go-to granola recipe! It's bursting with goodness–nuts and seeds, warming cinnamon, coconut oil, and maple syrup–and tastes about one thousand times better than store-bought varieties. Once you try homemade granola, you'll never go back.

MAKES 8 CUPS

1. Preheat the oven to 350°F. Line a large rimmed baking sheet with parchment paper. In a large bowl, combine the oats, pecans, pepitas, salt, and cinnamon. Stir to combine.

2. Pour in the coconut oil, maple syrup, and vanilla. Mix well, until every oat and nut is lightly coated. Pour the granola onto the prepared baking sheet and use a large spoon to spread it into an even layer. Bake until golden, 21 to 23 minutes, stirring halfway. Don't worry–the granola will continue to crisp up as it cools.

3. Let the granola cool completely, undisturbed, before breaking it into pieces and stirring in the dried cranberries. Store the granola in an airtight container at room temperature for 1 to 2 weeks, or in a sealed freezer bag in the freezer for up to 3 months.

4 cups old-fashioned rolled oats

1 cup raw pecan halves or roughly chopped walnuts

$1/2$ cup raw pepitas (hulled pumpkin seeds)

1 teaspoon fine sea salt

1 teaspoon ground cinnamon

$1/2$ cup melted coconut oil or extra-virgin olive oil

$1/2$ cup maple syrup or honey

1 teaspoon vanilla extract

$1/2$ cup dried cranberries

CHANGE IT UP

▶ This granola recipe is very flexible. Feel free to change up the nuts, spices, and dried fruit to make your own favorite granola.

GLUTEN FREE: *Use certified gluten-free oats* • **DAIRY FREE** • **VEGAN:** *Use maple syrup instead of honey.* • **EGG FREE** • **NUT FREE:** *Replace the nuts with additional pepitas.* • **SOY FREE**

Apple Crisp Breakfast Parfaits

Here's a great excuse to eat apple crisp for breakfast (not that you needed one). These deconstructed apple crisp parfaits are layered with cinnamon-spiked yogurt and chunky homemade applesauce. My Favorite Granola is a great stand-in for apple crisp topping. Unlike store-bought flavored yogurts, these hearty servings are only as sweet as you want them to be. **MAKES 6 SERVINGS**

1. *To make the applesauce:* Peel, core, and chop the apples into 1- to 2-inch chunks. In a medium Dutch oven or large stainless steel saucepan, combine the apple chunks, water, lemon juice, maple syrup, and cinnamon. Cover and bring the mixture to a simmer over medium heat. Simmer, stirring occasionally, until the apples are tender and falling apart, 15 to 20 minutes. Use the back of a sturdy spatula or wooden spoon to break up the largest chunks.

2. Remove the pot from the heat. At this point, the sweetness of the applesauce will depend entirely on your apples; taste, and if you would like sweeter applesauce, stir in some additional maple syrup or honey.

3. *To make the cinnamon yogurt:* In a medium bowl, combine the yogurt, lemon juice, and cinnamon. Whisk to combine and then add maple syrup or honey to taste, keeping in mind that the granola and applesauce are already on the sweeter side (if you like plain yogurt on its own, you might not want to add any at all).

4. To assemble the parfaits, line up six 1-pint mason jars, stemless wine glasses, or medium drinking glasses. Place about ⅓ cup yogurt at the base of each glass, then top the yogurt with ½ cup applesauce. Layer an additional ⅓ cup yogurt on top. If you will be serving immediately, layer about ⅓ cup granola on top. If not, wait to add the granola until just before serving so it stays crisp. The yogurt and applesauce will keep for 5 to 7 days, covered, in the refrigerator.

CHUNKY APPLESAUCE

3 Gala apples or your favorite red apples (about 1 pound)

3 Granny Smith or Golden Delicious apples (about 1 pound)

⅓ cup water

1 tablespoon lemon juice

1 tablespoon maple syrup or honey, or more to taste

1 teaspoon ground cinnamon

CINNAMON YOGURT

4 cups (32 ounces) plain Greek yogurt

1 tablespoon lemon juice

½ teaspoon ground cinnamon

Up to 4 tablespoons maple syrup or honey

2 cups My Favorite Granola (page 5)

TIP: *You can make these parfaits in advance and enjoy them Monday through Friday. For maximum portability, prepare them in mason jars or working jars with lids.*

GLUTEN FREE • DAIRY FREE: *Use your favorite nondairy yogurt.* • **VEGAN:** *Choose maple syrup instead of honey, use your favorite nondairy yogurt, and follow the vegan notes for the granola.* • **EGG FREE • NUT FREE:** *See dietary notes for the granola (page 5).* • **SOY FREE**

Quinoa Piña Colada Granola

4 cups old-fashioned rolled oats

$1/2$ cup raw cashews

$1/2$ cup uncooked quinoa (any color will do)

1 teaspoon fine sea salt

$1/2$ teaspoon ground cinnamon

$1/4$ teaspoon ground ginger

$1/2$ cup melted coconut oil

$1/2$ cup maple syrup

1 teaspoon vanilla extract

$1/2$ cup unsweetened coconut flakes or unsweetened shredded coconut

$2/3$ cup roughly chopped dried pineapple

Here's a tropical variation on My Favorite Granola (page 5) that almost rhymes, no less. This granola features toasted cashews, coconut flakes, chewy dried pineapple, and quinoa for a little extra crunch and color. On its own, it's an addictive snack, but it's even better on yogurt (sometimes I throw some sliced bananas or berries on top). Beware: This tropical treat may induce daydreams about sipping piña coladas on the beach. **MAKES 6 CUPS**

1. Preheat the oven to 350°F. Line a large rimmed baking sheet with parchment paper. In a large bowl, combine the oats, cashews, quinoa, salt, cinnamon, and ginger. Stir to combine.

2. Pour the coconut oil, maple syrup, and vanilla into the bowl. Mix well, until every oat and nut is lightly coated. Pour the granola onto the prepared baking sheet and use a large spoon to spread it into an even layer. Bake until golden, 18 to 20 minutes, mixing in the coconut and stirring halfway. The granola will further crisp up as it cools.

3. Let the granola cool completely, undisturbed, before adding the dried fruit. Store the granola in an airtight container at room temperature for 1 to 2 weeks, or in a sealed freezer bag in the freezer for up to 3 months.

TIP: *The freezer is the best place to store granola. Store it in a freezer bag with the air squeezed out, and your granola will taste fresh for several months. I just scoop frozen granola right from the bag into my yogurt. Be careful, though— some dried fruit freezes rock hard, and needs to rest for a few minutes at room temperature so you don't break a tooth on your first bite.*

GLUTEN FREE: *Use certified gluten-free oats.* • **DAIRY FREE** • **VEGAN** • **EGG FREE** • **NUT FREE:** *Substitute pepitas (hulled pumpkin seeds) for the cashews.* • **SOY FREE**

CHANGE IT UP

Feel free to use this recipe as a template and make your own custom blend by substituting different nuts or seeds (chop the nuts if they're larger than a peanut), dried fruit (chop the fruit if it's larger than a raisin), and/or spices. If you like your oatmeal on the sweeter side, add more sugar to the mix.

Make-Your-Own Instant Oatmeal Mix

Busy mornings still call for breakfast. This homemade mix is a healthier alternative to oatmeal packets, which are inevitably either flavorless or super sweet. Now you can make your own with high quality ingredients, for less than the cost of the store-bought variety. This oatmeal is great as is, or you can gussy up your bowl with prepared fresh fruit or a spoonful of nut butter, Coconut Whipped Cream (page 220), or your favorite jam.

MAKES 18 SERVINGS

4 cups quick-cooking oats *1 serving*

1 cup sliced almonds

1 cup chopped dried tart cherries, dried blueberries, or chopped dried apricots

$1/2$ cup flaxseeds or raw pepitas (hulled pumpkin seeds)

$1/3$ cup lightly packed coconut sugar

2 teaspoons ground cinnamon

$3/4$ teaspoon fine sea salt

1. In a large storage container or freezer bag, combine the oats, almonds, dried fruit, flaxseeds, coconut sugar, cinnamon, and salt. Stir to combine.

2. *To prepare a single serving of oatmeal on the stove:* Pour $2/3$ cup water into a small saucepan and bring to a boil over high heat. Stir the oatmeal mix again to ensure that it's evenly blended, then pour $1/3$ cup of the oatmeal mixture into the boiling water. Stir to combine, reduce the heat to medium-low, and simmer, uncovered, stirring occasionally, until the oats have absorbed most of the water and are creamy in texture, 5 to 7 minutes.

3. *To prepare a single serving of oatmeal in the microwave:* Stir the oatmeal mix again to ensure that it's evenly blended. Combine $1/3$ cup of the mix and $2/3$ cup water in a microwave-safe bowl (use a slightly larger bowl than you think you'll need, so the oatmeal doesn't bubble over). Microwave for $1^1/2$ to $2^1/2$ minutes, pausing to stir if necessary to prevent overflow, until the oats have absorbed most of the water and are creamy in texture.

4. The oatmeal will thicken up a bit more as it cools. Let the oatmeal rest for a few minutes, until it reaches a palatable temperature. Stir again, add any garnishes that you might like, and serve.

5. Leftover dry mix will keep at room temperature for up to 3 months, or in the freezer for up to 6 months.

TIP: *In the single-serving directions, I suggest using $1/3$ cup dry oatmeal mix because it is about the equivalent of a packet of oatmeal. If you would like to cook up more oatmeal at once, just follow the directions, using* twice as *much water as oatmeal.*

GLUTEN FREE: *Use certified gluten-free oats.* • **DAIRY FREE** • **VEGAN** • **EGG FREE** • **NUT FREE:** *Substitute pepitas for the sliced almonds.* • **SOY FREE**

Make-Ahead Green Smoothies

I'm not a morning person. I am, however, a breakfast person. I need my breakfasts to be easy enough to fumble together in the morning, because I don't have the energy to pull out a variety of smoothie ingredients before I've had coffee. Here's my solution—I portion the smoothie ingredients into mason jars and freeze them for later. Whenever I want a smoothie, I just dump the contents of the mason jar into the blender, add some liquids, and boom! Now I'm getting in some servings of greens and fruit before noon.

FOR EACH SMOOTHIE: In a wide-mouth mason jar or small freezer bag, combine all the ingredients under the "freeze" list. Screw on the lid or seal the bag, and place it in the freezer for up to 6 months.

When you're ready to serve, pour the contents of the jar or bag into the blender (if the frozen ingredients are frozen solid in your mason jar, let it rest at room temperature for 5 minutes and then use a sturdy butter knife to loosen around the edges). Add the remaining ingredients listed under "add." Blend until completely smooth using your blender's smoothie function, if it has one, or by starting on low speed and increasing to high as soon as you get enough traction. Pour into a glass and drink up.

PINEAPPLE-COCONUT GREEN SMOOTHIE

MAKES 1½ CUPS

FREEZE

1 cup packed spinach

½ medium banana, cut into 1-inch chunks

Heaping ½ cup frozen pineapple chunks

2 tablespoons unsweetened shredded coconut

1 tablespoon chia seeds (optional)

ADD

½ to ¾ cup water

Juice of 1 lime

Several ice cubes

GLUTEN FREE • DAIRY FREE • VEGAN • EGG FREE • NUT FREE • SOY FREE

CINNAMON-ALMOND GREEN SMOOTHIE

MAKES 1¼ CUPS

FREEZE

1 cup packed spinach

1 medium banana, cut into 1-inch chunks

1 tablespoon flaxseeds or flaxseed meal

1 tablespoon almond butter or peanut butter (Justin's works best)

¼ teaspoon ground cinnamon

ADD

¾ cup vanilla almond milk

GLUTEN FREE • DAIRY FREE • VEGAN • EGG FREE • SOY FREE

APPLE-GINGER GREEN SMOOTHIE

MAKES 2 CUPS

FREEZE

1 cup packed baby kale, curly green kale (tough ribs removed), or spinach

½ medium banana, cut into 1-inch chunks

½ Granny Smith apple, cored and roughly chopped

½-inch knob of peeled fresh ginger

Small handful of fresh cilantro

1 tablespoon hemp seeds or chia seeds (optional)

ADD

¾ to 1 cup water

Juice of 1 lemon

Several ice cubes

GLUTEN FREE • DAIRY FREE • VEGAN • EGG FREE • NUT FREE • SOY FREE

Trail Mix Granola Bites

2 cups quick-cooking oats (or old-fashioned rolled oats, pulsed briefly in a food processor or blender to break them up)

$1/2$ cup chopped raw pecans or walnuts

$1/2$ cup sliced almonds

$1/2$ cup raw pepitas (hulled pumpkin seeds)

$1/4$ cup flaxseeds

1 teaspoon ground cinnamon

$1/2$ teaspoon fine sea salt*

1 cup creamy peanut butter or almond butter*

$1/2$ cup honey or maple syrup

1 teaspoon vanilla extract

$1/2$ to $3/4$ cup unsweetened shredded coconut, as needed for rolling

Ingredient Note: If your nut butter is noticeably salty or if you are sensitive to salt, reduce the amount of salt to 1/4 teaspoon. If you are using unsalted nut butter, use the full amount, and add another pinch of salt if the mixture tastes bland.

These irresistible, coconut-dusted granola "bites" are lightly sweet, with a delicious combination of oats, nuts, and seeds inside. They are essentially my no-bake granola bars (a popular recipe on my blog) in ball form. I've learned that rolling the oats mixture into balls is way easier than slicing them into bars. Plus, they're more portable this way. **MAKES 32 BITES**

1. In a large bowl, combine the oats, pecans, almonds, pepitas, flaxseeds, cinnamon, and salt. Mix well using a large spoon or sturdy rubber spatula.

2. In a 2-cup liquid measuring cup or medium bowl, combine the peanut butter, honey, and vanilla. Whisk until thoroughly blended. (If you're having trouble mixing them together, which can happen with natural peanut butters, gently warm the mixture in the microwave or on the stove and try again.)

3. Pour the peanut butter mixture into the oat mixture. Mix well, until every oat is coated.

4. Pour the shredded coconut into a small bowl. Place a large airtight container or freezer bag nearby for the finished bites.

5. Working with a 1-tablespoon cookie dough scoop or with 2 spoons, scoop up about 1 tablespoon of dough at a time and roll it between your palms into a ball about 1 inch in diameter. (If the dough is too wet to roll easily, let it rest for 10 minutes to give the oats time to absorb some excess moisture. Don't wait too long, though, or you'll need to add a little more nut butter or sweetener to get the mixture to stick together.) Roll the ball in the shredded coconut and place it in the container. Repeat with the remaining dough, then refrigerate the balls for at least 1 hour to set.

6. Granola bites keep well for a few days at room temperature, but they are best stored in the refrigerator for up to 2 weeks. They also freeze well for up to 3 months.

GLUTEN FREE: *Use certified gluten-free oats.* • **DAIRY FREE** • **VEGAN:** *Use maple syrup instead of honey.* • **EGG FREE** •
NUT FREE: *Replace the pecans and almonds with additional pepitas and/or sunflower seeds. Use sunflower butter instead of peanut butter.* • **SOY FREE**

TIP: *Feel free to change up the nuts and seeds used here. Just be sure to chop any larger nuts and keep the total amounts the same. For a sweeter treat, replace some of the nuts or seeds with chocolate chips or small dried fruit, like dried cherries, cranberries, or raisins.*

CHANGE IT UP

For traditional banana pancakes, replace the coconut milk with your milk of choice and skip the shredded coconut.

Good (but a little too sweet)

Banana-Coconut Pancakes

These impossibly fluffy, whole-grain pancakes feature double the banana and triple the coconut! Mashed banana infuses the pancakes with banana flavor throughout, and slices of banana are icing on the cake. Coconut milk and coconut oil lend a tropical undertone to the batter, and shredded coconut toasts against the hot skillet for maximum coconut flavor. **MAKES 8 OR 9 MEDIUM PANCAKES; 2 LARGE OR 4 SIDE SERVINGS**

1. If you are using an electric skillet, preheat it to 350°F. In a medium bowl, combine the flour, baking powder, cinnamon, nutmeg, and salt. Whisk to blend.

2. In a small bowl, combine the coconut milk, mashed banana, egg, maple syrup, coconut oil, and vanilla. Whisk until blended. Pour the liquid mixture into the flour mixture and mix just until combined.

3. If you are not using an electric skillet, heat a heavy cast iron skillet or nonstick griddle over medium-low heat. You're ready to start cooking pancakes once a drop of water sizzles on contact with the hot surface. If necessary, lightly oil the cooking surface with additional coconut oil or cooking spray (nonstick surfaces likely won't require any oil).

4. Using a 1/3-cup measuring cup, scoop the batter onto the hot skillet, leaving a couple of inches around each pancake for expansion.

5. Sprinkle shredded coconut evenly over the raw tops of the pancakes while they cook. Cook until small bubbles form on the surface of the pancakes, 2 to 3 minutes (you'll know it's ready to flip when about 1/2 inch of the perimeter is matte instead of glossy). Flip the pancakes, then cook until lightly golden on both sides, 1 to 2 minutes more.

6. Repeat the process with the remaining batter, adding more oil and adjusting the heat as necessary. Serve immediately or keep warm in a 200°F oven. Top individual servings with sliced bananas and serve with more maple syrup or honey on the side.

7. Leftover pancakes can be stored in the refrigerator for up to 3 days, or frozen for up to 2 months. To reheat, stack leftover pancakes and wrap them in a paper towel before gently reheating in the microwave.

1 cup white whole wheat flour or regular whole wheat flour

1 tablespoon baking powder

1/2 teaspoon ground cinnamon

1/4 teaspoon ground nutmeg

1/4 teaspoon fine sea salt

3/4 cup light coconut milk

1/3 cup mashed ripe banana (from about 1 medium-large banana)

1 egg

2 tablespoons maple syrup or honey, plus more for serving

2 tablespoons coconut oil or unsalted butter, melted

1/2 teaspoon vanilla extract

1/4 cup unsweetened shredded coconut, for sprinkling

1 medium banana, thinly sliced, for garnish

GLUTEN FREE: *Substitute all-purpose gluten-free flour for the wheat flour.* • **DAIRY FREE:** *Use coconut oil instead of butter.* • **VEGAN:** *Omit the egg, use maple syrup instead of honey, and coconut oil instead of butter.* • **EGG FREE:** *Omit the egg.* • **NUT FREE • SOY FREE**

Fluffy Cinnamon Oat Pancakes

1 cup milk of choice

1 tablespoon apple cider vinegar or distilled white vinegar

1 cup white whole wheat flour or regular whole wheat flour

$^1/_3$ cup quick-cooking oats

$1^1/_2$ teaspoons baking powder

1 teaspoon ground cinnamon

$^1/_2$ teaspoon baking soda

$^1/_4$ teaspoon fine sea salt

1 egg

2 tablespoons unsalted butter, melted

2 tablespoons maple syrup or honey

1 teaspoon pure vanilla extract

Here's my go-to pancake recipe. These are nice and fluffy, with a hint of cinnamon and some creamy oats inside. The best part? They don't leave me with the jitters like pancakes made with regular all-purpose flour do. I like mine with a dollop of peanut butter on top for extra protein (you haven't lived until you've tried peanut butter on warm pancakes!), and a drizzle of maple syrup. You can also try adding slices of ripe banana or Strawberry Balsamic Sauce (page 202).

MAKES 7 OR 8 MEDIUM PANCAKES, ENOUGH FOR 2 TO 3 SERVINGS

1. In a 2-cup liquid measuring cup, combine the milk and vinegar. Stir to combine and let this homemade "buttermilk" mixture rest until it is lightly curdled, at least 5 minutes.

2. In a medium bowl, whisk together the flour, oats, baking powder, cinnamon, baking soda, and salt.

3. To the buttermilk mixture, whisk in the egg, melted butter, maple syrup, and vanilla. Whisk until thoroughly blended.

4. Pour the liquid mixture into the flour mixture. Stir just until combined (a few small lumps are okay). Let the batter rest for 5 minutes so your pancakes will be nice and fluffy.

5. Meanwhile, if you are using an electric skillet, preheat it to 375°F. Otherwise, heat a heavy cast iron skillet or nonstick griddle over medium-low heat. You're ready to start cooking pancakes once a drop of water sizzles on contact with the hot surface. If necessary, lightly oil the cooking surface with additional butter, oil, or cooking spray (nonstick surfaces likely won't require any oil).

6. Gently stir the batter one last time, in case the liquid has separated. Using a $^1/_3$-cup measuring cup, scoop a scant $^1/_3$ cup batter onto the warm skillet, leaving a couple of inches around each pancake for expansion. This batter is a little thick, so you might need to spread it out a bit by dabbing the edges with the back of your measuring cup immediately after pouring it onto the skillet.

7. Cook until small bubbles form on the surface of the pancakes, 2 to 3 minutes (you'll know it's ready to flip when about $^1/_2$ inch of the perimeter is matte instead of glossy). Flip the pancakes, then cook until lightly golden on both sides, 1 to 2 minutes more.

8. Repeat the process with the remaining batter, adding more oil and adjusting the heat as necessary. Serve the pancakes immediately with toppings of your choosing, or keep them warm in a 200°F oven.

9. Leftover pancakes can be stored in the refrigerator for up to 3 days, or frozen for up to 2 months. To reheat, stack leftover pancakes and wrap them in a paper towel before gently reheating in the microwave.

TIP: *To thaw frozen pancakes, the microwave works best. Stack up to 4 pancakes on top of each other, wrap in a paper towel, and microwave just until they are heated through the middle, 1 to 2 minutes. Don't overdo it, or you'll end up with tough pancakes.*

GLUTEN FREE: *Substitute certified gluten-free oat flour for the wheat flour, use certified gluten-free oats, and let the batter rest for 5 extra minutes.* • **DAIRY FREE:** *Use nondairy milk and olive oil instead of butter.* • **VEGAN:** *Use nondairy milk, replace the egg with 1 tablespoon ground flaxseed, and use olive oil instead of butter.* • **EGG FREE:** *Replace the egg with 1 tablespoon ground flaxseed.* • **NUT FREE** • **SOY FREE**

Best Waffles Ever

These waffles are everything I want a waffle to be, and tons of my blog readers say the same. They are perfectly crisp on the outside and fluffy on the inside. These waffles are made with oat flour, which you can easily make yourself (see Note). Oat flour lends a lightly creamy texture to the interiors of the waffles, and confers all of the health benefits of oats as well. This recipe yields a modest number of waffles (perfect for two servings), so double it if you're serving a family. **MAKES THREE 7-INCH ROUND BELGIAN WAFFLES OR 5 THINNER EGGO-STYLE WAFFLES**

1. In a medium bowl, whisk together the oat flour, baking powder, salt, and cinnamon.

2. In a small bowl, combine the milk, coconut oil, eggs, maple syrup, and vanilla. Whisk until well blended. (If your coconut oil solidifies on contact with the cold ingredients, gently warm the mixture in the microwave in 30-second intervals, just until it melts again.)

3. Pour the wet ingredients into the flour mixture. Stir with a big spoon just until combined (the batter will still be a little lumpy). Let the batter rest for 10 minutes so the oat flour has time to soak up some of the moisture. Preheat your waffle iron (if your waffle iron has a temperature/browning dial, set it to high).

4. Give the batter one more swirl with your spoon in case the liquid has separated. The batter will be thick, but don't worry! Pour enough batter onto the heated waffle iron to cover the center and most of the central surface area, and close the lid. Wait to check on the waffle until there is no more steam rising from the waffle iron.

5. Cook until the waffle is crisp and golden brown (you may need to cook these longer than your waffle iron's indicator light suggests). If you aren't serving the waffles right away, keep them warm on a baking sheet in a 200°F oven (don't stack them, or they'll lose crispness).

6. Repeat with remaining batter. Serve the waffles with maple syrup (or any other toppings that sound good). Leftover waffles refrigerate and freeze beautifully. Just store in freezer bags and pop individual waffles into the toaster until warmed through.

1½ cups oat flour* *(home-made)*

2 teaspoons baking powder

½ teaspoon fine sea salt

Pinch of ground cinnamon

¾ cup milk of choice

5 tablespoons coconut oil or unsalted butter, melted

2 eggs

2 tablespoons maple syrup, plus more for serving

1 teaspoon vanilla extract

*Ingredient Note: To make your own oat flour, simply blend old-fashioned rolled or quick-cooking oats in a food processor or blender until they are ground into a fine flour. After blending, I typically end up with a little more oat flour than the original measurement of oats. I like to make a few cups of oat flour at once and store the rest in an airtight bag for later. Once you've blended the flour, measure it using the "spoon and swoop" method (see page xxii) to make sure you have the right amount.

GLUTEN FREE: *Use certified gluten-free oats or certified gluten-free oat flour.* • **DAIRY FREE:** *Use your favorite nondairy milk and coconut oil instead of butter.* • **VEGAN:** *Use your favorite nondairy milk, coconut oil instead of butter, and omit the eggs.* • **EGG FREE:** *Omit the eggs.* • **NUT FREE** • **SOY FREE**

fair

or muffins

Banana Nut Bread

¾ cup roughly chopped raw walnuts or pecans

⅓ cup melted coconut oil or extra-virgin olive oil

½ cup honey or maple syrup

2 eggs

1 cup mashed overripe bananas (from about 2½ medium or 2 large bananas)

¼ cup milk of choice or water

1 teaspoon baking soda

1 teaspoon vanilla extract

½ teaspoon fine sea salt

½ teaspoon ground cinnamon, plus more to swirl on top

1¾ cups white whole wheat flour or regular whole wheat flour

nuts

This banana bread is one of the most popular recipes on my blog. Have you tried it yet? This bread is entirely naturally sweetened and made with whole grains, but no one will know that it's not grandma's recipe. For this version, I added freshly toasted nuts for traditional banana nut flavor. I love this banana bread for breakfast or as a snack, with a spread of peanut or almond butter on top.

MAKES 1 LOAF

1. Preheat the oven to 325°F. Line a small rimmed baking sheet with parchment paper for easy cleanup. Grease a 9 × 5-inch loaf pan.

2. Pour the chopped nuts onto the prepared baking sheet and bake until the nuts are fragrant and toasted, about 5 minutes, stirring halfway. Leave the oven on.

3. In a large bowl, beat the coconut oil and honey together with a whisk until combined. Add the eggs and beat well. Whisk in the mashed bananas and milk until blended. (If your coconut oil solidifies on contact with the cold ingredients, gently warm the mixture in the microwave in 30-second intervals until it melts again, or let the bowl rest in a warm place for a few minutes.)

4. Add the baking soda, vanilla, salt, and cinnamon and whisk to blend. Switch to a big spoon and stir in the flour, just until combined (some lumps are okay). Gently fold in the toasted nuts.

5. Pour the batter into the greased loaf pan and sprinkle the top lightly with additional cinnamon. If you'd like a pretty swirled effect, run the tip of a knife across the batter in a zigzag pattern.

6. Bake until a toothpick inserted into the center comes out clean, 1 hour to 1 hour 5 minutes. Let the bread cool in the loaf pan for 10 minutes, then transfer to a cooling rack to cool for 20 minutes before slicing.

7. This bread is moist, so it will keep for just 2 to 3 days at room temperature. Store it in the refrigerator for 5 to 7 days, or in the freezer for up to 3 months. I like to slice the bread before freezing and thaw individual slices, either by lightly toasting them or thawing them in the microwave.

GLUTEN FREE: *Substitute an all-purpose gluten-free flour blend for the wheat flour.* • **DAIRY FREE:** *Use nondairy milk (I used almond milk) or water.* • **VEGAN:** *Use maple syrup instead of honey, replace the eggs with Flax "Eggs" (see page 221), and choose nondairy milk or water.* • **EGG FREE:** *Replace the eggs with Flax "Eggs."* • **NUT FREE:** *Skip the nuts. Your banana bread may need only 55 to 60 minutes of baking time.* • **SOY FREE**

CHANGE IT UP

You can replace the nuts with
$1/2$ to $3/4$ cup mix-ins of your
choice, like chocolate chips,
raisins, chopped dried fruit,
or slices of banana. To make
banana nut muffins, spoon the
batter into 12 muffin cups
(greased or lined with muffin
liners if the muffin tin is not
nonstick) and bake at 325°F
until a toothpick inserted into
the center comes out clean,
22 to 25 minutes.

Blueberry Maple Muffins

These blueberry-studded beauties are my pride and joy. I set out to develop a healthier recipe with all the hallmarks of a classic blueberry muffin–impossibly fluffy and moist, with a sour cream-like tang, notes of vanilla, and plenty of jammy blueberries. Nine tries later, I finally got it. Here they are–whole-grain, naturally sweetened muffins that meet (no, *exceed*) all of my requirements. I top them with a light sprinkle of crunchy, shimmery raw sugar to throw off any suspicion that these muffins possess redeeming qualities.

MAKES 12 MUFFINS

1. Preheat the oven to 400°F. Grease 12 cups of a muffin tin (or use a nonstick muffin tin).

2. In a large bowl, combine $1^3/_4$ cups of the flour with the baking powder, baking soda, and salt. Blend well with a whisk.

3. In a medium bowl, combine the oil and maple syrup and beat together with a whisk until combined. Add the eggs and beat well. Then, add the yogurt and vanilla and mix well. (If the coconut oil solidifies on contact with the cold ingredients, gently warm the mixture in the microwave in 30-second intervals, just until it melts again.)

4. Pour the wet mixture into the flour mixture and mix with a big spoon, just until combined (a few lumps are okay). In a small bowl, toss the blueberries with the remaining 1 teaspoon flour (this helps prevent the blueberries from sinking to the bottom). Gently fold the blueberries into the batter.

5. Dividing evenly, spoon the batter into the 12 muffin cups. Sprinkle the tops of the muffins with turbinado sugar. Bake until the muffins are golden on top and a toothpick inserted into a muffin comes out clean, 16 to 19 minutes.

6. Place the muffin tin on a cooling rack to cool. You might need to run a butter knife along the outer edge of the muffins to loosen them from the pan. If you have leftover muffins, cover and store them at room temperature for up to 2 days, or in the refrigerator for up to 5 days. Freeze leftover muffins for up to 3 months; thaw individual muffins in the microwave as needed.

$1^3/_4$ cups plus 1 teaspoon white whole wheat flour or regular whole wheat flour

1 teaspoon baking powder

$^1/_2$ teaspoon baking soda

$^1/_2$ teaspoon fine sea salt

$^1/_3$ cup melted coconut oil or extra-virgin olive oil

$^1/_2$ cup maple syrup or honey

2 eggs

1 cup plain Greek yogurt

2 teaspoons vanilla extract

1 cup blueberries (fresh or frozen)

1 tablespoon turbinado (raw) sugar, for sprinkling on top

CHANGE IT UP

▸ You can substitute any other muffin-worthy fresh fruit for the blueberries. If you're using larger berries (like strawberries) or other fruit (like peaches), chop them into smaller pieces first.

GLUTEN FREE: *Substitute all-purpose gluten-free flour for the wheat flour.* • **DAIRY FREE/VEGAN:** *Replace the yogurt with vegan "buttermilk:" Combine $^2/_3$ cup nondairy milk (like almond milk) with 2 teaspoons vinegar and let rest for 5 minutes before proceeding. For vegan muffins, also substitute Flax "Eggs" (see page 221) for the eggs.* • **EGG FREE:** *Substitute Flax "Eggs" for the eggs.* • **NUT FREE** • **SOY FREE**

or apples
or zuchini

Carrot Cake Breakfast Cookies

1 cup quick-cooking oats

1 cup white whole wheat flour or regular whole wheat flour

1 teaspoon baking powder

1 teaspoon ground cinnamon

$\frac{1}{2}$ teaspoon fine sea salt

$\frac{1}{4}$ teaspoon ground ginger

$1\frac{1}{2}$ cups peeled grated carrots (about $\frac{1}{2}$ pound)

1 cup roughly chopped raw pecans or walnuts

$\frac{1}{4}$ cup raisins, preferably golden

$\frac{1}{2}$ cup honey or maple syrup

$\frac{1}{2}$ cup melted coconut oil

Breakfast cookies! Why not? These large breakfast cookies taste like carrot cake and are as hearty as a bran muffin. They include lots of nuts to stick with you for several hours. I prefer quick-cooking oats here because they disappear into the rest of the batter, but offer all of the same health benefits as old-fashioned oats. Cookie loves it when I make these cookies because she gets to eat some of the carrot scraps. I'm convinced that she can hear the vegetable peeler as it cuts through the air on the way toward a carrot. She comes running!

MAKES 10 LARGE COOKIES

1. Preheat the oven to 375°F. Line a large rimmed baking sheet with parchment paper.

2. In a large bowl, combine the oats, flour, baking powder, cinnamon, salt, and ginger. Whisk to blend. Add the carrots, pecans, and raisins and stir to combine.

3. In a medium bowl, combine the honey and coconut oil. Whisk until blended. Pour the liquid mixture into the flour mixture and stir just until combined. The dough might be rather wet, but don't worry.

4. Drop $\frac{1}{4}$-cup scoops of dough (an ice cream scoop with a wire scraper is perfect for this) onto the prepared baking sheet, leaving several inches of space around each one. Use the palm of your hand to gently flatten each cookie to about $\frac{3}{4}$ inch thick.

5. Bake until the cookies are golden and firm around the edges, 15 to 17 minutes. Cool the cookies on the baking sheet on a cooling rack for 10 minutes, then carefully transfer the cookies to the rack to cool completely (otherwise, the bottoms can brown too much). Leftover breakfast cookies will keep, covered, at room temperature for up to 2 days, in the refrigerator for up to 5 days, and in the freezer for up to 3 months.

GLUTEN FREE: *Substitute $1\frac{1}{4}$ cups oat flour for the wheat flour. Be sure to use certified gluten-free oats and oat flour.* • **DAIRY FREE** • **VEGAN:** *Use maple syrup instead of honey.* • **EGG FREE** • **NUT FREE:** *Replace the nuts with $\frac{2}{3}$ cup pepitas (hulled pumpkin seeds) or omit them altogether.* • **SOY FREE**

CHANGE IT UP
The carrot version of these cookies is my favorite, but you can replace the grated carrots with grated apples or zucchini (no need to peel either of them). If you're watching your fat or sugar intake, you can reduce the amount of coconut oil and sweetener somewhat by using 1/3 cup each coconut oil, sweetener, and unsweetened applesauce.

Creamy Cashew Chai Lattes

1 cup raw cashews

4 cups water, divided, plus more for soaking the cashews, as needed

6 chai tea bags

1/4 cup honey or maple syrup

1 tablespoon vanilla extract

1 teaspoon ground cinnamon

1/2 teaspoon ground ginger

1/4 teaspoon ground nutmeg

1/4 teaspoon ground cardamom or cloves

4 twists freshly ground black pepper

Fine sea salt

4 star anise or cinnamon sticks (optional), for garnish

TIME WARNING: *If you don't have a high-powered blender (like a Vitamix or Blendtec), you will need to soak the cashews for at least 4 hours.*

CHANGE IT UP

▸ You can use dates to sweeten this tea, if you prefer. Fresh, juicy dates blend right in, but older dates will require a 10-minute soak in warm water beforehand. I used 8 to 10 dates to reach the same level of sweetness as 1/4 cup honey.

These chai lattes are both ultra creamy and nutritious, thanks to the raw cashews that form the creamy base. Real chai tea and plenty of ground spices make it taste just like the coffee shop treat. If you have a decent or better blender, you probably won't have to strain the mixture at all. Enjoy these lattes warm in the winter, or poured over ice in the summer. They are both delicious!

MAKES 4 SERVINGS

1. If you do not have a high-powered blender such as a Vitamix or Blendtec, soak the cashews in water for at least 4 hours or overnight in the refrigerator. If you do have a high-powered blender, you can just skip the soaking step. (I am lazy and let my Vitamix do the work, but I feel obligated to mention that soaked cashews may be easier to digest.)

2. In a medium saucepan, bring 2 cups of the water to a simmer over high heat. Remove the pot from the heat, add the chai tea bags, and steep for 4 minutes. Discard the bags. Set the tea aside.

3. Meanwhile, if you soaked the cashews, drain them and rinse until the water runs clear. Place the cashews in a blender. Add the honey, vanilla, cinnamon, ginger, nutmeg, cardamom, black pepper, and a dash of salt.

4. Pour the tea into the blender, but keep the pot handy if you intend to drink warm tea soon. Securely fasten the lid. Start on the lowest setting and increase the speed until the cashews are totally pulverized. This could take 2 minutes in a high-powered blender, or longer in a regular blender.

5. Pour in the remaining 2 cups water. Secure the lid and blend again. Taste, and add more sweetener if desired. If you prefer a spicier chai, add up to an additional 1/2 teaspoon cinnamon and 1/4 teaspoon ginger. If your blender can't blend the cashews into creamy oblivion no matter how long you blend, strain the milk through a fine-mesh strainer or cheesecloth.

6. *For warm chai tea:* Use your blender's soup function until it's sufficiently heated. If you don't have a fancy-pants blender with a soup function, no problem—warm the tea in a saucepan on the stove over medium-high heat, stirring frequently, just until the mixture comes to a simmer. Pour into a mug and garnish with a star anise or cinnamon stick, if desired.

7. *For iced chai tea:* Fill a drinking glass with ice and pour the chai tea over it. Garnish as desired.

8. Store leftover chai tea in a covered container (a mason jar is perfect) in the refrigerator for up to 4 days. It settles over time, so you'll need to shake the jar or thoroughly whisk the contents again before serving.

TIP: *You can make these drinks caffeine-free by using a decaffeinated chai rooibos tea. I'm not too particular about my chai tea brands, but I can vouch for Numi, Tazo, and Trader Joe's.*

GLUTEN FREE • DAIRY FREE • VEGAN: *Use maple syrup instead of honey.* **• EGG FREE • SOY FREE**

Everything Avocado Toast

Creamy avocado on freshly toasted bread is one of life's simple pleasures, one that I didn't meet until I was an adult. Everything bagels were a childhood favorite of mine, so I mashed my two favorites together to make "everything" avocado toasts. It's hard to beat basic avocado toast with sea salt on top, but this toast wins!

MAKES 2 AVOCADO TOASTS

2 slices whole-grain bread

1 large or 2 small avocados, halved and pitted

Fine sea salt

Everything Spice Blend

Toast the bread in the toaster until golden. Using a spoon, scoop the flesh of the avocado onto a plate. Then, add a dash of salt and use a fork to mash the avocado until it is mostly smooth. Scoop the mashed avocado onto the bread and spread it into an even layer. Top with a sprinkle of Everything Spice Blend and serve immediately.

EVERYTHING SPICE BLEND

Toasting the seeds in a skillet brings out amazing fresh-from-the-oven, everything-bagel flavor. This everything spice blend is surprisingly great on peanut butter and unsurprisingly awesome on buttered toast. You can also sprinkle it over a toasted bagel with cream cheese, of course, and it's pretty tasty when lightly sprinkled over Creamy Roasted Cauliflower Soup (page 94). **MAKES ½ CUP**

2 tablespoons raw sunflower seeds

2 tablespoons sesame seeds

2 tablespoons poppy seeds

1 tablespoon dried minced onion

2 teaspoons dried minced garlic

1 teaspoon kosher salt

¼ teaspoon red pepper flakes (optional)

1. In a small skillet, combine the sunflower seeds, sesame seeds, poppy seeds, dried onion, dried garlic, salt, and red pepper flakes (if using) and toast over medium heat. Cook, stirring frequently, until the spices are fragrant and the sunflower seeds are turning lightly golden on the edges, about 5 minutes. (Keep an eye on the pan, as the seeds can burn if they are not stirred frequently, especially during the last couple of minutes.) Transfer the mix to a small bowl to cool.

2. Store cooled leftover spice blend in a jar at room temperature for up to 1 month.

GLUTEN FREE: *Use gluten-free bread.* • **DAIRY FREE** • **VEGAN** • **EGG FREE** • **NUT FREE** • **SOY FREE**

Spicy Breakfast Fajitas with Fried Eggs and Guacamole

VEGGIES

1 tablespoon extra-virgin olive oil

2 red, yellow, or orange bell peppers, sliced into ½-inch-wide strips

½ medium white onion, sliced into ½-inch-wide wedges

1 teaspoon ground cumin

½ teaspoon chili powder

Pinch of red pepper flakes

Fine sea salt

2 cloves garlic, pressed or minced

1 tablespoon lime juice

FAJITAS AND GARNISHES

6 corn tortillas or small flour tortillas

6 teaspoons extra-virgin olive oil, divided

6 eggs

Quick Guacamole (page 34)

⅓ cup crumbled feta cheese (about 2 ounces)

Handful of fresh cilantro, chopped

Freshly ground black pepper

Hot sauce and/or your favorite salsa

I'm a sucker for any combination of Mexican flavors with eggs, and these breakfast fajitas are no exception. They're a riff on all the breakfast tacos I enjoyed in Austin, Texas. I make them with a fried egg instead of steak, plenty of spicy sautéed peppers, and a generous spread of guacamole. While you can prepare your eggs however you'd like, I recommend frying them in olive oil to golden, caramelized, crispy-edged perfection, which coaxes out tons of extra flavor.

These fresh fajitas are a great meal on their own (plan on 2 to 3 fajitas per person), but you could also stretch them out with a side of seasoned black beans (from Taco Party!, page 189) or Shredded Brussels and Kale Hash with Crispy Parmsean (page 45).

MAKES 6 FAJITAS

1. *To prepare the veggies:* In a large skillet, heat the olive oil over medium heat. Once the oil is shimmering, add the bell peppers and onion, cumin, chili powder, red pepper flakes, and a few dashes of salt. Toss to combine, cover the pan, and cook, stirring occasionally, until the vegetables are easily pierced by a fork, 5 to 8 minutes. Uncover and continue cooking, stirring often, until the vegetables are lightly charred on the edges, about 5 minutes more. Add the garlic, toss well, and cook for another minute. Remove the pan from the heat and drizzle in the lime juice. Toss, season to taste with additional salt, and cover to keep warm.

2. *Meanwhile, to prepare the fajitas:* In a small skillet over medium heat, warm each tortilla on both sides until heated through. Stack the warmed tortillas on a plate as they are done and cover them with a kitchen towel to keep warm.

3. In the same skillet, heat 1 teaspoon of the oil over medium heat until shimmering. Carefully crack an egg and pour it into the skillet without breaking the yolk. Fry the egg, lifting and tilting the pan occasionally to redistribute the oil, until the whites are set and the yolk is cooked to your preferred level of doneness. Transfer the egg to a plate and repeat with the remaining eggs.

(CONTINUED)

(CONTINUED FROM PAGE 32)

4. To assemble the breakfast fajitas, place a fried egg on each tortilla, followed by a generous spread of guacamole down the length of the egg white. Top with some veggies. Sprinkle with feta, cilantro, and freshly ground pepper. Serve with hot sauce and/or salsa on the side.

QUICK GUACAMOLE

MAKES ABOUT 1¼ CUPS

2 avocados, halved and pitted

1 tablespoon lime juice, or more if needed

Kosher salt

Using a spoon, scoop the flesh of the avocados into a small bowl. Add the lime juice and ¼ teaspoon salt and mash with a pastry cutter, potato masher, or fork until the mixture is blended and no longer chunky. Taste and add additional lime juice and/or salt, if necessary.

GLUTEN FREE: *Use certified gluten-free corn tortillas.* • **DAIRY FREE:** *Skip the feta cheese.* • **NUT FREE** • **SOY FREE**

Simple Honey Scones

These simple scones are a sweet breakfast treat that you can whip up in no time flat. I have the recipe memorized already! They're tender, fluffy, and almost biscuit-like on the inside, just perfect for weekend brunches. Serve them with Strawberry Balsamic Sauce (page 200), your favorite jam, or citrus curd.

This recipe is based on traditional cream scones, which are butterless scones made with all-purpose flour, a little sugar, and lots of heavy cream. My version is made with white whole wheat flour (no one will know), honey, and regular coconut milk instead of the cream. The light honey flavor becomes a little more pronounced as they cool. These scones are faintly sweet as is, but a light sprinkle of raw sugar on top offers a sweet, irresistible crackle in every bite.

MAKES 8 SCONES

2½ cups white whole wheat flour or regular whole wheat flour, plus more as needed

2½ teaspoons baking powder

½ teaspoon fine sea salt

½ teaspoon ground cinnamon

1 cup canned coconut milk,* plus more for brushing on top

¼ cup honey

1 teaspoon vanilla extract

1 tablespoon turbinado (raw) sugar

1. Preheat the oven to 350°F. Line a large rimmed baking sheet with parchment paper. In a medium bowl, combine the flour, baking powder, salt, and cinnamon. Whisk to combine.

2. In a 2-cup liquid measuring cup or small bowl, combine the coconut milk, honey, and vanilla. Whisk to blend. Pour the wet ingredients into the flour mixture and mix with a big spoon until you have a cohesive dough. If the dough is sticky and unmanageable, add another tablespoon of flour and stir just until incorporated. Repeat if necessary.

3. Lightly flour your work surface and turn the dough over onto it. Knead the dough a few times, just enough to bring the dough together. Then press the dough into an even round about 1 inch thick all around.

4. Use a sharp chef's knife to cut the round into 8 even wedges, as you would a pizza. Separate the wedges and place each one on the prepared baking sheet several inches from the next. Brush the tops of the scones liberally with coconut milk and sprinkle them with the turbinado sugar.

5. Bake until the tops are lightly golden brown and firm to the touch, 25 to 27 minutes. Promptly transfer the scones to a cooling rack to cool. These scones are best enjoyed the day of, but can be stored for a couple of days at room temperature, or up to 3 months in the freezer.

Ingredient Note: Be sure to use regular (not light) coconut milk for the right texture; it's still lower in fat than heavy cream, and lighter milks of any variety won't work the same. If you open your can and find that the heavy cream component has separated from the coconut water, you'll need to gently warm the two together until you can whisk them back together, either in the microwave or on the stove.

CHANGE IT UP

▸ You can stir up to 1 cup fresh fruit or nuts (chopped if large) into the dry flour mixture. Your scones might require a few minutes longer in the oven, given the increase in volume.

DAIRY FREE • VEGAN: *Substitute maple syrup for the honey. The scones won't brown as nicely on top, but the baking time is not affected.* **• EGG FREE • NUT FREE • SOY FREE**

Spinach-Artichoke Quiche

THYME ALMOND MEAL CRUST

2 cups packed almond meal (8 ounces)

3 cloves garlic, pressed or minced

1 teaspoon dried thyme

$1/2$ teaspoon fine sea salt

Freshly ground black pepper

$1/3$ cup extra-virgin olive oil

1 tablespoon plus 1 teaspoon water

SPINACH-ARTICHOKE FILLING

2 teaspoons extra-virgin olive oil

3 cups packed baby spinach (about 3 ounces), roughly chopped

4 eggs

1 cup milk*

$1/2$ teaspoon fine sea salt

$1/4$ teaspoon red pepper flakes

1 cup drained and roughly chopped marinated artichokes

$1/2$ cup grated Parmesan cheese (about 1 ounce), divided

Ingredient Note: I used 2% milk here, but anything from fat-free to whole milk will work fine. Plain, unsweetened almond milk works, too.

The inside of this quiche tastes like my favorite spinach-artichoke dip, but the crisp, herbed crust might be the best part. It's made with almond meal instead of all-purpose flour, so it's full of savory, nutty flavor. The slices hold their shape, but the crust is tender and yields easily to a fork. You won't make a quiche with regular flour ever again! Serve this quiche with a green side salad tossed with my Liquid Gold Salad Dressing (page 52) for a simple, sophisticated breakfast, lunch, or dinner. **MAKES 6 TO 8 SERVINGS**

1. *To make the crust:* Preheat the oven to 400°F. Grease a 10-inch cast iron skillet or 9-inch pie pan with olive oil. In a medium bowl, stir together the almond meal, garlic, thyme, salt, and several twists of pepper. Pour in the olive oil and water and stir until the mixture is thoroughly combined.

2. Press the dough into the prepared skillet or pan until it is evenly dispersed across the bottom and up the sides (if you are using a cast iron skillet, make sure the dough goes at least $1^1/4$ inches up the sides). Bake until the crust is lightly golden and firm to the touch, 15 to 20 minutes.

3. *Meanwhile, to prepare the filling:* In a large skillet, warm the olive oil over medium heat until shimmering. Swirl the pan to coat, then toss in the spinach. Cook, stirring frequently, until the spinach has wilted and there is very little moisture left in the pan, 2 to 4 minutes. Transfer the mixture to a plate to cool.

4. In a bowl, whisk together the eggs, milk, salt, and pepper flakes. Stir in the slightly cooled spinach mixture, chopped artichokes, and most of the Parmesan, reserving a couple of tablespoons for sprinkling on top later.

5. Once the crust is done baking, pour in the egg mixture and top it with the remaining Parmesan. Return to the oven and bake until the center is firm to the touch and cooked through, 30 to 33 minutes. Let the quiche cool for 5 to 10 minutes before slicing it into 6 to 8 even wedges (depending on desired serving size) with a sharp knife. Serve immediately.

6. Leftovers keep well for up to 3 days in the refrigerator. You can serve leftovers chilled, but I prefer to warm them up a bit in a low oven or microwave.

GLUTEN FREE • SOY FREE

CHANGE IT UP

You can use this quiche as a template and substitute other veggies (about 2 cups) for the artichoke and spinach, and other cheeses for the Parmesan. Just be sure to cook the veggies until they're tender using your preferred method, then proceed with the recipe as written. One of my friends loves to make a broccoli-cheddar quiche with lightly steamed, chopped broccoli.

Burst Cherry Tomato, Basil, and Goat Cheese Scrambled Egg Toasts

Make ½?

Here's proof that simple can yield incredible results. These simple toasts feature contrasting textures that I just can't get enough of–creamy scrambled eggs and goat cheese, tender and saucy burst cherry tomatoes, and thick whole-grain toast that plays an essential supporting role but shatters in the most satisfying of ways.

MAKES 4 SERVINGS

1. In a large heavy-bottomed stainless steel saucepan, warm the olive oil over medium heat until shimmering. Add the tomatoes and ¼ teaspoon of the salt and cover the pot. Cook, shimmying the pot occasionally to redistribute the tomatoes, until most of the tomatoes are bursting out of their skins and the olive oil is reddish and somewhat saucy, 5 to 7 minutes. Remove the pot from the heat and set aside.

2. Meanwhile, toast the bread in a toaster until the outsides are lightly golden and crisp. Spread each piece of warm toast generously with goat cheese and set aside.

3. Crack the eggs into a medium bowl. Add the milk, the remaining ¼ teaspoon salt, and a few twists of pepper. Beat the mixture with a whisk until it's thoroughly combined and the mixture is pure yellow.

4. In a medium skillet, melt the butter over medium-high heat, swirling to coat the pan. Pour in the egg mixture, then use a heat-resistant spatula to scrape the eggs along the bottom and sides of the skillet until they begin to clump and the spatula leaves a trail on the bottom of the skillet, about 1½ minutes.

5. Reduce the heat to low and gently fold the eggs over on themselves until they are clumpy but still slightly wet, 30 to 60 seconds. Remove the pan from the heat and stir in half of the cherry tomatoes and half of the basil. Season to taste with additional salt and pepper, if necessary.

6. Divide the scrambled egg mixture on top of the prepared toasts. Top with the remaining tomatoes and basil. Serve immediately.

1 tablespoon extra-virgin olive oil

1 pint cherry or grape tomatoes

½ teaspoon fine sea salt, divided

4 large slices (½-inch thick) crusty whole-grain bread

4 ounces goat cheese, at room temperature

6 eggs

2 tablespoons neutral-flavored milk of choice

Freshly ground black pepper

A couple pats of unsalted butter or 2 teaspoons extra-virgin olive oil

2 tablespoons chopped fresh basil, divided

GLUTEN FREE: *Use gluten-free bread.* • **NUT FREE** • **SOY FREE**

Kale, Sweet Potato, and Feta Scramble

SAUTÉED SWEET POTATO AND KALE

2 tablespoons extra-virgin olive oil

Pinch of red pepper flakes

1 pound sweet potatoes (about 2 small or 1 large), peeled and cut into ¼-inch cubes

¼ teaspoon fine sea salt

½ medium bunch kale (about 4 ounces), preferably Tuscan (lacinato), tough ribs removed and leaves chopped into bite-size pieces

½ cup water

⅓ cup chopped green onion (2 to 4), plus more for garnish

SCRAMBLED EGGS

8 eggs

2 tablespoons neutral-flavored milk of choice

¼ teaspoon fine sea salt

Freshly ground black pepper

2 teaspoons extra-virgin olive oil

GARNISHES

⅓ cup crumbled feta cheese (about 2 ounces)

1 avocado, sliced into thin strips

Hot sauce (I love Cholula)

After a late night out, I'd gladly fork over 10 dollars for a serving of this veggie-packed, restorative scramble. Or, I could invite a few friends over for brunch and serve us all for the price of one. This scramble is a well-balanced breakfast (or lunch or dinner) option featuring tender cubes of sweet potato, savory kale, scrambled eggs, salty crumbled feta, and some creamy avocado, for good measure.

MAKES 4 SERVINGS

1. *To prepare the sweet potato and kale:* In a large skillet, heat the olive oil over medium heat until shimmering. Add the pepper flakes (more if you like heat, less if you don't) and cook until fragrant, about 30 seconds. Add the sweet potatoes and salt and toss to coat. Add a few handfuls of kale and toss to coat in the oil. Repeat until all of the kale has been added to the pan.

2. Pour the water into the pan, being careful to avoid oil splatters in the process. Cover the skillet, reduce the heat to medium-low, and cook for 5 minutes. Uncover and toss in the green onions. Cook, stirring occasionally, until all of the liquid has evaporated and the sweet potatoes are tender and easily pierced through by a fork, 9 to 11 minutes. Set aside.

3. *Meanwhile, to scramble the eggs:* Crack the eggs into a medium bowl. Add the milk, salt, and a few twists of pepper. Beat the mixture with a whisk until it's thoroughly combined and the mixture is pure yellow.

4. In a medium skillet, warm the oil over medium-high heat until shimmering. Swirl the pan to coat and pour in the egg mixture. Use a heat-resistant spatula to scrape the eggs along the bottom and sides of the skillet until they begin to clump and the spatula leaves a trail on the bottom of the skillet, about 1½ minutes.

5. Reduce the heat to low and gently fold the eggs over on themselves until they are clumpy but still slightly wet, 30 to 60 seconds. Scoot the eggs into the pan of cooked sweet potato and kale. Stir to combine, then season to taste with salt and pepper.

6. Spoon the mixture into bowls and garnish each one with a sprinkle of feta, a few slices of avocado, and chopped green onion. Serve immediately, with hot sauce on the side.

GLUTEN FREE • DAIRY FREE: *Use nondairy milk. Omit the feta and add some Quick-Pickled Red Onions (page 222) or pickled jalapeños to make up for it.* **NUT FREE • SOY FREE**

CHANGE IT UP

This recipe is flexible. You can use more of one type of veggie and less of another, which makes it a great way to use up leftover vegetables in your vegetable drawer.

Shredded Brussels and Kale Hash with Crispy Parmesan

O h, how I love extra crispy diner hash browns. Here's a more colorful and redeeming option, which is just as addictive. Shredded cabbage, sprouts, carrots, and kale are tossed with a little Parmesan cheese and olive oil. The combination becomes tender and crisp when roasted on a couple of large sheet pans. This hash is a great side for any savory breakfast in this book. It's also fantastic with a fried egg on top and a side of whole-grain toast, with your favorite hot sauce on the side.

The easiest way to shred all those veggies is by using a food processor. Otherwise, it can be a time-consuming endeavor. Use your food processor's slicing disc for the cabbage, sprouts, and kale; use the shredding disc for the carrots and cheese. You can also use a sharp knife or mandoline; please be careful. (Or else buy preshredded veggies at the grocery store.) It will seem like you have a ton of veggies, but they shrink down significantly in the oven. This recipe shares some of the same shredded vegetables as my Colorful Kale, Apple, and Fennel Slaw with Tart Cherries (page 68), so you might plan to shred extra veggies and make some slaw for lunch. **MAKES 4 SIDE SERVINGS**

8 cups shredded veggies (I like equal parts red cabbage, Brussels sprouts, kale, and carrots)

$3/4$ cup grated Parmesan cheese (about $1^1/_2$ ounces)

2 to 3 tablespoons extra-virgin olive oil

$1/4$ teaspoon fine sea salt

1. Preheat the oven to 425°F with racks in the middle and upper third of the oven. Line 2 large rimmed baking sheets with parchment paper to prevent sticking.

2. On one of the prepared sheets, combine all of the shredded vegetables. Top with the Parmesan, 2 tablespoons olive oil, and the salt. Toss until all of the vegetables are lightly coated in olive oil, adding another tablespoon of oil if necessary. Transfer half of the mixture to the other prepared baking sheet. Spread the mixture evenly over the pans.

3. Place one pan on the upper rack and the other on the middle rack. Bake until the hash is crisp and golden, 16 to 22 minutes, tossing and switching the pans halfway. Serve immediately. Leftovers keep in the refrigerator for up to 3 days.

GLUTEN FREE • DAIRY FREE/VEGAN: *Skip the cheese (for slightly less crispy results) and use the full 3 tablespoons of olive oil.* • **EGG FREE • NUT FREE • SOY FREE**

2 *Salads*

SALADS HAVE COME A LONG WAY. When I was little, my salad experiences typically featured pale green lettuce, a heavy pour of ranch or Italian dressing, and croutons that could nearly break a tooth. I liked them that way, too.

My salads have grown to cover my entire plate, and my appreciation for salads has transformed into an epic love affair. Salads made with fresh greens, loads of veggies, whole grains, and freshly toasted nuts are all that is good and delicious in this world! They qualify as a full meal and allow me to chomp on a big bowl of food with no ill side effects.

In this chapter, you will find satisfying salads that can serve as a full lunch or dinner. You can also serve them in smaller portions as side salads. Since a good side salad is my ideal side dish, I've offered a variety of simple side salad suggestions and salad dressings to help you improvise.

FIVE STEPS TO AN EPIC SALAD

1. **CHOOSE A THEME.** Even if you want to throw together a salad with what you have on hand, a theme helps narrow down your options.

   ▶ You could highlight a couple of your favorite in-season ingredients, like peaches and blackberries during the summer.

   ▶ Maybe you're craving a fresh take on your favorite dish (how about tacos in salad form?), or you want to re-create a salad that you enjoyed at a restaurant.

   ▶ If you're making side salads, look to your main dish for direction. Extra tomatoes? Use those!

2. **CHOOSE YOUR GREENS CAREFULLY.** Start with fresh, preferably organic greens, and make sure they're dry before you add dressing. Water repels oil, so you won't get a light and even coat of dressing on damp produce.

   ▶ Kale is the sturdiest option in the bunch, and it can hold up to dressing for a few days in the refrigerator. Since it is so sturdy and bitter, briefly massage before dressing (more on that later).

   ▶ Arugula is next, but is best consumed within a day or two in its dressed form; store the greens and dressing separately to be on the safe side. If you don't appreciate arugula's bold, peppery, bitter flavor, replace it with your favorite greens.

   ▶ The rest (romaine, spinach, red-leaf, butter lettuce, and more) are all fantastic options, but be sure to store leftover greens and dressing separately and toss just before serving.

3. **OPTIONAL: ADD SOME HEARTY INGREDIENTS FOR A SATISFYING, FULL MEAL.** Look to your theme to help you pick out harmonious flavors and textures.

   ▶ Consider leftover cooked whole grains; my favorites are farro, wild rice, brown rice, quinoa, and small pasta shapes.

   ▶ Cooked beans are good, too; chickpeas and black beans often work well, depending on the other flavors.

   ▶ Cruciferous vegetables add crunchy substance and mega antioxidants. Think thinly sliced cabbage, Brussels sprouts, and broccoli.

4. **ADD COMPLEMENTARY ACCENTS.** Start with veggies, fruits, and/or tender, leafy herbs that work with your salad's theme.

   ▶ Put some thought into how you prepare your produce. Contrasting textures make salads more interesting. Caramelized roasted vegetables are always amazing, sometimes carrot ribbons are more fun than chopped, and 1/2-inch cubes of apple offer more flavor and texture than thinly sliced.

   ▶ You can never go wrong with some sliced or diced avocado, and/or some shredded or crumbled cheese (I love goat cheese, feta, and Parmesan in salads).

   ▶ Dried fruit (chopped if large) and sun-dried tomatoes are awesome.

   ▶ Freshly toasted nuts or seeds offer lots of flavor and a big nutrition boost. Other crispy, crunchy add-ins include homemade whole-grain croutons, crispy tortilla strips, torn pieces of toasted pita, toasted large coconut flakes, and even granola.

5. **DRESS IT UP.** Store-bought dressings won't do your salad justice. I offer four dressing options in this chapter, so you can always keep one in the refrigerator. When in doubt, go with my Liquid Gold Salad Dressing (page 52).

Simple, Seasonal Side Salads

Combine your fresh greens of choice with my Liquid Gold Salad Dressing (page 52) and the seasonal accompaniments listed below.

SPRING

Chopped radishes

Sliced avocado

Toasted sunflower seeds

Crumbled feta cheese

SUMMER

Cherries (pitted and halved), raspberries, blackberries, or sliced strawberries

Toasted sliced almonds

Crumbled goat cheese

FALL

Thinly sliced apple or pear

Dried cranberries

Crumbled goat cheese

Toasted chopped pecans

WINTER

Carrot ribbons, made with a julienne peeler or vegetable peeler

Crumbled feta cheese

Diced avocado

Toasted chopped walnuts

Tangy Red Bell Pepper Dressing

Honey-Mustard Dressing

Jalapeño-Lime Dressing

*Liquid
Gold Salad
Dressing*

Four Salad Dressings

Often, when it comes to whipping up a side salad, my biggest obstacle is that I don't have a good dressing to go with it. Homemade dressings taste about one million times better than the store-bought variety, but I don't want to whisk one together at every meal. So, I designed four fantastic dressings that yield about 1 cup each. I keep one in the refrigerator at all times, and find that I eat a lot more greens this way. All of these dressings are olive oil–based. Olive oil actually helps the body absorb more nutrients from some common salad ingredients, like dark leafy greens and tomatoes.

These dressings all keep well in the refrigerator for up to 2 weeks. I like to store mine in a jar with a secure lid, so I can safely shake it to recombine the dressing before serving. You can also whisk it back together. If you find that the olive oil has solidified somewhat in the refrigerator, let it warm to room temperature for a few minutes, or help it along by warming it very briefly in the microwave, then shake or whisk to recombine.

LIQUID GOLD SALAD DRESSING

This lemony dressing is my go-to! I can't think of a single salad ingredient that it doesn't complement.

1/3 cup extra-virgin olive oil

1/3 cup lemon juice (from about 2 lemons)

2 tablespoons Dijon mustard

2 tablespoons honey or maple syrup

3 cloves garlic, pressed or minced

1/4 teaspoon fine sea salt

Generous amount of freshly ground black pepper

Pinch of red pepper flakes (optional)

Combine all of the ingredients and whisk to blend. The dressing should be pleasantly zippy; if it's too tart, whisk in a little more olive oil until it suits your taste buds. Taste and add additional salt and/or pepper if it doesn't knock your socks off.

TANGY RED BELL PEPPER DRESSING

This surprising, light dressing is a little sweet and a little tangy. Whatever I toss it with, I can't resist coming back for another bite. This dressing goes well with carrots, cilantro, corn, tomatoes, thinly sliced raw broccoli and cabbage, basil, goat cheese, Parmesan, leftover cooked pasta, chickpeas, and black beans.

1/4 cup extra-virgin olive oil

1 large red bell pepper, sliced into roughly 2-inch pieces

2 tablespoons lemon juice

1 tablespoon honey or maple syrup

1 teaspoon apple cider vinegar (omit for a sweeter dressing)

1 clove garlic, roughly chopped

1/4 teaspoon fine sea salt

Pinch of red pepper flakes

In a blender, combine all of the ingredients and blend until smooth. Taste and add another pinch of salt if the dressing needs a little something more.

HONEY-MUSTARD DRESSING

This savory honey-mustard dressing is a mayonnaise- and preservative-free alternative to the store-bought variety. Plus, it tastes so much better when it's made fresh! This dressing goes well with thinly sliced raw broccoli, Brussels sprouts, cabbage, kale, and carrots. It's also great with arugula, apples, bell peppers, shaved asparagus, goat cheese, sunflower seeds, pecans, and almonds.

$\frac{1}{2}$ cup extra-virgin olive oil

$\frac{1}{4}$ cup Dijon mustard

3 to 4 tablespoons honey, to taste

2 tablespoons lemon juice

2 tablespoons apple cider vinegar or more lemon juice

1 clove garlic, pressed or minced

$\frac{1}{2}$ teaspoon fine sea salt

Generous amount of freshly ground black pepper

Combine all of the ingredients and whisk to blend. This dressing is intentionally bold, but if the flavors are too intense, whisk in a little more olive oil until it suits your taste buds.

JALAPEÑO-LIME DRESSING

Don't worry, this blended lime and jalapeño dressing isn't too spicy! It's full of fresh flavor and goes great with Mexican ingredients, including tomatoes, corn, cilantro, pepitas (hulled pumpkin seeds), and crispy tortilla strips. It also plays nicely with arugula, romaine, kale, thinly sliced red cabbage, shredded carrots, apples, mango, feta cheese, and cheddar.

$\frac{1}{2}$ cup extra-virgin olive oil

$\frac{1}{2}$ cup lime juice (from about 4 limes)

1 small jalapeño, seeded, deribbed, and roughly chopped

1 tablespoon honey or maple syrup

1 teaspoon ground cumin

$\frac{1}{2}$ teaspoon Dijon mustard

1 clove garlic, roughly chopped

$\frac{1}{4}$ teaspoon fine sea salt

Pinch of red pepper flakes (optional)

In a blender, combine all of the ingredients (except the pepper flakes) and blend until smooth. Taste and blend in additional salt if the dressing needs a little more oomph. If you'd like a spicier dressing, blend in the pepper flakes. If the dressing is too bold for your liking, dilute it with a little more olive oil and blend again.

Thai-Style Mango Slaw

This slaw is sweet, savory, chewy, crispy, and nutty all at the same time, which is to say that it is utterly irresistible. Fresh mango lends a tropical Thai vibe and wild rice adds some welcome earthy undertones. I like to keep a salad like this in the fridge and take a fork to it when hunger strikes.

This colorful and refreshing slaw is special diet–friendly and keeps well for several hours at room temperature, so it's perfect for potlucks or pack-for-lunch leftovers. I actually brought this slaw with me to a friend's Mexican-themed potluck and apologized for missing the mark, but it was received with oohs and aahs that got louder after the first bite. No regrets! **MAKES 4 LARGE OR 8 SIDE SALADS**

1 cup wild rice, rinsed

SLAW
4 cups thinly sliced red cabbage (about 1 pound), roughly chopped into 2-inch-long strips

2 ripe mangoes, diced

1 red bell pepper, chopped

$1/2$ cup chopped green onions (about 4)

$1/2$ cup chopped fresh cilantro

SESAME-LIME DRESSING
$1/4$ cup lime juice (from about 2 limes)

1 tablespoon extra-virgin olive oil

1 tablespoon toasted sesame oil

2 cloves garlic, pressed or minced

$1/2$ teaspoon fine sea salt

$1/4$ teaspoon red pepper flakes

1. Bring a large pot of water to boil. Add the rinsed rice and continue boiling, reducing the heat as necessary to prevent overflow, until the rice is pleasantly tender but still offers a light resistance to the bite, 40 to 55 minutes. Remove the pot from the heat, drain the rice, and return it to the pot. Cover and let the rice rest for 10 minutes, then uncover and set aside while you assemble the slaw.

2. *Meanwhile, to prepare the slaw:* In a large serving bowl, combine the cabbage, mangoes, bell pepper, green onions, and cilantro.

3. *To prepare the dressing:* In a small bowl, combine all of the dressing ingredients and whisk until blended.

4. Add the warm rice to the bowl of slaw ingredients and toss to combine. Drizzle in the dressing and toss again. Season to taste with additional salt, if necessary.

5. Serve immediately, or chill the salad until you're ready to serve. This salad keeps well, chilled, for 3 to 4 days. You might want to wake up the flavors with an extra squeeze of lime juice.

GLUTEN FREE • DAIRY FREE • VEGAN • EGG FREE • NUT FREE • SOY FREE

Fresh Taco Salad with Creamy Avocado-Lime Dressing

TACO FILLING

1 tablespoon extra-virgin olive oil

4 cloves garlic, pressed or minced

1 1/2 teaspoons chili powder

1 teaspoon ground cumin

1 tablespoon tomato paste

1/2 cup quinoa, rinsed

1 cup water

1 can (15 ounces) black beans, rinsed and drained, or 1 1/2 cups cooked black beans

1/4 teaspoon fine sea salt

Freshly ground black pepper

CRISPY TORTILLA STRIPS*

1 1/2 teaspoons extra-virgin olive oil

3 corn tortillas, cut into 2-inch-long, 1/4-inch-wide strips

Fine sea salt

CREAMY AVOCADO-LIME DRESSING

1/4 cup lime juice (from about 2 limes)

1 tablespoon extra-virgin olive oil

1 tablespoon water

1/2 medium-large avocado, pitted

(CONTINUED)

This taco salad is very different from the taco salads that my mom used to order at Mexican restaurants. They were the lightest option on the menu, but I always found myself wondering, how do those giant fried tortillas hold up to all the cheese and sour cream?

Here's my fresher, vegetarian version of those taco salads, which serves as a balanced, full meal in a bowl. Crisp romaine and peppery arugula tossed in a creamy, intentionally zippy avocado-lime dressing form the base. Chili-flavored quinoa and black beans make it plenty hearty, while tomatoes, radishes, and avocado lend some color and pops of flavor. The ode to my mom's taco salads wouldn't be complete without some crispy tortilla strips on top. **MAKES 4 LARGE SALADS**

1. To make the taco filling: In a medium saucepan, warm the olive oil over medium heat until shimmering. Add the garlic, chili powder, and cumin. Cook until fragrant, stirring constantly, about 30 seconds. Add the tomato paste and sauté for another minute, stirring constantly. Add the rinsed quinoa and water, and stir to combine. Bring the mixture to a gentle boil, then cover the pot and reduce the heat as necessary to maintain a gentle simmer. Cook until the liquid is absorbed, 15 to 20 minutes (the quinoa might not be fluffy yet, but don't worry).

2. Remove the pot from the heat and let it rest, still covered, for 5 minutes. Then, uncover and fluff the quinoa with a fork. Gently stir in the black beans and salt. Season to taste with pepper and additional salt, if necessary. Cover and set aside for a couple of minutes to warm up the beans.

3. To make the tortilla strips: In a large skillet, warm the olive oil over medium heat until shimmering. Toss in the tortilla strips, sprinkle them with salt, and stir. Cook until the strips are crispy and turning golden, stirring occasionally, 5 to 10 minutes. Drain the tortilla strips on a plate covered with a piece of paper towel.

4. To make the dressing: In a small food processor or blender, combine the lime juice, olive oil, and water. Using a spoon, scoop in the half avocado and add the cilantro, jalapeño, garlic, and salt. Process until the dressing is nice and smooth. The dressing should be zippy, but if it's

(CONTINUED)

CHANGE IT UP
You can incorporate this protein-rich taco filling into a number of Mexican recipes, including nachos, enchiladas, and, of course, tacos.

(CONTINUED FROM PAGE 56)

$^1/_4$ cup lightly packed fresh cilantro (some stems are okay)

1 small-medium jalapeño, seeded, deribbed, and roughly chopped

1 clove garlic, roughly chopped

$^1/_4$ teaspoon fine sea salt

SALAD

1 small head romaine lettuce, chopped (or 5 ounces chopped romaine)

3 cups packed baby arugula (about 3 ounces)

1 cup thinly sliced grape or cherry tomatoes

$^1/_3$ cup thinly sliced and roughly chopped radishes (3 to 4), or chopped red onion

$^1/_3$ cup crumbled feta cheese (about 2 ounces)

$^1/_2$ medium-large avocado

*Ingredient Note: If you're in a hurry, you can replace the crispy tortilla strips with a small handful of crumbled tortilla chips. Sprinkle them over the salads just before serving.

unpleasantly tart or difficult to blend, dilute it with 1 to 2 tablespoons of water and blend again.

5. *To assemble the salads:* Combine the romaine and arugula in a large bowl. Wait to dress the salad until you are ready to serve, as the greens wilt fairly quickly once dressed. (If you won't be consuming all 4 servings of this salad right away, portion off the greens you'd like to save for later, and dress only the greens you intend to eat now.)

6. When you're ready, drizzle the mixture with just enough dressing to lightly coat the greens (you might have extra). Toss until the dressing is evenly distributed.

7. Arrange the dressed greens in 4 individual salad bowls (or dinner plates, if your bowls are on the small side). Top each salad with taco filling, tomatoes, radishes, crispy tortilla strips, and feta. Slice the remaining avocado half into long strips and place a couple of strips on each salad. Serve immediately.

8. If you have leftover dressing, press plastic wrap against the surface to prevent browning and store it in the refrigerator for later. Leftover tortilla strips tend to become unpalatably tough within a couple of hours, so you might want to skip those and add a few crushed tortilla chips to leftovers.

GLUTEN FREE: *Be sure to use certified gluten-free corn tortillas.* • **DAIRY FREE/VEGAN:** *Omit the feta cheese.* • **EGG FREE** • **NUT FREE** • **SOY FREE**

Kale and Quinoa Salad with Crisp Celery, Plumped Cranberries, and Lemon Dressing

This kale salad is simple, redeeming, and delicious by design. It's a great picnic salad, or more realistically, a great pack-for-work or dinner-after-indulgent-vacation salad. Don't skip the celery–it's a totally underrated component that offers some necessary crunch. Kale, quinoa, dried cranberries, almonds, and a mustard-spiked lemon dressing make for a wholesome and delicious salad.

MAKES 4 MEDIUM SALADS

1. In a small saucepan, combine the rinsed quinoa and water. Bring the mixture to a boil over medium-high heat, then reduce the heat as necessary to maintain a gentle simmer. Simmer, uncovered, until all of the water is absorbed, 11 to 14 minutes. Remove the pot from the heat, stir in the dried cranberries (so they can get nice and plump), and cover the pot. Let the quinoa and cranberries steam with the lid on for 10 minutes, then fluff the quinoa with a fork and set aside.

2. *Meanwhile, to make the dressing:* In a small bowl, combine the olive oil, lemon juice, mustard, maple syrup, garlic, salt, and pepper and whisk until blended.

3. *To assemble the salad:* Place the chopped kale in a big salad bowl. Sprinkle a small pinch of salt over the kale and massage the leaves with your hands by scrunching big handfuls at a time, until the leaves are darker in color and fragrant, and reduced in volume by about one-third. Add the celery to the bowl.

4. In a small skillet, combine the almonds and olive oil and cook over medium heat, stirring frequently, until the almonds are fragrant and golden on the edges, 5 to 8 minutes. (Be careful, it's easy to burn those delicate almonds!) Pour the almonds into the salad bowl.

5. While the quinoa mixture is warm, add it to the salad bowl. Drizzle in all of the dressing and toss to coat. Wait until the salad has cooled to nearly room temperature before gently tossing in the crumbled goat cheese so it doesn't melt. Serve immediately. This salad keeps well, chilled, for up to 4 days.

1/2 cup quinoa, rinsed

1 cup water

1/3 cup dried cranberries or dried tart cherries

DRESSING

1/4 cup extra-virgin olive oil

2 tablespoons lemon juice

2 teaspoons Dijon mustard

2 teaspoons maple syrup or honey

1 large clove garlic, pressed or minced

1/2 teaspoon fine sea salt

Several twists of freshly ground black pepper

SALAD

1 medium bunch curly kale (about 8 ounces), tough ribs removed and leaves chopped into bite-size pieces

Fine sea salt

2 ribs celery, chopped

1/2 cup sliced almonds

1/2 teaspoon extra-virgin olive oil

1/3 cup crumbled goat cheese (about 2 ounces)

GLUTEN FREE • **DAIRY FREE/VEGAN:** *Skip the cheese. For a vegan salad, use maple syrup instead of honey.* • **EGG FREE** • **NUT FREE:** *Replace the almonds with pepitas (hulled pumpkin seeds).* • **SOY FREE**

Kale and Quinoa Salad with
Crisp Celery, Plumped Cranberries,
and Lemon Dressing (page 59)

Moroccan Roasted Carrot, Arugula, and Wild Rice Salad

WILD RICE

1 cup wild rice, rinsed

¼ teaspoon fine sea salt

ROASTED CARROTS

1 pound carrots,* peeled and cut on the diagonal into ½-inch-thick slices

1 tablespoon extra-virgin olive oil

1 teaspoon chili powder

¼ teaspoon ground cinnamon

¼ teaspoon fine sea salt

LEMON CITRONETTE

¼ cup extra-virgin olive oil

2 tablespoons lemon juice

1 teaspoon Dijon mustard

1 teaspoon honey or maple syrup

1 clove garlic, pressed or minced

¼ teaspoon fine sea salt

Freshly ground black pepper

SALAD

⅓ cup raw pistachios, roughly chopped, or pepitas (hulled pumpkin seeds)

5 to 6 ounces baby arugula

⅓ cup crumbled goat or feta cheese (about 2 ounces)

3 tablespoons raisins, preferably golden

Middle Eastern flavors collide with Minnesota-grown wild rice in this hearty roasted carrot salad. It's like they were meant to be together all along. Roasted carrots taste downright exotic once they combine with chili powder, pistachios, golden raisins, and goat cheese. I love how wild rice always retains its slightly chewy texture, no matter how long it soaks in dressing. You'll be pleasantly surprised by the flavors here. **MAKES 4 LARGE SALADS OR 6 MEDIUM SIDE SALADS**

1. *To cook the wild rice:* Bring a large pot of water to boil. Add the rinsed rice and continue boiling, reducing the heat as necessary to prevent overflow, until the rice is pleasantly tender but still offers a light resistance to the bite, 40 to 55 minutes. Remove the pot from the heat, drain the rice, and return it to the pot. Cover and let the rice rest for 10 minutes, then uncover and stir in the salt. Set aside.

2. *To roast the carrots:* Preheat the oven to 400°F. Line a large rimmed baking sheet with parchment paper for easy cleanup.

3. Place the carrots on the baking sheet and drizzle them with the olive oil. Sprinkle the chili powder, cinnamon, and salt on top. Toss until the carrots are lightly coated in oil and spices. Arrange in a single layer and roast until they are caramelized on the edges and easily pierced through by a fork, 25 to 40 minutes (see Note), tossing halfway.

4. *To make the lemon citronette:* In a small bowl, whisk together the olive oil, lemon juice, mustard, honey, garlic, salt, and pepper to taste.

5. *To prepare the salad:* In a medium skillet, toast the chopped pistachios over medium heat, stirring frequently, until fragrant and turning golden on the edges, 4 to 6 minutes. Set aside to cool.

6. In a large serving bowl, combine the cooked wild rice and arugula. When you're ready to serve, drizzle the mixture with just enough dressing to lightly coat the salad (you might have a little extra) and toss to combine. Arrange the roasted carrots down the center and sprinkle the toasted pistachios, crumbled goat cheese, and raisins on top. Serve immediately. This salad is best the day it's prepared, but it keeps well, chilled, for 2 to 3 days.

GLUTEN FREE • DAIRY FREE/VEGAN: *Skip the cheese. For a vegan salad, use maple syrup instead of honey.* **• EGG FREE •**
NUT FREE: *Substitute pepitas for the pistachios.* **• SOY FREE**

Ingredient Note: If you make this with heirloom carrots from the farmers' market, they may roast in as little as 25 minutes. Regular carrots are denser and require more time in the oven.

Southwestern Roasted Veggie Salad with Chipotle-Balsamic Dressing

ROASTED VEGGIES

1 medium sweet potato (about ³/₄ pound), peeled and cut into ³/₄-inch cubes

1 red bell pepper, cut into 1-inch squares

2 tablespoons extra-virgin olive oil, divided

1 teaspoon chili powder

Fine sea salt

12 ounces broccoli florets (from 1 large bunch), cut into bite-size pieces

CHIPOTLE-BALSAMIC DRESSING

¹/₄ cup extra-virgin olive oil

1 tablespoon balsamic vinegar

1 tablespoon lime juice

1 teaspoon adobo sauce (from a can of chipotle peppers in adobo)*

¹/₂ teaspoon maple syrup or honey

1 small clove garlic, pressed or minced

¹/₄ teaspoon fine sea salt

SALAD

¹/₂ cup raw pepitas (hulled pumpkin seeds)

5 to 6 ounces baby arugula (5 to 6 packed cups)

¹/₂ cup crumbled feta cheese (about 2¹/₂ ounces)

Oh my word, this salad. If you try only one salad from this book, let it be this one. Caramelized, roasted bell peppers and sweet potatoes are balanced by spicy, bitter arugula and smoky chipotle. Plenty of toasty pepitas, creamy feta cheese, and ripe avocado make it truly irresistible. It's a wholesome salad that could qualify as lunch or a light dinner. **MAKES 2 LARGE SALADS OR 4 GENEROUS SIDE SALADS**

1. *To roast the veggies:* Preheat the oven to 425°F with racks in the middle and upper third of the oven.

2. On a large rimmed baking sheet, combine the sweet potato and bell pepper. Drizzle with 1 tablespoon of the olive oil, sprinkle with the chili powder and a few dashes of salt, and toss until evenly coated. Arrange them in a single layer. On a second large rimmed baking sheet, toss the broccoli florets with the remaining 1 tablespoon olive oil until evenly coated. Arrange the florets in a single layer and sprinkle with salt.

3. Roast the broccoli on the upper rack and the pan of sweet potatoes and peppers on the middle rack until the vegetables are tender and caramelized on the edges. The broccoli will be done around the 20-minute mark, which is perfect timing for tossing the sweet potato/pepper pan. Return the sweet potato/pepper pan to the oven and continue roasting until the sweet potatoes and peppers are tender and deeply caramelized, 15 to 20 minutes longer.

4. *Meanwhile, to make the dressing:* In a small bowl, combine the olive oil, balsamic vinegar, lime juice, adobo sauce, maple syrup, garlic, and salt and whisk until blended. Taste and add a pinch of salt if necessary.

5. *To prepare the salad:* In a medium skillet, toast the pepitas over medium heat, stirring frequently, until they are turning golden on the edges and making little popping noises, about 5 minutes.

6. In a large bowl, combine the arugula, roasted veggies, toasted pepitas, feta, and sun-dried tomatoes. Wait until you're ready to serve to add the dressing, as the arugula wilts if it's in contact with the dressing for too long. (If you plan to have leftovers, store the dressing separately from the remaining ingredients, and toss them together just before serving.)

7. When you're ready to serve, drizzle enough dressing on top to lightly coat (you might not need all of it) and toss everything together. Dice the avocado, add it to the bowl, and gently toss a couple more times. Serve immediately.

Ingredient Note: Look for canned chipotle peppers in adobo sauce in the international/Hispanic aisle of your grocery store. Or, use 1 teaspoon smoked paprika instead.

$1/_3$ cup oil-packed sun-dried tomatoes, rinsed and drained

1 avocado, halved and pitted

GLUTEN FREE • DAIRY FREE/VEGAN: *Skip the feta cheese. For a vegan salad, use maple syrup instead of honey.* **• EGG FREE • NUT FREE • SOY FREE**

Green Goddess Kale Salad

Now this is a garden salad! This chopped kale salad wonder is crispy, chewy, and zingy all at once. It's full of fresh-from-the-garden flavors, including carrots, cucumbers, radishes, and a creamy, herbed avocado dressing. The tarragon lends a lemony and light licorice-flavored note that I just can't resist. I dare you not to eat all of it in one sitting. I know Cookie would, if I turned my head for long. She loves kale! **MAKES 2 LARGE SALADS OR 4 GENEROUS SIDE SALADS**

1. *To prepare the salad:* Transfer the chopped kale to a big salad bowl. Sprinkle a small pinch of salt over the kale and massage the leaves with your hands by scrunching big handfuls at a time, until the leaves are darker in color and fragrant, and reduced in volume by about one-third. Add the cucumber, carrots, and radishes to the bowl.

2. In a small skillet, combine the sunflower seeds, olive oil, and a few dashes of salt. Toast over medium heat, stirring frequently, until the seeds are fragrant and turning lightly golden on the edges, 4 to 5 minutes. Pour the seeds into the salad bowl.

3. *To make the dressing:* In a food processor or blender, combine the lemon juice, olive oil, water, avocado, parsley, green onions, tarragon, garlic, salt, and several twists of black pepper. Blend or process, starting on low speed and slowly increasing to medium, until the dressing is smooth and creamy, pausing to scrape down the sides as necessary. The dressing should be pretty zippy, so taste it and blend in more lemon juice if necessary. If it needs more oomph, add up to 1/4 teaspoon more salt.

4. When you're ready to eat, drizzle the dressing over the salad (you might not need all of it, although I recommend adding more dressing to kale salads than you would for other salads). Toss until the salad is lightly coated in dressing. Serve immediately. This salad keeps well, chilled, for up to 2 days.

SALAD
1 medium bunch curly kale (about 8 ounces), tough ribs removed and leaves chopped into bite-size pieces

Fine sea salt

1 cup seeded and chopped cucumber (about 1/2 medium)

1 cup finely chopped carrots (about 3)

1/2 cup finely chopped radishes (about 4)

1/3 cup raw sunflower seeds

1/4 teaspoon extra-virgin olive oil

DRESSING
3 tablespoons lemon juice (from 1 to 1 1/2 lemons), or more if needed

2 tablespoons extra-virgin olive oil

2 tablespoons water

1 avocado, diced

1/3 cup lightly packed fresh flat-leaf parsley (some stems are okay)

2 tablespoons chopped green onions (1 to 2)

1 tablespoon fresh tarragon leaves or roughly chopped fresh basil or cilantro

1 clove garlic, roughly chopped

1/4 teaspoon fine sea salt

Freshly ground black pepper

GLUTEN FREE • DAIRY FREE • VEGAN • EGG FREE • NUT FREE • SOY FREE

Colorful Kale, Apple, and Fennel Slaw with Tart Cherries

SLAW

2 cups packed chopped Tuscan (lacinato) kale leaves, tough ribs removed (about $1/_2$ medium bunch)

2 cups thinly sliced red cabbage (about $1/_2$ pound)

2 cups thinly sliced Brussels sprouts (about $1/_2$ pound), tough ends trimmed

1 cup thinly sliced raw fennel (about $1/_2$ medium bulb)*

1 medium-large Granny Smith apple, cut into $1/_2$-inch cubes

$1/_2$ cup chopped dried tart cherries

ZIPPY LIME DRESSING

3 tablespoons extra-virgin olive oil

3 tablespoons lime juice (from about $1^1/_2$ limes), or more if needed

1 tablespoon plus 1 teaspoon honey or maple syrup

1 tablespoon apple cider vinegar

1 tablespoon Dijon mustard

$1/_4$ teaspoon fine sea salt

Meet my slaw soulmate. It's a vibrant, hefty, slightly sweet slaw that is great on its own. It's also fantastic with sandwiches, burgers, and heavier entrees that need some balance. Thinly sliced fennel elevates this slaw with its light licorice flavor and delicate crunch. If you haven't tried raw fennel before, you're in for a treat!

Unlike my other kale salads that call for massaging the kale, this one just needs a 15-minute rest to break down the kale and meld the flavors. Tart dried cherries play particularly well with the other ingredients, so they are definitely worth using over dried cranberries. If you would like to turn this into a more substantial meal on its own, add up to $1/_2$ cup freshly toasted, salted sunflower seeds.

MAKES 4 LARGE OR 8 SIDE SALADS

1. *To prepare the slaw:* In a large salad bowl, combine the kale, cabbage, Brussels sprouts, fennel, apple, and dried cherries.

2. *To make the dressing:* In a small bowl, whisk together the olive oil, lime juice, honey, vinegar, mustard, and salt until blended. Taste and adjust as necessary. For more acidity, add a little more lime juice, or to mellow the flavors a bit, add a little more honey.

3. Drizzle the dressing over the salad and toss to combine. For best flavor, let the salad marinate for 15 to 20 minutes before serving. This slaw keeps well, chilled, for 2 to 3 days.

TIP: *The easiest way to shred the kale, cabbage, and sprouts is to run them through your food processor using the slicing attachment. Use a mandoline to finely slice the fennel, if you have one. If not, a sharp knife will work well.*

Ingredient Note: *If you love fennel, you can add the full bulb for a more pronounced fennel slaw. If you don't love raw fennel, just replace it with 1 additional cup of kale, cabbage, or Brussels sprouts. Leftover fennel is best used quickly. I like to toss finely sliced raw fennel with a light drizzle of olive oil, a squeeze of lemon juice, and a sprinkle of salt and pepper for a simple salad or snack.*

GLUTEN FREE • DAIRY FREE • VEGAN: *Use maple syrup instead of honey.* **• EGG FREE • NUT FREE • SOY FREE**

Outrageous Herbaceous Chickpea Salad

T make ½

Here's a simple chickpea salad that I could eat every single day. It's bursting with fresh Mediterranean flavors, thanks to chopped bell pepper, parsley, red onion, and celery. Lemon and garlic take it from tasty to transcendent. This salad packs well, so it's perfect for potlucks and picnics. It's also a great lunch option, so long as your serving is large enough. You can also pile it onto greens and drizzle some Liquid Gold Salad Dressing (page 52) on top for a quick and substantial green salad. **MAKES 4 SIDE SALADS**

1. In a medium bowl, combine the chickpeas, bell pepper, parsley, onion, celery, olive oil, lemon juice, garlic, salt, and pepper to taste. Toss until combined. Taste and add additional lemon juice, salt, or pepper if necessary.

2. Serve immediately, or chill until you're ready to serve. Leftovers keep well, chilled, for up to 4 days.

2 cans (15 ounces each) chickpeas, rinsed and drained, or 3 cups cooked chickpeas

1 medium red bell pepper, chopped

1½ cups chopped fresh flat-leaf parsley (about 1 bunch)

½ cup chopped red onion (about ½ small)

½ cup chopped celery (about 2 ribs)

3 tablespoons extra-virgin olive oil

3 tablespoons lemon juice (from 1 to 1½ lemons), or more if needed

2 cloves garlic, pressed or minced

½ teaspoon fine sea salt

Freshly ground black pepper

GLUTEN FREE • DAIRY FREE • VEGAN • EGG FREE • NUT FREE • SOY FREE

Tahini Kale Caesar Salad with Whole-Grain Croutons

CROUTONS

6 ounces crusty whole-grain bread, cut into $^3/_4$-inch cubes (about 3 cups)

2 tablespoons extra-virgin olive oil

Fine sea salt

TAHINI CAESAR DRESSING

$^1/_4$ cup tahini

3 tablespoons lemon juice (from 1 to 1$^1/_2$ lemons)

1 tablespoon extra-virgin olive oil

2 cloves garlic, pressed or minced

1 teaspoon Dijon mustard

$^1/_4$ teaspoon fine sea salt

2 tablespoons water

Freshly ground black pepper

SALAD

1 medium bunch (about 8 ounces) Tuscan (lacinato) kale, tough ribs removed and leaves chopped into bite-size pieces

Fine sea salt

5 ounces romaine (about $^1/_2$ small–medium head), chopped into bite-size pieces

$^1/_3$ cup finely grated Parmesan cheese (about $^2/_3$ ounce)

Tahini is the peanut butter of sesame seeds. It's also my secret sauce. It has an irresistible tang and reminds me of Parmesan in its ability to take a good recipe into gimme-that-now territory.

To me, garlicky tahini dressings have always tasted remarkably similar to Caesar dressings, even without any anchovies or Parmesan. The similarity becomes even more pronounced with the addition of Dijon mustard, which is standard in Caesar dressings. Here is a healthier Caesar salad featuring fresh, crisp whole-grain croutons and kale, for extra flavor, color, and health bonus points. **MAKES 4 TO 6 SIDE SALADS**

1. *To make the croutons:* Preheat the oven to 400°F.

2. Place the cubed bread on a large rimmed baking sheet and drizzle with the olive oil. Toss until the cubes are lightly and evenly coated in oil, then arrange them in a single layer. Sprinkle the cubes with several dashes of salt. Bake until golden brown and crisp, 7 to 9 minutes, stirring halfway.

3. *To make the dressing:* In a small bowl, combine the tahini, lemon juice, olive oil, garlic, mustard, and salt. Whisk until blended, then add the water and whisk until you have a smooth, blended tahini sauce. Season generously with black pepper (about 10 twists). The dressing should be tangy, like classic Caesar dressings. If it's overwhelmingly tart or too thick to pour, whisk in an additional tablespoon of water.

4. *To prepare the salad:* Transfer the chopped kale to a big salad bowl. Add a dash of salt and massage the leaves with your hands by scrunching big handfuls at a time, until the leaves are darker in color and the volume has reduced by about one-third.

5. Add the chopped romaine to the bowl. Wait to dress the salad until you are ready to serve, since the romaine and croutons get soggy if they're in contact with the dressing for too long. (If you plan to have leftovers, store individual components separately, and toss them together just before serving.)

6. When you're ready, drizzle enough dressing over the greens to lightly coat (you might not need all of it). Toss until the dressing is evenly distributed. Add the croutons and Parmesan and toss again. Serve immediately.

DAIRY FREE/VEGAN: *Use 2 tablespoons nutritional yeast instead of the Parmesan.* • **EGG FREE** • **NUT FREE** • **SOY FREE**

Creamy Arugula, Goat Cheese, and Tomato Pasta Salad

This simple pasta salad is basically a big bowl of my favorite things–whole-grain pasta, goat cheese, lemon, and arugula. Combined, they look and taste like the most gourmet of pasta salads. It's a wonderful potluck side and packs great for picnics. The recipe was actually passed from friend to friend by word of mouth 5 years ago. I absolutely loved it, and it became one of the very first recipes I ever posted to my blog. I didn't know how to write a proper recipe back then, so now I'm doing it justice. **MAKES 4 MEDIUM OR 6 SIDE SALADS**

1. Bring a large pot of salted water to boil over high heat. Cook the pasta until al dente, according to package directions. Before draining, reserve about 1 cup of the pasta cooking water. Drain the pasta and pour it into a large serving bowl.

2. Sprinkle the crumbled goat cheese over the pasta, then drizzle in the olive oil and lemon juice. Sprinkle the salt, pepper flakes, and several twists of black pepper on top. Pour about $1/3$ cup of the reserved pasta cooking water over the pasta and toss until the pasta is evenly coated.

3. Add the arugula, cherry tomatoes, and olives (if using) and toss to combine. If the pasta seems dry, add small splashes of cooking water and toss until it's nice and creamy. Taste and adjust if necessary–add more olive oil for richness, lemon juice for extra zing, and salt and/or pepper for seasoning. Serve immediately.

4. This salad is best consumed soon after making, but it keeps well, chilled, for 2 to 3 days. I like to gently reheat my leftover salad for just a few seconds in the microwave, which loosens up the goat cheese again.

---

8 ounces whole-grain fusilli or rotini pasta

4 ounces goat cheese, crumbled (about $2/3$ cup)

2 tablespoons extra-virgin olive oil, or more if needed

2 tablespoons lemon juice, or more if needed

$1/2$ teaspoon fine sea salt

$1/4$ teaspoon red pepper flakes

Freshly ground black pepper

5 to 6 ounces baby arugula (5 to 6 packed cups)

1 pint cherry tomatoes, sliced into thin rounds

$1/3$ cup pitted and thinly sliced Kalamata olives (optional)

FAIR WARNING: *This salad probably isn't for you if you don't enjoy arugula and goat cheese (although, my Cashew Sour Cream is a great alternative). You can definitely leave out the olives if you don't like them.*

GLUTEN FREE: *Use certified gluten-free pasta.* • **DAIRY FREE/VEGAN:** *Substitute $1/2$ cup Cashew Sour Cream (page 217) for the goat cheese. You may not need to add any reserved pasta cooking water to the dish.* • **EGG FREE** • **NUT FREE** • **SOY FREE**

Roasted Cauliflower, Farro, and Arugula Salad with Lemony Tahini Dressing

ROASTED VEGGIES AND FARRO

1 large head cauliflower (about 2 pounds), cut into bite-size florets

1 large red bell pepper, cut into 1-inch squares

2 tablespoons extra-virgin olive oil, or more if needed

$1/4$ teaspoon ground cumin

Pinch of ground cinnamon

Fine sea salt and freshly ground black pepper

1 cup farro, rinsed

LEMONY TAHINI DRESSING

$1/4$ cup extra-virgin olive oil

2 tablespoons lemon juice

2 to 3 tablespoons tahini

2 cloves garlic, pressed or minced

$1/2$ teaspoon fine sea salt

Freshly ground black pepper

SALAD

4 cups packed baby arugula (about 4 ounces)

1 can (15 ounces) chickpeas, rinsed and drained, or $1^{1}/2$ cups cooked chickpeas

$1/2$ cup chopped fresh flat-leaf parsley

$1/2$ cup chopped fresh cilantro

This salad draws inspiration from an amazing roasted cauliflower and falafel pita sandwich I ordered at a local Mediterranean restaurant. I unraveled the falafel into its most basic parts–chickpeas, parsley, cilantro, and spices–and combined them all with roasted cauliflower and plenty of greens to make this salad. Chewy, tender farro (a distant relative to wheat) is my abstract take on pita, and the light, lemony tahini dressing ties everything together. I'm in love.

MAKES 4 LARGE OR 6 MEDIUM SALADS

1. *To roast the veggies:* Preheat the oven to 425°F.

2. On a large rimmed baking sheet, combine the cauliflower florets and bell pepper. Drizzle the olive oil over the veggies. Sprinkle the cumin and cinnamon on top, followed by a few dashes of salt and a few twists of black pepper. Toss until the veggies are lightly coated in olive oil and spices (add another drizzle of olive oil if necessary). Arrange the veggies in a single layer and roast until they are tender and deeply golden on the edges, about 35 minutes, tossing halfway. Set aside.

3. *To cook the farro:* In a medium saucepan, combine the farro with enough water to cover by a couple of inches. Bring the water to a boil over high heat, then reduce to a gentle simmer and cook, stirring occasionally, until the farro is tender to the bite but still pleasantly chewy (pearled farro will take around 15 minutes; unprocessed farro will take 25 to 40 minutes). Drain off the excess water and return the farro to the pot.

4. *Meanwhile, to prepare the dressing:* In a small bowl, combine the olive oil, lemon juice, tahini, garlic, salt, and pepper to taste. Whisk until blended. If you would prefer a creamier consistency, whisk in an additional tablespoon of tahini.

5. Once you have drained the cooked farro, pour all of the dressing into the pot and stir to combine. Taste and add additional salt or pepper if desired.

6. *To assemble the salad:* Pour the farro mixture into a large serving bowl or onto a large serving platter. Add the arugula and toss to combine. Top with the roasted cauliflower and red bell pepper, then

evenly distribute the chickpeas, parsley, cilantro, feta, and green onions on top. Gently toss the salad a few times. Serve immediately. Leftovers keep well, chilled, for 2 to 3 days.

$^1/_2$ cup crumbled feta cheese (about $2^1/_2$ ounces)

$^1/_3$ cup chopped green onions (2 to 3)

GLUTEN FREE: *Omit the farro, or replace it with long-grain brown rice (see page 224 for cooking instructions).* • **DAIRY FREE/VEGAN:** *Skip the feta cheese.* • **EGG FREE** • **NUT FREE** • **SOY FREE**

3 *Soups*

WHEN IT'S COLD OUTSIDE, THERE'S NOTHING BETTER THAN SNUGGLING UP ON THE COUCH WITH COOKIE AND A WARM BOWL OF SOUP. The soups and stews you'll find in this chapter are nourishing and hearty, but not heavy. I hope they warm you up on cool fall and winter evenings.

Most of these recipes (the blended soups excluded) yield quite a bit of soup, 6 to 8 servings each. They all make for great leftovers, and will keep well in the refrigerator for up to 4 days. These soups all freeze well for later, too. When hunger strikes, it's always a relief to find wholesome backup meals in the freezer.

To freeze soup, let it cool down until it is safe to handle. Then, divide the soup into individual portions to speed the cooling process (a key food-safety element). Spoon the soup into 1-pint, wide-mouth mason jars, leaving at least 1 inch of space at the top of the jar to allow for expansion. When freezing liquids, it's important to use wide-mouth mason jars rather than the jars with sloping sides, because they're less likely to break as liquids expand and contract.

Let the soup cool to room temperature, stirring occasionally to speed the process, before screwing on the lids (otherwise, you'll trap heat in the container, which is counterproductive). Screw on the lids just halfway at first, to allow room for expansion. Place the jars in the freezer. Once they have frozen solid, screw the lids on completely to help prevent freezer burn. For best flavor and texture, frozen soups are generally best consumed within 3 months, although frozen soups reheated after that mark do not pose any health risks.

If you have the foresight, transfer jars of frozen soup to the refrigerator to thaw for a day or two before reheating the soup in the microwave or in a pot on the stove. More often than not, I take advantage of the defrost function on my microwave. Be careful–those mason jars get very hot. Use oven mitts to remove hot jars from the microwave, and be sure not to slosh hot soup over the sides onto your hands.

Black Bean Tortilla Soup with Sweet Potatoes

2 tablespoons plus 2 teaspoons extra-virgin olive oil

1 large yellow onion, chopped

1 small sweet potato (about ½ pound), peeled and cut into ¼-inch dice

1 medium red bell pepper, chopped

1 medium jalapeño, seeded, deribbed, and finely chopped

Fine sea salt

4 cloves garlic, pressed or minced

2 teaspoons ground cumin

1½ teaspoons chili powder

2 cans (15 ounces each) black beans, rinsed and drained, or 3 cups cooked black beans

1 can (14.5 ounces) diced tomatoes, preferably fire-roasted, with their liquid

4 cups (32 ounces) vegetable broth

4 corn tortillas, cut into 2-inch-long, ¼-inch-wide strips

¼ cup chopped fresh cilantro, divided

2 tablespoons lime juice

¼ teaspoon red pepper flakes (optional)

Freshly ground black pepper

Here's a delightful vegetarian version of the chicken tortilla soup I used to order at restaurants. Tortilla soup is a traditional Mexican soup made with a chili- and lime-spiked, tomato-y broth and crispy tortilla strips. The tortilla soup I knew growing up included chicken, lots of crushed fried tortilla chips, shredded cheese, and sour cream. This version is light and fresh, but sticks with you, thanks to hearty black beans and sweet potatoes. Oven-baked crispy tortilla strips are placed in the bowl and on top of the soup, so you get both tender and crunchy tortillas in each bite. It's a fiesta in a bowl!

MAKES 5 TO 6 HEARTY BOWLS

1. In a large Dutch oven, warm 2 tablespoons of the olive oil over medium heat until shimmering. Add the onion, sweet potato, bell pepper, jalapeño, and ¼ teaspoon salt. Cook, stirring occasionally, until the onions are translucent and the sweet potatoes are easily pierced through by a fork, 10 to 15 minutes.

2. Stir in the garlic, cumin, and chili powder and cook until fragrant, about 30 seconds. Pour in the beans, tomatoes, and broth. Increase the heat to medium-high and bring the mixture to a simmer. Cook, reducing the heat as necessary to maintain a gentle simmer, until the broth is flavorful and the sweet potatoes and beans are very tender, about 30 minutes.

3. Meanwhile, to make the crispy tortilla strips: Preheat the oven to 400°F. Line a large baking sheet with parchment paper for easy cleanup

4. On the prepared baking sheet, toss the tortilla strips with the remaining 2 teaspoons olive oil until lightly and evenly coated. Arrange them in a single layer and sprinkle with salt. Bake until crisp, about 8 minutes, flipping halfway.

5. Once the soup is done cooking, stir in most of the cilantro (reserve about 1 tablespoon for garnishing) and the lime juice. Season to taste with additional salt, if necessary (I usually add another ¼ teaspoon salt), pepper flakes (if you want more spice), and black pepper to taste.

6. To serve, divide about half of the baked tortilla strips into individual soup bowls, reserving the other half for topping the bowls. Ladle the soup over the tortilla strips. Top each bowl of soup with additional

tortilla strips, radishes, feta, and a light sprinkle of the reserved cilantro.

TIP: *Leftover crispy tortilla strips don't always keep well, so you might want to crumble tortilla chips over reheated bowls of soup. That said, I really prefer the clean flavor of freshly baked tortilla strips, so they're worth the effort to make fresh.*

GARNISHES

2 radishes, thinly sliced and roughly chopped

$1/4$ cup crumbled feta cheese (about $1^1/_2$ ounces)

GLUTEN FREE: *Use certified gluten-free tortillas.* • **DAIRY FREE/VEGAN:** *Skip the feta cheese.* • **EGG FREE** • **NUT FREE** • **SOY FREE**

CHANGE IT UP

If you're in a hurry, buy pre-cut cubed butternut squash, and instead of making your own tortilla strips, just use a handful of crumbled tortilla chips.

Ingredient Note: If you can't find chipotle peppers in adobo sauce (check the international/Hispanic aisle of your grocery store), replace them with an equal amount of smoked paprika.

Butternut Squash Chipotle Chili

This hearty chili is a little spicy and a little sweet. It's absolutely perfect for serving at game-day watch parties, since it's gluten free, vegan, and satisfies conventional carnivore taste buds too. In summary, this chili makes everyone happy! This recipe is one of the most popular recipes on my blog, and readers report that it has won more than a few chili cook-offs. **MAKES 5 TO 6 HEARTY BOWLS**

1. In a Dutch oven or soup pot, warm the olive oil over medium heat until shimmering. Add the onion, bell peppers, butternut squash, and a pinch of salt. Cook, stirring occasionally, until the onions are translucent, about 10 minutes.

2. Reduce the heat to medium-low and add the garlic, chili powder, 1 1/2 teaspoons adobo sauce, the cumin, and cinnamon. Cook, stirring constantly, until fragrant, about 30 seconds. Add the bay leaf, black beans, tomatoes, and broth. Stir to combine, then increase the heat to medium-high and bring the mixture to a simmer.

3. Cover and cook, reducing the heat as necessary to maintain a gentle simmer and stirring occasionally, for about 1 hour. You'll know your chili is done when the butternut squash is nice and tender and the liquid has reduced somewhat. Remove the bay leaf and discard it.

4. For a thicker chili, mash the chili with a potato masher until you reach a more hearty consistency. (Alternatively, transfer 2 cups of the chili to a blender, blend until smooth–beware hot steam escaping from the lid–and stir it back into the pot.) Add salt to taste. If your chili isn't spicy enough, add more adobo sauce (I usually add another 1 1/2 teaspoons, but I like spicy chili).

5. *To make the tortilla strips:* Heat a large skillet over medium heat and add the olive oil. Once the oil is shimmering, toss in the tortilla strips, sprinkle them with salt, and stir. Cook until the strips are crispy and turning golden, stirring occasionally, 5 to 10 minutes. Cover a plate with a piece of paper towel and place it near the stove. Once the strips are done, scoot them onto the covered plate to drain and cool.

6. Ladle the chili into bowls (this chili is very hearty, so I usually aim for about 1 1/2 cups of chili per bowl), then top with crispy tortilla strips, plenty of diced avocado, and a small sprinkle of chopped cilantro.

2 tablespoons extra-virgin olive oil

1 medium red onion, chopped

2 red bell peppers, chopped

3 cups cubed butternut squash (1/2-inch cubes)

Fine sea salt

4 cloves garlic, pressed or minced

1 tablespoon chili powder

1 1/2 to 3 teaspoons adobo sauce, from a can of chipotle peppers in adobo*

1 teaspoon ground cumin

1/4 teaspoon ground cinnamon

1 bay leaf

2 cans (15 ounces each) black beans, rinsed and drained, or 3 cups cooked black beans

1 can (14.5 ounces) diced tomatoes, with their liquid

2 cups vegetable broth

CRISPY TORTILLA STRIPS

1 1/2 teaspoons extra-virgin olive oil

3 corn tortillas, cut into 2-inch-long, 1/4-inch-wide strips

Fine sea salt

ADDITIONAL GARNISHES

1 large or 2 small avocados, diced

Handful of chopped fresh cilantro

GLUTEN FREE: *Use certified gluten-free corn tortillas.* • **DAIRY FREE** • **VEGAN** • **EGG FREE** • **NUT FREE** • **SOY FREE**

West African Peanut Soup

2 tablespoons extra-virgin olive oil

1 medium red onion, chopped

1 medium sweet potato (about ¹⁄₂ pound), peeled and cut into ¹⁄₄-inch dice

1 medium jalapeño, seeded, deribbed, and finely chopped

Fine sea salt

2 tablespoons peeled and finely grated or minced fresh ginger

4 cloves garlic, pressed or minced

4 cups (32 ounces) vegetable broth

2 cups water

³⁄₄ cup creamy peanut butter*

6 ounces tomato paste

1 medium bunch collard greens or kale (about 8 ounces), tough ribs removed and leaves chopped into bite-size pieces

1 can (15 ounces) chickpeas, rinsed and drained, or 1¹⁄₂ cups cooked chickpeas

Hot sauce, preferably Sriracha

GARNISHES
¹⁄₄ cup roughly chopped roasted peanuts

Handful of chopped fresh cilantro

I t's true. I put peanut butter in soup, and I'm not one bit sorry. If you're apprehensive about the idea, I get it. I was hesitant, too. An old friend convinced me to try it, and I'm so glad he did. Now, I hope you'll take my endorsement and make it!

We certainly weren't the first to put peanut butter in soup—it's commonplace in West Africa. Peanut butter makes the soup rich and luxurious, and offers more redeeming qualities than heavy cream. This recipe is a reworked version of the recipe on my blog. I added sweet potato, jalapeño, and chickpeas to make it even more hearty and delicious. If you want to make it more substantial, serve it over some cooked brown rice (page 224). **MAKES 5 TO 7 HEARTY BOWLS**

1. In a Dutch oven or soup pot, warm the olive oil over medium heat until shimmering. Add the onion, sweet potato, jalapeño, and a dash of salt. Cook, stirring occasionally, until the onions are translucent and the sweet potatoes are tender, about 10 minutes. Add the ginger, garlic, and 1 teaspoon salt. Cook, stirring frequently, until fragrant, about 1 minute.

2. Pour in the vegetable broth and water, increase the heat to medium-high, and bring the mixture to a simmer. Cook for 15 minutes, stirring occasionally and reducing the heat as necessary to maintain a gentle simmer.

3. Meanwhile, in a heatproof medium bowl, combine the peanut butter and tomato paste. Transfer 1 to 2 cups of hot broth from the pot to the bowl. Whisk the mixture together until smooth, then pour the peanut mixture into the soup and mix well.

4. Stir the collard greens and chickpeas into the soup and continue cooking until the soup is nice and thick, with sufficiently softened greens, 15 to 25 minutes longer. Season the soup with hot sauce to taste (I usually add over 1 tablespoon Sriracha, but I like spicy soups). Remove the pot from the heat and add more salt to taste, if necessary (I often add up to ¹⁄₂ teaspoon more).

5. Serve the soup in bowls with a sprinkle of chopped peanuts and cilantro on top. Serve with additional hot sauce on the side.

GLUTEN FREE • DAIRY FREE • VEGAN • EGG FREE • SOY FREE

Ingredient Note: I use unsweetened natural peanut butter in this recipe (salted or unsalted both work). If you're allergic to peanuts, substitute almond butter or sunflower butter and skip the peanut garnish.

Tuscan White Bean, Kale, and Farro Stew

I like to pretend I'm curled up by a fire in a cozy Italian countryside home while I sip this substantial stew. It features classic Tuscan flavors, including white beans, tomatoes, kale, garlic, and rosemary. Nutty, whole-grain farro is often found in Italian recipes and makes the soup a complete meal. This soup is perfect for when you need a hearty, warming lunch or dinner that won't weigh you down. It yields quite a bit of soup, which makes great leftovers for the next few days. Like all of my soups, it also freezes well for more long-term storage. **MAKES 6 TO 8 HEARTY BOWLS**

1. In a Dutch oven or soup pot, warm 2 tablespoons of the olive oil over medium heat until shimmering. Add the onion, carrots, celery, and ¼ teaspoon salt. Cook, stirring occasionally, until the vegetables are tender and the onion is translucent, about 10 minutes.

2. Add the garlic and pepper flakes and cook, stirring frequently, until fragrant, about 1 minute. Add the bay leaves, farro, beans, tomatoes, vegetable broth, and water. Stir to combine.

3. Increase the heat to medium-high and bring the mixture to a simmer. Continue cooking, reducing the heat as necessary to maintain a gentle simmer, for 30 minutes. Add the chopped kale and rosemary sprig. Stir to combine and continue cooking until both the farro and kale are tender, about 10 minutes longer.

4. Remove the pot from the heat and discard the bay leaves and rosemary sprig. Stir in the lemon juice and season to taste with additional salt (I usually add another ¼ teaspoon) and plenty of black pepper. Lastly, stir in the remaining 1 tablespoon olive oil for extra richness (trust me!).

5. Serve the soup in bowls with a sprinkle of Parmesan on top. Serve immediately.

TIP: *The fresh rosemary sprig helps differentiate this soup's flavor from other tomato-based soups, so please don't skip it. Did you know that you can easily freeze extra rosemary? Just wash it, pat dry, and freeze in a freezer bag with the air squeezed out.*

- 3 tablespoons extra-virgin olive oil, divided
- 1 large yellow onion, chopped
- 3 carrots, chopped
- 3 ribs celery, chopped
- Fine sea salt
- 6 cloves garlic, pressed or minced
- ½ teaspoon red pepper flakes
- 2 bay leaves
- 1 cup farro, rinsed
- 2 cans (15 ounces each) cannellini beans or Great Northern beans, rinsed and drained, or 3 cups cooked beans
- 1 can (14.5 ounces) diced tomatoes, with their liquid
- 4 cups (32 ounces) vegetable broth
- 2 cups water
- 1 medium bunch kale (about 8 ounces), preferably Tuscan (lacinato), tough ribs removed and leaves chopped into bite-size pieces
- 1 sprig (about 6 inches) fresh rosemary
- 1 tablespoon lemon juice
- Freshly ground black pepper
- Finely grated Parmesan cheese, for garnish

GLUTEN FREE: *Replace the farro with long-grain brown rice, or omit the farro altogether for a lighter, grain-free soup.* • **DAIRY FREE/VEGAN:** *Omit the Parmesan garnish.* • **EGG FREE** • **NUT FREE** • **SOY FREE**

Moroccan Butternut, Chickpea, and Couscous Stew

Morocco is near the tippy-top of my list of countries to visit. For now, I have this stew. I love to stand over the stove as it's cooking so I can savor the smell of warming Moroccan spices. This thick veggie stew is flavorful, but not too spicy. It's well-balanced thanks to tender cubes of sweet butternut squash. Chickpeas, whole wheat couscous, and hardy greens make it a simple, but true, feast in a bowl. Please don't be intimidated by the long list of ingredients here. They are all pretty basic, and the soup is easy to make. **MAKES 6 TO 8 SERVINGS**

3 tablespoons extra-virgin olive oil, divided

2 cups cubed butternut squash ($^1/_2$-inch cubes)

1 medium yellow onion, chopped

2 carrots, chopped

1 rib celery, chopped

Fine sea salt

6 cloves garlic, pressed or minced

1 tablespoon smoked paprika

$1^1/_2$ teaspoons curry powder

$^1/_4$ teaspoon ground cinnamon

$^1/_4$ teaspoon red pepper flakes

1 can (28 ounces) diced tomatoes, with their liquid

4 cups (32 ounces) vegetable broth

2 cups water

Freshly ground black pepper

1 can (15 ounces) chickpeas, rinsed and drained, or $1^1/_2$ cups cooked chickpeas

1 cup whole wheat couscous*

2 cups chopped fresh collards or kale (tough ribs removed)

1 tablespoon lemon juice, or more if needed

Handful of chopped fresh cilantro (optional), for garnish

1. In a Dutch oven or soup pot, warm 2 tablespoons of the olive oil over medium heat until shimmering. Add the butternut squash, onion, carrots, celery, and a pinch of salt. Cook, stirring often, until the squash is tender and the onion is translucent, 10 to 15 minutes.

2. Add the garlic, smoked paprika, curry powder, cinnamon, and pepper flakes. Cook until fragrant, stirring constantly, about 1 minute.

3. Pour in the diced tomatoes, broth, and water. Add 1 teaspoon salt and season generously with black pepper. Increase the heat to medium-high and bring the mixture to a boil, then partially cover the pot with the lid, leaving about a 1-inch gap for steam to escape. Reduce the heat as necessary to maintain a gentle simmer and cook for 20 minutes.

4. Uncover, add the chickpeas, couscous, and chopped greens and cook, uncovered, for 10 minutes more, or until the couscous and greens have cooked to your liking.

5. Remove the pot from the heat and stir in the lemon juice and the remaining 1 tablespoon olive oil. Taste and season with more salt (I usually add another $^1/_2$ teaspoon), pepper, and/or lemon juice until the flavors really sing. Serve the soup in bowls with a sprinkle of cilantro on top, if desired.

GLUTEN FREE: *Substitute $^1/_2$ cup quinoa (rinsed) for the couscous and cook for an additional 10 minutes; or omit the couscous completely for a lighter soup.* • **DAIRY FREE** • **VEGAN** • **EGG FREE** • **NUT FREE** • **SOY FREE**

Ingredient Note: Look for whole wheat couscous in the pasta aisle or bulk bin section of the grocery store. I usually buy mine at Trader Joe's.

Hearty Lentil Minestrone *VG*

This minestrone is a riff on the blog's most popular soup, lentil soup! It's a classically flavored minestrone, with lentils added for even more depth and substance. Minestrone was traditionally a soup full of leftover veggies, so feel free to use whichever seasonal vegetables you have on hand. This soup is made extra luxurious and authentic with olive oil; ¼ cup might seem like a lot of oil for a soup, but it's really not that much per serving. Promise! **MAKES 6 TO 8 SERVINGS**

¼ cup extra-virgin olive oil

1 medium yellow onion, chopped

2 carrots, chopped

2 ribs celery, chopped

2 tablespoons tomato paste

Fine sea salt

1 cup chopped seasonal vegetables (yellow squash, zucchini, butternut squash, potatoes, or peas)

4 cloves garlic, pressed or minced

½ teaspoon dried oregano

½ teaspoon dried thyme

1 can (28 ounces) diced tomatoes, with their liquid

¾ cup French green lentils or brown lentils, picked over for debris and rinsed

4 cups (32 ounces) vegetable broth

2 cups water

2 bay leaves

Pinch of red pepper flakes

Freshly ground black pepper

1 cup whole-grain orecchiette, elbow, or small shell pasta*

1 can (15 ounces) Great Northern beans or cannellini beans, rinsed and drained, or 1½ cups cooked beans

2 cups chopped Tuscan (lacinato) or curly kale, tough ribs removed

2 teaspoons lemon juice, or more if needed

Freshly grated Parmesan cheese, for garnish

1. In a Dutch oven or soup pot, warm the olive oil over medium heat until shimmering. Add the onion, carrots, celery, tomato paste, and a pinch of salt. Cook, stirring often, until the vegetables have softened and the onions are turning translucent, 7 to 10 minutes.

2. Add the seasonal vegetables, garlic, oregano, and thyme. Cook, stirring frequently, until fragrant, about 2 minutes. Pour in the tomatoes, lentils, broth, and water. Add 1 teaspoon salt, the bay leaves, and pepper flakes. Season generously with black pepper.

3. Increase the heat to medium-high and bring the mixture to a simmer, then partially cover the pot with the lid, leaving about a 1-inch gap for steam to escape. Reduce the heat as necessary to maintain a gentle simmer and cook for 15 minutes.

4. Uncover and add the pasta, beans, and chopped kale. Continue simmering uncovered until the lentils are tender and the pasta is cooked al dente, about 20 minutes.

5. Remove the pot from the heat, then remove and discard the bay leaves. Stir in the lemon juice. Taste and season with more salt (I usually add another ½ teaspoon), pepper, and/or lemon juice until the flavors really sing. Serve the soup in bowls with grated Parmesan on top.

GLUTEN FREE: *Use gluten-free pasta.* • **DAIRY FREE/VEGAN:** *Omit the Parmesan.* • **EGG FREE** • **NUT FREE** • **SOY FREE**

*Ingredient Note: My favorite pasta for this soup is DeLallo organic whole wheat orecchiette, which has a lovely texture and never gets too soggy. Orecchiette means "little ears" in Italian. Cute, right?

Classic Tomato Soup

Good

O nce I started making homemade soups, I realized just how much better homemade soups are than the store-bought kind. I'd been soup-deprived my whole life! Soon thereafter, I decided to conquer tomato soup. I bought ripe summer tomatoes, cranked up the oven to roast them, and discovered one of life's unfortunate realities: Tomato season and oven boycott season are one and the same.

I was reluctant to use canned tomatoes as the base of a tomato soup recipe, but practicality won out as my craving for homemade tomato soup grew to impossible proportions. Here we are! This recipe makes use of canned tomatoes, but tastes super fresh, perhaps simply because it's freshly made. I honestly prefer it to the soup I made that hot September day. You'll never guess, but instead of heavy cream, I used white beans to thicken and mellow the flavors of the soup. The soup is classic as is, but I love to add fresh basil when I have it, for tomato-basil soup. **MAKES 4 MODEST BOWLS**

1. In a Dutch oven or soup pot, warm the olive oil over medium heat until shimmering. Add the onion and salt and cook, stirring occasionally, until the onions are tender and turning translucent, 7 to 10 minutes. Add the tomato paste and cook, stirring constantly, until fragrant, about 30 seconds.

2. Add the tomatoes and vegetable broth and stir to combine. Increase the heat to medium-high, and bring the mixture to a simmer. Cook for 30 minutes, reducing the heat as necessary to maintain a gentle simmer, and stirring occasionally.

3. Remove the pot from the heat and let it cool for a few minutes. Carefully transfer the mixture to a blender, being sure not to fill past the maximum fill line (blend in batches if necessary). Add the beans, butter, sugar, and several twists of black pepper. Securely fasten the lid and blend the soup until smooth, being careful to avoid hot steam escaping from the lid.

4. Since canned tomatoes vary in flavor, I always end up tinkering with this soup a bit at the end. Taste and, if necessary, add a little more sugar (to balance out the acidity of the tomatoes), butter (for richness and to mellow the flavors a bit), pepper, and salt (I usually add another $1/2$ teaspoon). If you're adding basil, add it now. Blend again and serve.

---

2 tablespoons extra-virgin olive oil

1 medium yellow onion, chopped

$1/2$ teaspoon fine sea salt

2 tablespoons tomato paste

1 can (28 ounces) whole tomatoes, with their liquid

2 cups vegetable broth

$1/2$ cup cooked Great Northern beans or cannellini beans

1 tablespoon unsalted butter

1 teaspoon coconut sugar or brown sugar

Freshly ground black pepper

10 to 15 roughly chopped fresh basil leaves (optional), to taste

TIP: *This recipe yields 4 modest bowls of soup. You might want to double the recipe if you're serving a crowd, or if you would like to have leftovers.*

GLUTEN FREE • DAIRY FREE/VEGAN: *Use 1 tablespoon olive oil instead of the butter.* **• EGG FREE • NUT FREE • SOY FREE**

Creamy Roasted Cauliflower Soup

1 large head cauliflower (about 2 pounds), cut into bite-size florets

4 tablespoons extra-virgin olive oil, divided

Fine sea salt

1 medium red onion, chopped

2 cloves garlic, pressed or minced

4 cups (32 ounces) vegetable broth

2 cups whole-grain bread cubes (½-inch thick)

¼ cup sliced almonds

2 tablespoons unsalted butter

1 teaspoon lemon juice, or more if needed

Pinch of ground nutmeg

2 tablespoons finely chopped fresh flat-leaf parsley, for garnish

Cauliflower soup is not the prettiest of soups, but it sure is tasty. I had no interest in it until my friend Tessa made it for a girls' night a couple of years ago, and then I was hooked.

Here's the cauliflower soup of my dreams, made with caramelized roasted cauliflower for maximum flavor. It's super creamy, yet cream-less. A little bit of butter does the trick! You can also make a great vegan version with cashews instead. The bowls aren't complete without freshly toasted croutons and almonds, for an irresistible nutty crunch, and parsley, for a hint of fresh green flavor.

MAKES 4 MODEST BOWLS

1. Preheat the oven to 425°F.

2. On a large rimmed baking sheet, toss the cauliflower with 2 tablespoons of the olive oil until lightly and evenly coated in oil. Arrange the cauliflower in a single layer and sprinkle with salt. Bake until the cauliflower is tender and caramelized on the edges, 25 to 35 minutes, tossing halfway. Leave the oven on.

3. Meanwhile, once the cauliflower is almost done, in a Dutch oven or soup pot, warm 1 tablespoon of the olive oil over medium heat until shimmering. Add the onion and ¼ teaspoon salt. Cook, stirring occasionally, until the onion is softened and turning translucent, 5 to 7 minutes.

4. Add the garlic and cook, stirring constantly, until fragrant, about 30 seconds, then add the broth. Reserve 4 of the prettiest roasted cauliflower florets for garnish, then transfer the cauliflower to the pot. (Reserve the baking sheet for the croutons.) Increase the heat to medium-high and bring the mixture to a simmer, then reduce the heat as necessary to maintain a gentle simmer. Cook, stirring occasionally, for 20 minutes, to give the flavors time to meld.

5. Meanwhile, on the baking sheet, combine the bread cubes and almonds. Drizzle with the remaining 1 tablespoon olive oil and toss until the mixture is lightly coated. Arrange the mixture in a single layer and sprinkle lightly with salt. Bake until the croutons and almonds are nice and golden on the edges, 7 to 9 minutes, tossing halfway.

6. Once the soup is done cooking, remove the pot from the heat and let it cool for a few minutes. Then, carefully transfer the hot soup to a

blender, working in batches if necessary. (Do not fill past the maximum fill line or the soup will overflow!)

7. Add the butter and blend until smooth. Add the lemon juice and nutmeg and blend again. Taste and add additional salt if necessary (I usually add another $1/4$ to $1/2$ teaspoon) and a little more lemon juice, if it needs more zing. Blend again.

8. Top individual bowls of soup with 1 roasted cauliflower floret, a handful of the crouton and almond mixture, and a sprinkle of parsley.

GLUTEN FREE: *Skip the croutons.* • **DAIRY FREE/VEGAN:** *Use cashews instead of butter. Soak $1/4$ cup cashews for 4 hours. Drain and rinse before proceeding (if you have a high-powered blender like a Vitamix or Blendtec, you can skip the soaking step). Add the cashews when you would add the dairy butter.* • **EGG FREE** • **NUT FREE:** *Skip the almonds.* • **SOY FREE**

4 *Happy Hour*

I LOVE NOTHING MORE THAN LAUGHING WITH CLOSE FRIENDS AROUND A DINNER TABLE. My girlfriends and I try to get together every couple of weeks for ladies' night, which might start at 8 p.m. and carry on until midnight. Sometimes, the host will offer an elaborate spread; other times, we pass around a bowl of popcorn, some chocolate, and a bottle of wine. It's always so much fun.

Here are 20 reasons to invite friends over and break out those cocktail glasses. In this chapter, you'll find fresh appetizers and snacks, including spring rolls, salsas, and my favorite hummus. I've also included a few simple cocktails that are great for parties, or for sipping after a long day. Cheers!

Fresh Sesame Soba Spring Rolls with Peanut Dipping Sauce

4 ounces soba noodles*

1 tablespoon sesame seeds

2 teaspoons toasted sesame oil

PEANUT DIPPING SAUCE

$1/3$ cup creamy peanut butter

2 tablespoons rice vinegar or white wine vinegar

2 tablespoons reduced-sodium tamari or soy sauce

2 tablespoons honey

1 tablespoon lime juice, or more if needed

2 teaspoons toasted sesame oil

1 teaspoon grated fresh ginger or $1/4$ teaspoon ground ginger

2 medium cloves garlic, pressed or minced

Pinch of red pepper flakes

SPRING ROLLS

1 large carrot ($1/4$ pound)

2 Persian cucumbers or 1 small cucumber

6 to 8 rice papers*

2 medium jalapeños, seeded, deribbed, and cut lengthwise into long, thin strips

1 avocado, cut into long, thin strips

$1/4$ cup chopped green onions (about 2)

Handful of fresh cilantro leaves, chopped

F resh spring rolls are Vietnamese. Soba noodles are Japanese. I'm sure I'm upsetting someone by mixing the two cuisines, but they go so well together! Rice noodles are common spring roll fillings, but I opted for soba noodles instead, which are made with buckwheat flour. They add some nutritious, nutty flavor to the rolls.

Don't worry about the rice papers–they seem intimidating at first, but they're fairly easy to manage. Working one by one, you'll soak each brittle, translucent round in warm water for just a few seconds, and they'll turn into pliable and stretchy skins right before your eyes. If you are already a pro at rolling burritos or swaddling babies, you have great potential when it comes to wrapping spring rolls.

MAKES 6 TO 8 SPRING ROLLS

1. Bring a large pot of salted water to boil and cook the soba noodles just until al dente, according to package directions. Rinse them under cold water, drain, and return them to the pot. Toss the noodles with the sesame seeds and toasted sesame oil. Set aside.

2. *Meanwhile, to make the dipping sauce:* In a small bowl, whisk together the peanut butter, vinegar, tamari, honey, lime juice, sesame oil, ginger, garlic, and pepper flakes until well combined. If the sauce is too thick for dipping, stir in a little more lime juice. Set aside.

3. *To prepare the spring rolls:* Run a julienne peeler or vegetable peeler down the length of the carrot and cucumber(s) repeatedly, turning halfway, to create long "noodles." Toss the carrot and cucumber noodles with the soba noodles.

4. Fill a shallow pan larger than your rice papers (a pie pan works great) with warm water. Fold a lint-free tea towel in half and place it next to the dish. Make sure your prepared fillings are within reach.

5. Place one rice paper in the water and let it rest for about 20 seconds. You'll learn to go by feel here–wait until the sheet is pliable but not super floppy. Carefully lay it flat on the towel.

6. Leaving about 1 inch of open rice paper around the edges, cover the lower third of the paper with a handful of soba, carrot, and cucumber noodles. Top with a few strips of jalapeño and avocado in a row on top of the noodles, then sprinkle with green onions and chopped cilantro.

7. Fold the lower edge over the fillings, then fold over the short sides like you would to make a burrito. Lastly, roll it up, stretching the remaining long side around the roll to seal it. Repeat with the remaining ingredients. Halve the rolls on the diagonal with a sharp chef's knife (or serve whole) with the peanut dipping sauce on the side. If you have any peanut sauce left over, it makes a great veggie dip.

PEANUT ALLERGY NOTE: *If you're serving someone with a peanut allergy, substitute almond butter or sunflower butter for the peanut butter.*

*Ingredient Note: Look for soba noodles and rice papers (also called spring roll wrappers or spring roll skins) in the Asian section of well-stocked grocery stores.

GLUTEN FREE: *Be sure to use gluten-free tamari. Either use 100% buckwheat gluten-free soba noodles (which can be difficult to find) or triple the amount of carrot and cucumber.* • **DAIRY FREE** • **VEGAN:** *Use maple syrup instead of honey.* • **EGG FREE**

Everyday Red Salsa

If tomatoes aren't in season, or you don't want to crank up the oven, or you're just in a hurry, make this salsa! You can get amazing flavor from a can of quality fire-roasted tomatoes (I highly recommend Muir Glen brand here). This quick salsa recipe is ready in less than 10 minutes, and it is 100 percent worth the effort.

MAKES 2 CUPS

1 can (15 ounces) diced fire-roasted tomatoes

1 clove garlic, roughly chopped

$1/2$ cup roughly chopped white onion (about $1/2$ small onion)

$1/4$ cup lightly packed fresh cilantro leaves

$1/2$ medium jalapeño, seeded, deribbed, and roughly chopped

1 tablespoon lime juice, or more if needed

$1/2$ teaspoon fine sea salt

1. Drain off about half of the tomato juice from the can (about $1/3$ cup) and discard it.

2. In a food processor, pulse the garlic to chop it more finely. Add the tomatoes and all of the remaining juice from the can. Add the onion, cilantro, jalapeño, lime juice, and salt. Process the mixture until it is mostly smooth and no big chunks of tomato or onion remain, scraping down the sides as necessary. Season to taste with additional lime juice and salt, if necessary.

3. Serve the salsa immediately or store it for later. This salsa keeps well in the refrigerator, covered, for about 10 days.

GLUTEN FREE • DAIRY FREE • VEGAN • EGG FREE • NUT FREE • SOY FREE

Roasted Summertime Salsa

1 pound tomatoes
(about 3 medium)

$1/2$ medium jalapeño,
seeded and deribbed

1 clove garlic, roughly
chopped

$1/2$ cup roughly chopped
white onion (about
$1/2$ small)

$1/4$ cup lightly packed
fresh cilantro leaves

1 tablespoon lime juice,
or more if needed

$1/2$ teaspoon fine sea salt

Fair warning: Once you start making your own salsa, you can't go back. Homemade salsa is infinitely more flavorful than the jarred stuff, even when you have to resort to canned tomatoes. Fresh ingredients make all the difference!

When I was working on my salsa technique for this book, I quickly realized that the concentrated flavor of roasted tomatoes is key. If it's too hot outside to turn on the oven, see my Everyday Red Salsa (page 101), which uses canned tomatoes. **MAKES 2 CUPS**

1. Preheat the broiler with a rack about 4 inches below the heat source. Place the tomatoes and jalapeño on a rimmed baking sheet and broil until they're blackened in spots, about 5 minutes.

2. Remove the baking sheet from the oven and use tongs to carefully flip over the tomatoes and jalapeño. Broil until the tomatoes are splotchy-black and blistered, 4 to 6 minutes more.

3. Meanwhile, in a food processor, pulse the garlic to chop it more finely. Add the onion, cilantro, lime juice, and salt. Set aside.

4. Once the tomatoes have cooled enough to handle, slice them into large pieces. Remove any rough bits where the tomato met the stem and discard them. Slice the roasted jalapeño into a few smaller pieces.

5. Add the tomato and jalapeño to the food processor. Process the mixture until it is mostly smooth and no big chunks of tomato or onion remain, scraping down the sides as necessary. Season to taste with additional lime juice and salt, if necessary. Serve the salsa immediately or store it for later. This salsa keeps well in the refrigerator, covered, for about 10 days.

GLUTEN FREE • DAIRY FREE • VEGAN • EGG FREE • NUT FREE • SOY FREE

CHANGE IT UP

You can make creamy avocado salsa verde by blending in 1 to 2 diced avocados. Just let the salsa cool before adding the diced avocado to the food processor and blending it in. The more avocado you add, the creamier it gets.

Roasted Salsa Verde

What is your condiment of choice? Ketchup, mustard, pesto, salsa, pickled onions? Tough call, I know. Salsa verde is my top choice. I put it on almost all of my Mexican creations, especially when black beans, sweet potatoes, or bell peppers are involved. It's a little spicy, a little sweet, and bursting with freshly roasted tomatillo flavor. It complements, rather than overwhelms, other Mexican flavors. **MAKES 2½ CUPS**

1½ pounds tomatillos (about 12 medium), husked and rinsed

1 small jalapeño, stem end removed (omit for mild salsa)

½ cup chopped white onion (about ½ small)

¼ cup lightly packed fresh cilantro leaves

2 to 4 tablespoons lime juice (from 1 to 2 limes)

Fine sea salt

1. Preheat the broiler with a rack about 4 inches below the heat source. Place the tomatillos and jalapeño (if using) on a rimmed baking sheet (do not line with parchment paper–it will burn) and broil until they're blackened in spots, about 5 minutes.

2. Remove the baking sheet from the oven and use tongs to carefully flip over the tomatillos and jalapeño. Put them back in the oven to broil until the tomatillos are splotchy-black and blistered, 4 to 6 minutes more.

3. Meanwhile, in a food processor or blender, combine the chopped onion, cilantro, 2 tablespoons lime juice, and ½ teaspoon salt.

4. Carefully transfer the hot tomatillos, jalapeño, and all of their juices into the food processor or blender. Pulse until the mixture is mostly smooth and no big chunks of tomatillo remain, scraping down the sides as necessary. Season to taste with additional lime juice and salt (I usually add another ½ teaspoon), if desired.

5. This salsa keeps well in the refrigerator, covered, for about 10 days.

GLUTEN FREE • DAIRY FREE • VEGAN • EGG FREE • NUT FREE • SOY FREE

Pineapple Pico de Gallo

3 cups diced fresh pineapple (about 1 medium)

1 red bell pepper, chopped

$1/2$ cup chopped red onion (about $1/2$ small)

$1/4$ cup chopped fresh cilantro

1 medium jalapeño, seeded, deribbed, and finely chopped

3 tablespoons lime juice (from about $1^1/_2$ limes), or more if needed

$1/4$ teaspoon fine sea salt

The summer after my freshman year of college, my family and I flew south to Mexico for vacation. I was still a picky eater back then, but my taste buds had loosened up a little during my first year away. I got my first taste of super fresh pico de gallo in Mexico, and I proceeded to pile it on everything I ate for the next 5 days. Pico de gallo on eggs, spaghetti, salads, and chips, of course. So many chips.

Traditional pico de gallo is made with chopped tomatoes, but I made this version with fresh pineapple and threw in some red bell pepper for good measure. It might seem strange to replace tomato with pineapple, but they are both fruits, after all! **MAKES 3½ CUPS**

1. In a serving bowl, combine the pineapple, bell pepper, onion, cilantro, and jalapeño. Add the lime juice and salt and stir to combine. Season to taste with additional lime juice and/or salt if it doesn't taste utterly awesome yet.

2. For best flavor, let the pico de gallo rest for 10 minutes or longer before serving. It's best served fresh but keeps well, chilled, for 3 to 4 days.

GLUTEN FREE • DAIRY FREE • VEGAN • EGG FREE • NUT FREE • SOY FREE

Best-Ever Guacamole with Toasted Pepitas and Chipotle Sauce

Guacamole wasn't on the original recipe list for this book. *Too basic*, I thought. Then I perfected my guacamole game, and I couldn't keep it from you. It's the perfect party dip and topping for tacos, burritos, nachos, and all of your favorite Mexican entrees.

Here's the kicker, though–this guacamole gets even better with a couple more Mexican grocery staples. A heavy sprinkle of freshly toasted pepitas and a drizzle of spicy adobo sauce make it otherworldly. They're the perfect contrast to creamy, fresh guacamole, and you can scoop up as much or as little of each as you'd like. If you're sensitive to spice or want basic guacamole, you can leave off the toppings. Either way, this guacamole goes great with tortilla chips, carrot sticks, and wide strips of bell pepper. **MAKES ABOUT 4 CUPS**

¼ cup raw pepitas (hulled pumpkin seeds)

½ teaspoon extra-virgin olive oil

4 medium avocados, halved and pitted

½ cup finely chopped white onion (about ½ small onion)

¼ cup finely chopped fresh cilantro

1 small jalapeño, seeded, deribbed, and finely chopped

3 tablespoons lime juice (from about 1½ limes), or more if needed

¼ teaspoon ground coriander

1 teaspoon kosher salt

1 tablespoon adobo sauce, from a can of chipotle peppers in adobo*

Ingredient Note: Look for canned chipotle peppers in adobo sauce in the international/Hispanic aisle of well-stocked grocery stores. If you can't find them, use a chipotle-flavored hot sauce.

1. To toast the pepitas, combine the pepitas and olive oil in a small skillet. Cook over medium heat, stirring frequently, until the pepitas turn golden on the edges and start making little popping noises, about 5 minutes. Set aside to cool for a few minutes.

2. Using a spoon, scoop the flesh of the avocados into a low serving bowl, discarding any bruised, browned areas. Using a pastry cutter, potato masher, or fork, mash up the avocado until it reaches your desired texture (I like my guacamole to have some texture, so I stop mashing once there are just small chunks remaining).

3. Promptly add the onion, cilantro, jalapeño, lime juice, coriander, and salt. Stir to combine. Taste and add additional salt (I often add up to ½ teaspoon more) and/or lime juice, if needed.

4. Top the guacamole with the toasted pepitas and drizzle the adobo sauce over the top. To store leftovers, press plastic wrap against the surface of the guacamole and refrigerate for later. Leftovers will keep well for 3 days. If the top turns light brown, just scoop off the browned bits and you should find bright green guacamole underneath.

TIP: *Your guacamole can only be as good as your avocados, so be sure to use ripe avocados (but not overripe–they should just barely yield to light pressure, and be free of any squishy areas).*

GLUTEN FREE • DAIRY FREE • VEGAN • EGG FREE • NUT FREE • SOY FREE

Roasted Cherry Tomato Crostini with White Bean Pesto

TOASTS AND ROASTED TOMATOES

1 whole-grain baguette or small loaf of crusty whole-grain bread (about 14 ounces), cut into $1/2$-inch slices

3 tablespoons extra-virgin olive oil, divided

1 pint (2 cups) cherry or grape tomatoes, halved lengthwise

Fine sea salt and freshly ground black pepper

WHITE BEAN PESTO

1 can (15 ounces) cannellini beans, rinsed and drained, or $1^1/2$ cups cooked beans

1 cup lightly packed fresh basil leaves, plus a few more small or torn basil leaves for garnish

$1/3$ cup raw almonds

1 tablespoon lemon juice, or more if needed

1 clove garlic, roughly chopped

$1/2$ teaspoon fine sea salt

Pinch of red pepper flakes

$1/4$ cup extra-virgin olive oil, or more if needed

$3/4$ cup finely grated Parmesan cheese (about $1^1/2$ ounces)

Freshly ground black pepper

I am unabashedly in love with roasted cherry tomatoes. They're a little sweet, a little tart, and full of rich, concentrated tomato flavor. When tomatoes are in season (okay, and even when they aren't), I can't get enough cherry tomatoes.

These crostini are a riff on the summertime mainstays of Italian cooking–basil pesto and tomatoes. I blended white beans and Parmesan into the mixture for a rich, creamy spread, which goes great with roasted cherry tomatoes. **MAKES ABOUT 2 DOZEN CROSTINI**

1. *To make the toasts and roasted tomatoes:* Preheat the oven to 400°F with racks in the middle and upper third of the oven. Line one large rimmed baking sheet and one small rimmed baking sheet with parchment paper for easy cleanup.

2. On the large baking sheet, brush both sides of the bread slices with olive oil (you'll need about 2 tablespoons of oil for this). On the small baking sheet, toss the tomatoes with the remaining 1 tablespoon olive oil and a sprinkle of salt and pepper.

3. Place the pan of toasts on the middle rack and the pan of tomatoes on the upper rack. Remove the toasts once they are nice and golden on top, 9 to 10 minutes. Continue roasting the tomatoes until they are juicy, tender, and collapsing on themselves, 8 to 9 minutes longer.

4. *Meanwhile, to make the white bean pesto:* In a food processor, combine the beans, basil, almonds, lemon juice, garlic, salt, and pepper flakes. While running the food processor, drizzle in the olive oil and process until the mixture is smooth, pausing to scrape down the sides as necessary. Add the Parmesan and process again to blend. Taste and add more lemon juice or salt if necessary. If the mixture seems dry, add a splash of olive oil and blend again.

5. To assemble the crostini, top each slice of toast with a generous spread of pesto and several roasted tomatoes. Sprinkle with black pepper and garnish each toast with a small basil leaf or some torn fresh basil. Crostini are best served immediately. You'll have around 1 cup of leftover pesto, which makes a great sandwich spread or dip for vegetables or pita chips.

GLUTEN FREE: *Serve the white bean pesto in a bowl and top with the roasted tomatoes, a few leaves of torn basil, and black pepper. Serve it as a dip with sturdy gluten-free crackers.* • **DAIRY FREE/VEGAN:** *Replace the Parmesan with $1/3$ cup nutritional yeast.* • **EGG FREE** • **NUT FREE:** *Omit the almonds.* • **SOY FREE**

TIP: *Feel free to prepare the spread the day before, but wait to toast the bread and roast the tomatoes until you're ready to serve.*

Roasted Strawberry, Basil, and Goat Cheese Crostini

If you haven't experienced roasted strawberries yet, you've been missing out—they're sweet and jammy, like the inside of a strawberry pie. Roasted strawberries collide with tangy goat cheese and fresh basil to create this simple and sophisticated summertime appetizer. You could also serve these with a big green salad for a light summer meal. **MAKES ABOUT 2 DOZEN CROSTINI**

1. Preheat the oven to 350°F with racks in the middle and upper third of the oven. Line two large rimmed baking sheets with parchment paper for easier cleanup. Set the goat cheese on the counter to soften up a bit.

2. On one baking sheet, toss the strawberries with the honey, then spread the strawberries into a single layer. Bake on the upper rack until the fruit is tender, juicy, and collapsing on itself, 20 to 25 minutes, tossing halfway. Watch the fruit on the edges of the pan, as the honey can burn quickly.

3. Meanwhile, on the remaining baking sheet, brush the olive oil lightly over both sides of each slice of bread. Bake on the middle rack until the toasts are golden on top, 10 to 12 minutes.

4. Once the toasts are cool enough to safely handle, top each one with a smear of goat cheese, followed by a spoonful of roasted strawberries and their juices. Finish off the crostini with a sprinkling of torn basil and black pepper. Crostini are best served immediately.

4 to 5 ounces goat cheese

1 pound strawberries, hulled and cut into bite-size pieces

2 tablespoons honey

2 tablespoons extra-virgin olive oil

1 whole-grain baguette or small loaf of crusty whole-grain bread (about 14 ounces), cut into $1/_2$-inch slices

Small handful of fresh basil leaves, torn into little pieces

Freshly ground black pepper

TIP: *If you don't love goat cheese, alternatives include mascarpone, cream cheese, or ricotta.*

GLUTEN FREE: *Top room-temperature goat cheese with warm roasted strawberries, torn basil, and black pepper. Serve it as a dip with sturdy gluten-free crackers.* • **DAIRY FREE/VEGAN:** *Substitute Cashew Sour Cream (page 217) for the goat cheese. For vegan crostini, use maple syrup instead of honey.* • **EGG FREE** • **NUT FREE** • **SOY FREE**

Fresh Greek Nachos with Herbed Tahini Sauce

TOASTED PITA WEDGES

4 whole wheat pitas (7-inch)

Extra-virgin olive oil, for brushing

Fine sea salt

MEDITERRANEAN SALAD

1 can (15 ounces) chickpeas, rinsed and drained, or $1^1/_2$ cups cooked chickpeas

1 medium tomato, finely chopped

1 small cucumber, finely chopped

$^1/_4$ cup chopped green onions (about 2)

$^1/_4$ cup chopped fresh flat-leaf parsley, plus more for garnish

$^1/_4$ cup pitted and thinly sliced Kalamata olives

2 tablespoons lemon juice

1 large clove garlic, pressed or minced

1 tablespoon extra-virgin olive oil

$^1/_2$ teaspoon fine sea salt

HERBED TAHINI SAUCE

$^1/_3$ cup tahini

$^1/_4$ cup lemon juice (from $1^1/_2$ to 2 lemons)

$^1/_4$ cup mixed fresh leafy herbs (I like half flat-leaf parsley and half basil or cilantro)

2 tablespoons water, plus more as needed

$^1/_4$ teaspoon fine sea salt

Let's just get it out there: There is no cheese in these "nachos." But freshly toasted pita wedges, topped with a simple Greek chickpea salad and drizzled with herbed tahini sauce, are so nacho-like that I couldn't resist. The tangy tahini sauce offers the same level of indulgent, creamy texture and rich flavor as gooey nacho cheese, without the cheese coma. **MAKES 4 TO 6 SERVINGS**

1. *To toast the pita wedges:* Preheat the oven to 400°F. Line a large rimmed baking sheet with parchment paper for easy cleanup. Brush both sides of the pitas with olive oil and lightly sprinkle with salt. Stack 1 pita evenly on top of another and use a sharp chef's knife to slice them into 8 small wedges, like you would a pizza. Repeat with the remaining 2 pitas. Arrange the wedges evenly across the baking sheet and bake until they are lightly crisp and golden, about 10 minutes, flipping halfway.

2. *To assemble the salad:* In a medium bowl, combine the chickpeas, tomato, cucumber, green onions, parsley, olives, lemon juice, garlic, olive oil, and salt. Toss, then taste and add more salt, if necessary. Set aside to marinate.

3. *To make the tahini sauce:* In a small food processor, combine the tahini, lemon juice, herbs, water, and salt and blend until smooth, pausing to scrape down the sides as necessary. (Alternatively, you can finely chop the leafy herbs and whisk together the sauce in a liquid measuring cup.) The sauce should be nice and creamy, but drizzle easily off the back of a spoon–if not, blend in a bit more water. Taste and add more salt, if necessary.

4. To assemble the nachos, arrange the toasted pita wedges across a large serving plate (some overlap is fine). Stir the salad once more, then use a slotted serving spoon to scoop the salad onto the pita wedges, leaving the messy salad juices in the bowl. Generously drizzle the herbed tahini sauce over the salad, then finish off the nachos with a light sprinkle of chopped fresh parsley. Serve immediately.

5. These nachos are best consumed soon after assembling, as they get soggy over time, but I have enjoyed leftovers from the refrigerator the next day.

TIP: *If you don't like olives, omit them. To replace the olives' salty punch, you might appreciate a light sprinkle of feta cheese instead.*

DAIRY FREE • VEGAN • EGG FREE • NUT FREE • SOY FREE

Olive Oil and Black Pepper Popcorn

Someone, somewhere, declared that you cannot pop popcorn in olive oil, and I'm here to prove that person wrong. You most certainly *can* pop popcorn in olive oil, as long as you use extra-virgin olive oil and don't crank up the heat too high. You will be rewarded with a rich, flavorful, heart-healthy snack. Once it's popped, I add another drizzle of olive oil for rich flavor, followed by salt and freshly ground black pepper. It's a simple snack that tastes incredibly complex. Stovetop popcorn might seem a little intimidating if you're accustomed to the microwave variety, but it's really easy to make and tastes infinitely better. **MAKES 10 TO 11 CUPS**

4 tablespoons extra-virgin olive oil, divided

$1/2$ cup popcorn kernels, divided

Fine sea salt and freshly ground black pepper

SAFETY TIP: *Never leave the kitchen with hot oil on the stove! If a pot or pan ever starts smoking, remove it from the heat immediately. If a pot of oil ever catches on fire, turn off the heat immediately, and if it's not already covered with a lid, carefully cover the pot with a metal lid or baking sheet. Do not move the pot, and whatever you do, do NOT remove the lid—oxygen will fuel the fire.*

1. In a large, heavy-bottomed saucepan, combine 2 tablespoons of the olive oil and 2 popcorn kernels over medium heat. Cover the pot and wait for the kernels to pop, which might take a few minutes. In the meantime, place a large serving bowl near the stove so it's ready when you need it.

2. Once the kernels pop, remove the pot from the heat and pour in the remaining popcorn kernels. Cover the pot again, still off the heat, and give the pot a little shimmy to distribute the kernels evenly. Let the pot rest for 30 seconds to make sure the oil doesn't get too hot before the kernels are ready to pop.

3. Return the pot to medium heat and continue cooking the popcorn, carefully shimmying the pot occasionally to cook the kernels evenly. Once the kernels start popping, continue cooking until the popping sound slows down to about one pop per every few seconds. (If the popcorn tries to overflow the pot, just tip the upper portion of popcorn into your bowl and return it to the heat.) Remove the lid and dump the popcorn into your serving bowl.

4. Drizzle the remaining 2 tablespoons olive oil (if you have a special jar of fancy olive oil, now is the time to use it) over the popcorn. Sprinkle the popcorn with salt and lots of black pepper. Toss the popcorn, taste, and add more salt and pepper as necessary. Serve immediately for best flavor and texture. The popcorn will taste good for several hours, though.

CHANGE IT UP

▶ You can use this recipe as a base for all kinds of toppings. Try cooking the popcorn in coconut oil for a slight movie theater popcorn effect. Or, drizzle infused olive oil on top for extra flavor. Additional topping options include finely grated Parmesan cheese, nutritional yeast, and dried herbs and spices, such as garlic powder.

GLUTEN FREE • DAIRY FREE • VEGAN • EGG FREE • NUT FREE • SOY FREE

Green Goddess Hummus

1/4 cup tahini

1/4 cup lemon juice
(from 1 1/2 to 2 lemons)

2 tablespoons extra-
virgin olive oil, plus
more for serving

1 clove garlic, roughly
chopped

1/2 teaspoon fine sea salt

1/2 cup lightly packed
fresh flat-leaf parsley
(some stems are okay)

1/4 cup lightly packed
fresh tarragon leaves,
basil, or cilantro

2 tablespoons roughly
chopped fresh chives
or green onions

1 can (15 ounces)
chickpeas, rinsed and
drained, or 1 1/2 cups
cooked chickpeas

Chopped fresh herbs
(whatever you have left),
for garnish

I'm so glad to have hummus in my life. It wasn't long ago that hummus was an obscure celery dip for hippies and health fanatics. Hummus is here to stay, and for good reason—it's a healthy snack and spread that is far more redeeming than most.

Most of the big-brand, store-bought hummuses skimp on tahini, which means that they aren't rich, thick, or flavorful enough to do hummus proper justice. This homemade hummus has just the right amount of tahini, plus it's free of preservatives. It's ultra creamy thanks to the blending method (basically, you make sure the tahini is nice and fluffy before adding the chickpeas). Serve this herbed hummus with pita wedges (page 116), crackers, or veggies.

MAKES 1¾ CUPS

1. In a food processor or high-powered blender (i.e., Vitamix or Blendtec), combine the tahini, lemon juice, olive oil, garlic, and salt. Process for about 1 1/2 minutes, pausing to scrape down the sides as necessary, until the mixture is well blended.

2. Add the herbs and process for about 1 minute, pausing to scrape down the sides as necessary, until the herbs have blended into the mixture and the mixture is nice and smooth.

3. Add half of the chickpeas to the food processor and process for 1 minute. Scrape down the bowl, then add the remaining chickpeas and process until the hummus is thick and quite smooth, 1 to 2 minutes more.

4. If your hummus is too thick or hasn't yet blended into creamy oblivion, run the food processor while drizzling in 1 to 2 tablespoons of water, until it reaches your desired consistency. Taste and season with additional salt, if necessary.

5. Scrape the hummus into a small serving bowl. Lightly drizzle olive oil over the top and sprinkle with some chopped herbs. Leftover hummus keeps well, chilled, for 4 to 6 days.

GLUTEN FREE • DAIRY FREE • VEGAN • EGG FREE • NUT FREE • SOY FREE

CHANGE IT UP
You can skip the herbs
(parsley, tarragon, and chives)
altogether for extra creamy,
classic hummus, or use this as
a base recipe for any number
of variations. Try adding
some sun-dried tomatoes,
chopped roasted red peppers,
or pitted olives.

Zesty Black Bean and Corn Salad in Lettuce Cups

These zesty lettuce cups are meant to be light summertime lunches, happy hour snacks, or dinner party appetizers. You can also eat the filling as a salad or serve it as a dip for tortilla chips. I love to spoon it into sturdy butter lettuce or Little Gem leaves for a fun handheld option.

These salad cups would make a wonderful spread with chips and salsa (pages 101–105) and a pitcher of margaritas (page 131). You'll invite me to all of your summer parties, won't you, please?

MAKES 16 TO 20 LETTUCE CUPS

1. *To make the salad:* In a large bowl, combine the beans, corn, feta, cilantro, radishes, jalapeño, and lime zest. Drizzle the lime juice, olive oil, and vinegar over the salad and add the salt. Stir to combine. Taste and add additional salt, if necessary.

2. *To assemble the lettuce cups:* Gently tug each leaf from the base until you have 16 to 20 leaves (the innermost leaves will be too small, but save those for a green salad). Place a couple slices of avocado on each leaf, then spoon the black bean and corn salad into each lettuce leaf (the more you fill them, the messier they are to eat!) and set them on a large serving platter.

3. Lettuce cups are best consumed promptly, but leftover black bean and corn salad will keep well on its own, chilled, for 3 to 4 days.

ZESTY BLACK BEAN AND CORN SALAD

2 cans (15 ounces each) black beans, rinsed and drained, or 3 cups cooked black beans

Kernels from 2 large ears of corn or 2 cups thawed frozen corn kernels

$1/2$ cup crumbled feta cheese (about $2^{1}/_{2}$ ounces)

$1/3$ cup chopped fresh cilantro

5 medium red radishes, thinly sliced, then roughly chopped

1 large jalapeño, seeded, deribbed, and finely chopped

$1/2$ teaspoon grated lime zest

$1/4$ cup lime juice (from about 2 limes)

$1/4$ cup extra-virgin olive oil

1 tablespoon red wine vinegar

$3/4$ teaspoon fine sea salt

LETTUCE CUPS

2 heads butter lettuce or Little Gem

2 avocados, cut into long thin strips

GLUTEN FREE • DAIRY FREE/VEGAN: *Skip the feta cheese in the salad. You could add some chopped pickled jalapeño to make up for it.* **• EGG FREE • NUT FREE • SOY FREE**

Avocado, Spinach, and Artichoke Dip with Toasted Pita Wedges

TOASTED PITA WEDGES

4 whole-grain pitas (7-inch)

2 tablespoons extra-virgin olive oil

Fine sea salt

DIP

1 large or 2 small avocados (about ½ pound total), halved and pitted

1 tablespoon extra-virgin olive oil

1 tablespoon lemon juice, or more if needed

1 clove garlic, roughly chopped

¼ teaspoon fine sea salt

Pinch of red pepper flakes

Freshly ground black pepper

1½ cups packed baby spinach (about 1½ ounces)

½ cup well-drained marinated artichokes (from one 5-ounce jar)

One day, I opened up my vegetable drawer to find an avocado resting on a bag of spinach, and this avocado, spinach, and artichoke dip happened next. It's like guacamole crossed with spinach artichoke dip. How can you go wrong?

Consider this dip a dairy-free and vegan alternative to classic spinach-artichoke dip that tastes just as awesome, in its own right. It's easier to make, with no warming required. Serve it with toasted pita wedges (see below), store-bought pita chips, tortilla chips, or raw veggies, like carrot sticks and cucumber slices. **MAKES 1½ CUPS DIP; 6 SERVINGS**

1. To make the pita wedges: Preheat the oven to 400°F. Line a large rimmed baking sheet with parchment paper for easy cleanup.

2. Brush the pitas with olive oil on both sides, then lightly sprinkle salt on top. Stack 2 pitas evenly on top of each other and use a sharp chef's knife to slice them into 8 small wedges, like you would a pizza. Repeat with the remaining 2 pitas. Arrange the wedges on the baking sheet in a single layer. Bake until the pita wedges are crisp and lightly golden, about 10 minutes, flipping halfway.

3. To make the dip: Using a spoon, scoop the avocado flesh into a food processor. Add the olive oil, lemon juice, garlic, salt, pepper flakes, and several twists of black pepper. Blend until smooth, pausing to scrape down the sides as necessary. Add the spinach and artichokes and pulse until they are roughly chopped, 15 to 20 times, pausing to scrape down the sides if necessary. Season to taste with additional salt or lemon juice, if needed.

4. Transfer the dip to a small serving bowl and serve with the toasted pita wedges on the side. This dip stores surprisingly well—just press plastic wrap against the surface to prevent it from browning. It keeps well, chilled, for up to 4 days. Unfortunately, leftover pita wedges tend to get tough fairly quickly.

GLUTEN FREE: *Serve with gluten-free chips or crackers instead of the pita wedges.* • **DAIRY FREE** • **VEGAN** • **EGG FREE** • **NUT FREE** • **SOY FREE**

Elderflower Champagne Cocktail

I love to order the occasional $12 cocktail at a swanky bar, but homemade cocktails don't need to be so complicated. Because by the time you're making a cocktail, you just need a cocktail, right?

Here is a delightful three-ingredient cocktail that is light, bubbly, and not too sweet. It's a simple combination of Champagne, St-Germain elderflower liqueur, and a splash of fresh lemon juice that reminds me of a French 75. St-Germain is hard to describe–it's a delicately flavored French liqueur that tastes a little like honeysuckle. It would be a great choice for a fancy lady brunch or girls' night. I've never met a man who doesn't enjoy St-Germain, so your fellow might want one as well! **MAKES 1 COCKTAIL**

3 ounces brut Champagne or Prosecco, chilled

$^1/_2$ ounce St-Germain elderflower liqueur

$^1/_2$ ounce lemon juice

Lemon twists, for garnish*

Ingredient Note: To make lemon twists: Before you juice your lemon, use a vegetable peeler to peel off 2-inch-long strips of zest, avoiding the bitter pith as much as possible (you'll need 1 strip per cocktail).

Gently pour the sparkling wine into a glass. (Pro Tip: 3 ounces is about half the capacity of a standard Champagne flute.) Pour in the St-Germain and lemon juice. Twist the lemon peel over the drink before dropping it in. Tweak your amounts of St-Germain or lemon juice if desired. Cheers!

TIPS: *Be sure to stash your bubbly in the refrigerator in advance, so it's nice and cold when you are ready to pour.*

St-Germain is readily available at liquor stores these days. It's somewhat pricy at around $35 per 750 ml bottle, but it is so worth it (it's also available in very small 50 ml bottles, if you'd like to try it before you take the plunge).

You can make up to 8 of these cocktails with one standard bottle (750 ml) of Champagne. If you will only be making a few, one option is to buy a half bottle or single serving bottles. Or, use a Champagne sealer to seal the bottle for later in the week. I bought a Metrokane brand sealer for around $5 and it works well!

GLUTEN FREE • DAIRY FREE • VEGAN • EGG FREE • NUT FREE • SOY FREE

Spicy Cucumber Margarita

Chili-salt rim: 1 part kosher salt to 1 part ancho chile powder or regular chili powder

1 lime wedge

One 2-inch piece peeled cucumber, quartered lengthwise and cut crosswise into ¼-inch-thick pieces

1½ ounces silver or blanco tequila

1½ ounces lime juice (from about 1½ limes)

¾ ounce orange juice (from ¼ to ½ orange)

1 teaspoon Simple Syrup (page 131)

1 thin jalapeño slice (⅛- to ¼-inch thick; a little goes a long way!)

Small cucumber rounds, for garnish

Cucumber cocktails are about as refreshing as cocktails get. These sweet and spicy numbers are inspired by my favorite margarita in Austin, Texas (if you're in town, be sure to go to Rainey Street and order one on the patio at Lucille's). They have a pleasant little kick to them, thanks to some jalapeño and chili powder.

For the most pronounced cucumber flavor, use a fresh, juicy garden cucumber. Serve these with a side of homemade salsa (pages 101–105) and tortilla chips and pretend you're soaking up some sun on a south-of-the-border vacation. **MAKES 1 COCKTAIL**

1. *To rim your glass:* On a small rimmed plate, mix together equal parts salt and chile powder. I like to use my fingers to rub the powder into the salt (be sure to wash your hands afterward). Run a wedge of lime around the top of the glass. Dip the top of the glass into the salt blend at a 45-degree angle and roll it from side to side to catch the salt.

2. In a cocktail shaker or 1-quart mason jar (you can make a few cocktails at once), add the cucumber, tequila, lime juice, orange juice, Simple Syrup, and jalapeño. Top off the shaker with ice. Fasten the lid securely and shake it like crazy for 30 seconds. Strain the liquid into an ice-filled cocktail glass and garnish with a slice of cucumber. Start sipping immediately.

GLUTEN FREE: *Use 100% agave tequila.* • **DAIRY FREE** • **VEGAN** • **EGG FREE** • **NUT FREE** • **SOY FREE**

If you're sensitive to spice, or
are not in the mood for it, skip
the jalapeño and chili powder.
You'll end up with a basic
cucumber margarita, and by
basic, I mean still super tasty.

MARGARITA TIPS: *For the best flavor, and for less risk of a hangover, choose a quality 100% agave tequila.*

I used to use agave nectar in margaritas, but now that I've learned that it has more fructose than high-fructose corn syrup, I use simple syrup in my drinks instead; it's made with sugar, which is lower in liver-damaging fructose. (If you really want to use agave nectar for the pitcher of margaritas, start with ¼ cup.)

Pitcher of Margaritas

Margaritas and fun are synonyms in my vocabulary. Just say the word, and I get a little giddy. I'll probably even break out into a little margarita dance once they hit the table. I can't help myself!

Margaritas are citrusy, refreshing, and strong, which is basically everything that I want a cocktail to be. Here's a recipe for a whole pitcher of margaritas to serve at your next party. Margaritas go great with any and all of the Mexican recipes in this book.

MAKES 10 MARGARITAS

1. To rim the glasses: Place about a tablespoon of kosher salt on a small, rimmed plate. Run a wedge of lime around the top of each glass. Dip the top of each glass into the salt at a 45-degree angle and roll it from side to side to catch the salt. Set the glasses aside and place a bowl of lime wedges nearby for guests to add to their drinks.

2. In a large pitcher, combine the tequila, lime juice, orange juice, and Simple Syrup. Stir until blended. Fill the pitcher with ice, stir again, and let the mixture rest for 5 minutes to dilute a bit (these margaritas aren't kidding around). Pour into individual glasses and serve.

Kosher salt

Lime wedges, for rimming the glass and for garnish

$2^1/_2$ cups silver or blanco tequila

2 cups lime juice (from 12 to 25 limes, depending on their size; about 3 pounds total)

1 cup orange juice (from 2 to 4 oranges)

Simple Syrup

TO MAKE JUST 1 MARGARITA: *First, rim your glass with salt. Fill a cocktail shaker with ice and add 2 ounces tequila, $1^1/_2$ ounces lime juice, 1 ounce fresh orange juice, and 2 teaspoons Simple Syrup. Securely fasten the lid, shake like crazy, and strain into an ice-filled cocktail glass.*

SIMPLE SYRUP

MAKES ½ CUP

$^1/_3$ cup sugar (I use organic cane sugar)

$^1/_3$ cup water

In a small saucepan, combine the sugar and water. Warm the mixture over high heat, stirring often, just until the sugar dissolves. Let it cool to room temperature before using. If making ahead, store covered in the refrigerator for up to 1 month.

GLUTEN FREE: *Use 100% agave tequila.* • **DAIRY FREE** • **VEGAN** • **EGG FREE** • **NUT FREE** • **SOY FREE**

Brown Derby Cocktail

2 ounces grapefruit juice (from about ½ large grapefruit)

1½ ounces Canadian rye whiskey,* such as Wiser's

½ ounce Honey Simple Syrup

Grapefruit peel, for garnish

CHANGE IT UP

▸ If you'd like to experiment with other liquors, gin and vodka also go nicely with grapefruit and honey. If you prefer lighter, fizzier drinks, try adding a splash of chilled grapefruit-flavored sparkling water after pouring this cocktail into your glass. LaCroix makes one called pamplemousse.

Meet my very favorite cocktail. It's an ice-cold, shaken drink featuring an unlikely combination of flavors. Grapefruit, whiskey, and honey? I only wish I'd thought of it myself! As rumor has it, the Brown Derby was the signature drink at a glamorous Los Angeles nightclub on Sunset Boulevard in the 1930s called the Vendôme Club. The Vendôme Club named the drink after a popular diner down the street, which was named The Brown Derby and operated out of a funny, derby hat–shaped building. You can Google pictures of the building, if you don't believe me.

This drink works so well because grapefruit juice softens the flavor of whiskey (or any liquor, really) and makes a refreshing, citrusy drink with some redeeming vitamin C. Honey Simple Syrup offers some light sweetness and warm honey flavor, and couldn't be easier to make. (You do need to make it, though–honey doesn't mix into cold liquids very well.) If whiskey cocktails aren't your first pick, this one just might change your mind. **MAKES 1 COCKTAIL**

1. Before juicing your grapefruit, use a vegetable peeler to peel off strips of zest roughly 2 inches long, avoiding the bitter pith as much as possible. You'll need 1 strip per cocktail.

2. To make a cocktail (you can make a few cocktails at once), fill a cocktail shaker with ice. Pour in the grapefruit juice, whiskey, and Honey Simple Syrup. Fasten the lid securely and shake it like crazy for 30 seconds. Strain the liquid into a martini glass. Gently twist the grapefruit peel over the drink, peel side down, to release the zest's fragrant oils. Drop the twist into the glass and start sipping immediately.

*Ingredient Note: Whiskey aficionados will probably scoff at me for specifying Canadian whiskey here, but it's smooth and easy to sip. If you are using a more strongly flavored whiskey, like Bulleit bourbon, you'll probably want to add some more grapefruit juice and Honey Simple Syrup to balance the flavors.

GLUTEN FREE: *Substitute 100% agave reposado tequila for the whiskey.* • **DAIRY FREE** • **VEGAN:** *This drink is good (although not quite as good) with maple syrup. Use ¼ ounce instead of the Honey Simple Syrup.* • **EGG FREE** • **NUT FREE** • **SOY FREE**

HONEY SIMPLE SYRUP

MAKES ½ CUP

 ¼ cup honey

 ¼ cup water

1. *To make the syrup on the stove:* Combine the honey and water in your smallest saucepan over medium heat. Warm the mixture, stirring often, just until the honey has fully blended into the water (this won't take long). Remove the pot from the heat and set aside.

2. *To make the syrup in the microwave:* Combine the honey and water in a glass measuring cup or microwave-safe bowl. Microwave the mixture until it's warm enough that you can stir the honey into the water, about 30 seconds to 1 minute.

3. Refrigerate leftover honey simple syrup for up to 1 month.

Pineapple-Tini

2 ounces Pineapple-Infused Vodka

1½ teaspoons lime juice, or more if needed

1 teaspoon Simple Syrup (page 131), or more if needed

Small wedges of fresh pineapple (optional), for garnish

🕐 **TIME WARNING:** *The infused pineapple vodka requires a 2-week waiting period.*

Here's a fresh and fruity cocktail that's just sweet enough to delight. I should warn you right away that it requires a 2-week waiting period, but it is so worth it! During those 2 weeks, fresh pineapple transfers its delicious, tropical flavor to vodka, and you end up with the most delightful infused liquor.

The infusion process makes the very best pineapple martinis (it's also a fun project), but I've included a muddled pineapple version in Change It Up that is almost as good. Either way, fresh pineapple is key to making a tasty cocktail. I tried making them with canned pineapple juice, but they tasted like suntan lotion on spring break. **MAKES 1 COCKTAIL**

Fill a large cocktail shaker with ice. Pour in the pineapple vodka, lime juice, and Simple Syrup. Securely fasten the lid and shake until the outside of the cocktail shaker is so cold you can shake no more, about 20 seconds. Taste and add additional lime juice or Simple Syrup, if necessary. Strain the mixture into a martini glass (or pour into a rocks glass and add a couple of ice cubes to keep it cold). If you'd like, garnish the glass with a wedge of pineapple. Just slice each pineapple wedge about two-thirds up the center and slide it onto the rim of the glass.

PINEAPPLE-INFUSED VODKA

Use quality vodka and a juicy, ripe pineapple so the pineapple flavor can shine through. My favorite brand is Tito's, out of Austin, Texas. Pineapple-infused vodka is great over ice with club soda and lime. **MAKES 2 CUPS, ENOUGH FOR 8 COCKTAILS**

3 cups cubed (¾ inch) fresh pineapple (from a 3-pound or larger pineapple)

2 cups vodka

1. Transfer the cubed pineapple to a 1-quart mason jar (or any 1-quart glass jar with a secure lid) and pour the vodka over the pineapple. Screw on the lid tightly and place the jar in a cool, dark place (like inside a cupboard). Let it rest for 14 days, shaking occasionally. I'm forgetful, so I set a reminder on my calendar for the end date.

2. When the vodka is ready, place a fine-mesh strainer over a large liquid measuring cup (at least 2-cup capacity) or medium bowl. Pour the pineapple vodka through the strainer. Discard the pineapple; all of its flavor has transferred to the vodka, so it's useless to us now.

3. Leftover pineapple-infused vodka will keep well in the refrigerator for a month or so. Store it in an appropriately sized mason jar with the lid securely fastened.

GLUTEN FREE: *Be sure to choose a vodka that is made from corn or potatoes, rather than grains. Tito's vodka is gluten free.* • **DAIRY FREE • VEGAN • EGG FREE • NUT FREE • SOY FREE**

CHANGE IT UP

If you need a pineapple-tini sooner, rather than later: In a cocktail shaker, muddle ⅓ cup chopped juicy ripe pineapple until it has released all of its juices. Add 2 ounces vodka, 1½ teaspoons lime juice, and 1 teaspoon Simple Syrup (page 131). Fill the shaker with ice, fasten the lid securely, and shake it like crazy for 30 seconds. Strain the liquid into a martini glass and serve immediately.

Strawberry Rosé Sangria

Sangria reminds me of Spain, which reminds me of tapas and siestas. I'd like all three, please. Sangria is typically made with red wine and brandy, but I'm wild about this version with rosé and St-Germain. It's fruity, refreshing, and a hit at girls' night.

Please don't judge the pink wine; rosé is not necessarily any sweeter than any other shade of wine. I opt for dry rosé, but you can choose a sweeter one if you'd like. **MAKES 6 SERVINGS**

1 medium orange, halved from stem to blossom end

1 Honeycrisp apple, chopped

1 cup hulled and thinly sliced strawberries (about 4 ounces)

$1/4$ cup St-Germain elderflower liqueur

1 bottle (750 ml) dry rosé wine

Ice, for serving

1. Squeeze the juice of one orange half into a pitcher. Slice the remaining orange half into $1/4$-inch-thick half-moons, then slice those down the center to make smaller wedges. Add them to the pitcher.

2. Add the apple and strawberries to the pitcher, followed by the St-Germain. Pour in the wine and stir it all together. For best flavor (although it's plenty tasty at this point), let the sangria chill in the refrigerator for several hours, or overnight, before serving. Serve in glasses over ice.

CHANGE IT UP

▸ For a more traditional sangria flavor, you can substitute brandy for the St-Germain. Since St-Germain is sweet, you might want to stir in a couple tablespoons of Simple Syrup (page 131) in its absence.

GLUTEN FREE • DAIRY FREE • VEGAN: *Use a vegan-friendly wine.* **• EGG FREE • NUT FREE • SOY FREE**

Hibiscus Pink Lemonade

5 cups water, divided

2 hibiscus tea bags*

1 cup lemon juice (from 5 to 7 lemons, about 1½ pounds total)

⅓ cup mild honey

⅓ cup sugar (I use organic cane sugar), or more if needed

*Ingredient Note: You can find hibiscus tea in the tea aisle of most grocery stores these days. Tazo Passion tea is a great option. If you can only find loose-leaf hibiscus tea, steep 2 teaspoons in place of the 2 tea bags.

This pink lemonade is naturally colored with hibiscus tea! This tea is made from the petals of hibiscus flowers, which are pleasantly tart in flavor, and usually contains some orange peel and rose hips as well—all of which play nicely with fresh lemon juice. It's an incredibly refreshing drink that tastes as lovely as it looks.

I tried to rely entirely on natural sweeteners for this lemonade, but my all-honey version just tasted like honey, maple syrup didn't offer an authentic lemonade taste, and agave nectar is beside the point (see the tip on page 130). I compromised by using equal parts honey and organic cane sugar. **MAKES 6 CUPS**

1. Bring 2 cups of the water to a boil. Place the tea bags in a 2-cup or larger liquid measuring cup and pour the boiling water over the tea bags. Let the tea steep for 3 minutes, then discard the tea bags.

2. Pour the brewed tea, lemon juice, honey, and sugar into a blender. Secure the lid and blend until the honey and sugar have disappeared into the liquid.

3. Add the remaining 3 cups water to the blender and stir to combine. Taste, and if it's too tart for your liking (keep in mind that serving the lemonade over ice will dilute the flavors), add additional sugar and blend again.

4. If you're serving a crowd, fill a pitcher with ice and pour in the lemonade. For individual portions, just pour the lemonade into individual glasses over ice and refrigerate the rest. The lemonade keeps well, chilled, for up to 5 days.

GLUTEN FREE • DAIRY FREE • VEGAN: *Replace the honey with an additional ⅓ cup sugar.* **• EGG FREE • NUT FREE • SOY FREE**

CHANGE IT UP
If you're in the mood for
something boozy, try adding
a splash of vodka or gin.

5 *Let's Feast*

WHO'S HUNGRY FOR DINNER? This chapter is full of savory, satisfying main dishes that just so happen to be meatless (which is not to imply that they are missing anything). Whereas traditional dinner plates tend to follow the basic protein-veggie-starch formula, you'll find that vegetarian main dishes tend to incorporate all of those components in one big, creative, and colorful bowl. I love to eat this way, and I hope you will, too.

I designed the recipes in this chapter to appeal to hungry carnivores, vegetarians, vegans, and everyone in between. They make use of wholesome ingredients like whole grains, beans, tofu, edamame, and hearty roasted vegetables to keep your belly happy from dinner to bedtime. You will find some veggie-packed spins on familiar comfort food favorites (pizza, lasagna, and enchiladas, oh my!), as well as some vibrant new dishes with diverse flavors to stretch your repertoire.

While this chapter includes most of my hearty main dishes, don't forget about the meals that qualify for dinner throughout earlier chapters in the book. All of the egg dishes in the breakfast chapter make fantastic evening meals, as do the big green salads made with whole grains and beans. They might not look like your average dinner, but that's a good thing!

Colorful Weeknight Burrito Bowls

I know you're wondering, and the answer is yes: This cilantro-lime rice tastes like the rice at everyone's favorite burrito place! I had Chipotle's burrito bowls in mind when I crafted this colorful dinner recipe. It's fresh, satisfying, and packs great for lunch the next day.

I am a crazy person and request *all* of the salsas when I'm in line at Chipotle, but these burrito bowls are perfect with the easiest of guacamoles plus some salsa verde, whether it's homemade (page 105) or store-bought. **MAKES 4 SERVINGS**

CILANTRO-LIME RICE

1½ cups long-grain brown rice or brown basmati rice, rinsed

1 bay leaf

¼ cup chopped fresh cilantro

2 tablespoons lime juice (from about 1 lime)*

1½ teaspoons lemon juice (from 1 small lemon)

1 tablespoon plus 1 teaspoon extra-virgin olive oil

½ teaspoon fine sea salt

CABBAGE AND BLACK BEAN SLAW

3 cups thinly sliced red cabbage (about ¾ pound), roughly chopped into 2-inch-long pieces

2 cans (15 ounces each) black beans, rinsed and drained, or 3 cups cooked black beans

1 red bell pepper, chopped

½ cup chopped green onions (about 4)

½ cup chopped fresh cilantro

¼ cup lime juice (from about 2 limes), or more if needed

1 clove garlic, pressed or minced

1 tablespoon extra-virgin olive oil

½ teaspoon fine sea salt

GARNISHES

Quick Guacamole (page 225)

Salsa verde, homemade (page 105) or store-bought

Toasted pepitas (page 111), optional

Crumbled feta cheese (optional)

1. *To prepare the rice:* Bring a large pot of water to boil over high heat. Pour in the rice and drop in the bay leaf. Give the mixture a brief stir and let it boil for 30 minutes, reducing the heat if necessary to prevent overflow. Drain the rice, return it to the pot, cover, and let it rest for 10 minutes off the heat. Discard the bay leaf and fluff the rice with a fork.

2. Add the cilantro, lime juice, lemon juice, olive oil, and salt and stir to combine. Taste and add additional salt if necessary (I usually add an extra ¼ teaspoon). Cover until you're ready to serve

3. *Meanwhile, to assemble the slaw:* In a medium bowl, combine the cabbage, black beans, bell pepper, green onions, cilantro, lime juice, garlic, olive oil, and salt. Toss to combine, then taste and add more lime juice if necessary. Set aside to marinate.

4. Serve individual portions in bowls, with rice on the bottom, slaw in the middle, and a scoop of guacamole on top. Don't forget to add at least 1 spoonful of salsa verde. If desired, sprinkle with toasted pepitas and/or crumbled feta cheese.

5. Leftover rice and slaw will keep well for up to 4 days. Store the guacamole in a small bowl with plastic wrap pressed against the top to help prevent browning.

GLUTEN FREE • DAIRY FREE/VEGAN: *Skip the feta cheese.* **• EGG FREE • NUT FREE • SOY FREE**

Alternative Burrito Bowl Menus

Homemade burrito bowls are one of my favorite meals to whip up, so here are a few more options for you. Be sure to garnish your burrito bowl with guacamole and salsa.

KALE AND BLACK BEANS

Cilantro-Lime Rice (page 142)

Refried Black Beans (page 189)

Kale Slaw (page 189)

SUMMERTIME CORN

Cilantro-Lime Rice

Zesty Black Bean and Corn Salad (page 123)

Guacamole is mandatory!

HEARTY BEER BEANS AND FAJITA VEGGIES

Cilantro-Lime Rice

Beer Beans (page 180)

Fajita Veggies (page 32)

Ingredient Note: This recipe calls for a lot of fresh lime juice. You may need as many as 4 medium limes for the full recipe.

Quinoa-Stuffed Sweet Potatoes

4 medium sweet potatoes (about 2½ pounds total), scrubbed clean

1 cup quinoa, rinsed

2 cups water

½ cup raw pepitas (hulled pumpkin seeds)

½ teaspoon plus 3 tablespoons extra-virgin olive oil

1 can (15 ounces) chickpeas, rinsed and drained, or 1½ cups cooked chickpeas

½ cup chopped green onion (about 4)

½ cup chopped fresh flat-leaf parsley

2 cloves garlic, pressed or minced

3 tablespoons lemon juice (from 1 to 1½ lemons), or more if needed

Fine sea salt

½ cup crumbled goat cheese (about 2½ ounces)

My dad always tried to convince me to try his sweet potatoes growing up. "They taste like candy!" he claimed, but I couldn't wrap my little head around the idea of sweet vegetables. I finally discovered the joy of spicy sweet potatoes as an adult, and the balance of sweet and savory always leaves me hungry for more.

These stuffed sweet potatoes taste like magic. There is something truly enchanting about the combination of tender sweet potato, toasted pepitas, pungent green onions, and tangy goat cheese. Fluffy quinoa and hearty chickpeas play supporting roles, turning what would be a side dish into a potential entree. The recipe yields about twice as much quinoa salad as you need for stuffing the potatoes, which is perfect for spilling over the sides. The quinoa salad is also great on its own, as a side dish or packed lunch. **MAKES 4 SERVINGS**

1. Preheat the oven to 400°F. Line a rimmed baking sheet with parchment paper to catch any sweet potato drippings.

2. Pierce each sweet potato several times with a fork to allow steam to escape while cooking. Place the sweet potatoes on the prepared sheet and bake until they yield to a gentle squeeze and are cooked through, 45 minutes to 1 hour.

3. In a medium saucepan, combine the quinoa and water. Bring the mixture to a boil over medium-high heat, then reduce the heat as necessary to maintain a gentle simmer. Simmer, uncovered, until all of the water is absorbed, 15 to 20 minutes. Remove the pot from the heat, cover, and let the quinoa steam for 5 minutes. Uncover and fluff the quinoa with a fork.

4. In a medium skillet, combine the pepitas and ½ teaspoon of the olive oil. Cook over medium heat, stirring frequently, until the pepitas are turning golden on the edges and making little popping noises, about 5 minutes. Pour the toasted pepitas into a large bowl.

5. To the bowl, add the chickpeas, green onion, parsley, garlic, lemon juice, ½ teaspoon salt, and the remaining 3 tablespoons olive oil. Toss to combine. Add the fluffed quinoa to the bowl and stir until the ingredients are evenly distributed. Taste and add additional salt, if necessary (I usually add another ¼ teaspoon), and more lemon juice if you would like a more tangy flavor.

6. Wait to add the goat cheese until you're ready to serve, so it doesn't melt into the quinoa. When it's time, add the crumbled goat cheese to the bowl and gently stir to combine.

7. To assemble, use a small paring knife to slice down the middle of the sweet potatoes, leaving about 1 inch intact on each end. Squish the ends toward the middle a bit to open them up. Transfer each sweet potato to its own plate. Sprinkle the interiors of the sweet potatoes with a dash of salt and use a fork to gently mash up the insides a bit, which will make room for more filling. Fill the sweet potatoes with the quinoa mixture, letting extra filling overflow to the sides. Serve immediately.

8. Leftover stuffed sweet potatoes keep well, chilled, for up to 4 days. Gently reheat in the microwave or oven before serving.

GLUTEN FREE • DAIRY FREE/VEGAN: *Omit the goat cheese and top the stuffed sweet potatoes with a dollop of Cashew Sour Cream (page 217).* **• EGG FREE • NUT FREE • SOY FREE**

Beans and Greens Quesadillas

Trust me on these quesadillas. They're a Southern/Tex-Mex mash-up that taste far greater than their humble ingredients might suggest. I stuff them with garlicky, quick-cooked collard greens (one of my favorite simple sides) and pinto beans. Wrapped in melted cheese and a crispy tortilla, you have one fine quesadilla. I love these for a quick lunch or dinner! **MAKES 4 SERVINGS**

1. *To prepare the collard greens:* Use a sharp chef's knife to cut out the center rib of each collard leaf. Stack a few leaves at a time and roll them up into a cigar-like shape. Slice across the roll as thinly as possible to yield collard ribbons about $1/4$ inch wide. Shake up the greens and give them a few chops so the strands aren't too long.

2. In a large skillet, warm the olive oil over medium heat until shimmering. Add the collard greens and a pinch of salt. Cook, stirring often, until they are wilting, dark green, and some are starting to lightly char on the edges, 4 to 6 minutes. Add the garlic, pepper flakes, and a few twists of black pepper. Cook, stirring constantly, until fragrant, about 1 minute. Stir the vinegar into the greens and remove the pan from the heat. Scoop the contents of the pan into a bowl to cool.

3. *To make the quesadillas, one at a time:* Heat a medium skillet over medium heat. Warm 1 tortilla for about 30 seconds, flipping halfway. Flip once more and sprinkle one-half of the tortilla with about $1/4$ cup shredded cheese. Cover the cheese with one-fourth of the cooked collard greens and $1/4$ cup pinto beans. Sprinkle about $1/4$ cup cheese over the fillings and fold over the empty side of the tortilla to enclose the fillings.

4. Quickly brush the top of the quesadilla with a light coating of oil, then flip it with a spatula. Let the quesadilla cook until golden and crispy on the bottom, 1 to 2 minutes. Brush the top with a light coating of oil, then carefully flip it and cook until the second side is golden and crispy. Transfer it to a cutting board. Repeat to make 3 more quesadillas.

5. Slice each quesadilla into 3 pieces with a chef's knife. Serve immediately with salsa, guacamole, and/or sour cream on the side, if you'd like. Leftovers store well, chilled, for up to 4 days. Gently reheat in the microwave or oven before serving.

SEASONED COLLARD GREENS

1 bunch collard greens (8 to 12 ounces)

1 tablespoon extra-virgin olive oil

Fine sea salt

2 cloves garlic, pressed or minced

Pinch of red pepper flakes

Freshly ground black pepper

$1/2$ teaspoon apple cider vinegar or lemon juice

QUESADILLAS

4 whole-grain tortillas (8-inch)

2 cups grated mild cheddar or Monterey Jack cheese (about 8 ounces)

1 cup cooked pinto beans (from one 15-ounce can), rinsed and drained

Refined avocado oil or other quality high-heat vegetable oil, for brushing

OPTIONAL GARNISHES

Salsa, homemade (pages 101–105) or store-bought

Quick Guacamole (page 225)

Sour cream or Cashew Sour Cream (page 217)

TIP: *If you can't find collard greens, Tuscan (lacinato) kale or chard will work as well.*

GLUTEN FREE: *Use certified gluten-free "flour" tortillas or make smaller (and more) quesadillas out of certified gluten-free corn tortillas.* • **DAIRY FREE/VEGAN:** *Omit the cheese and spread $1/4$ cup Cashew Sour Cream (page 217) over each tortilla instead.* • **EGG FREE • NUT FREE • SOY FREE**

Sweet Potato, Poblano, and Black Bean Enchiladas

ROASTED VEGGIES

1 large sweet potato (³/₄ to 1 pound), peeled and cut into ¹/₂-inch cubes

2 poblano peppers or red bell peppers, cut into 1-inch squares

1 tablespoon extra-virgin olive oil, or more if needed

Fine sea salt and freshly ground black pepper

HOMEMADE RED ENCHILADA SAUCE

3 tablespoons whole wheat flour

1 tablespoon chili powder

1 teaspoon smoked paprika

1 teaspoon ground cumin

¹/₂ teaspoon garlic powder

¹/₄ teaspoon fine sea salt

Pinch of ground cinnamon

2 tablespoons tomato paste

2 cups vegetable broth

3 tablespoons extra-virgin olive oil

1 teaspoon apple cider vinegar or distilled white vinegar

Freshly ground black pepper

(CONTINUED)

🕐 **TIME WARNING:** *These enchiladas take about 1¹/₂ hours from start to finish, but half of it is passive baking time.*

Golden, bubbling cheese is my love language. When I was growing up, my mom had just a few recipes in her repertoire that we would all eat, and chicken enchiladas was one of them. She filled flour tortillas with rotisserie chicken, sour cream, and green chiles and poured canned enchilada sauce on top. They weren't complete without a big sprinkle of cheese on top, which melted into golden oblivion in the oven. I loved those enchiladas.

Here is my vegetarian version of Mom's enchiladas, which is somewhat more redeeming. Instead of chicken, I stuff them with roasted sweet potato and poblano peppers, black beans, and just a little bit of sour cream. I use whole-grain tortillas, which aren't traditional (Mexicans use corn tortillas), but I just love the contrast of those crispy flour tortilla edges with the tender interiors. Then, I top them with my absolute favorite homemade enchilada sauce, and just enough cheese to turn golden and delicious. **MAKES 4 SERVINGS**

1. Preheat the oven to 400°F with racks in the middle and upper third of the oven. Line a large rimmed baking sheet with parchment paper for easy cleanup. Lightly grease a 9 × 13-inch baking dish.

2. *To roast the veggies:* On the prepared baking sheet, combine the sweet potato and poblanos. Drizzle the olive oil over them and toss until all sides are lightly and evenly coated, adding more oil if necessary. Lightly sprinkle with salt and pepper and arrange the ingredients in a single layer. Bake on the middle rack until the sweet potato and poblanos are tender and caramelized on the edges, 40 to 45 minutes, tossing halfway. Leave the oven on for the enchiladas.

3. *To make the enchilada sauce:* This sauce comes together quickly once you get started, so measure the dry ingredients (the flour, chili powder, paprika, cumin, garlic powder, salt, and cinnamon) in a small bowl and place it near the stove. Place the tomato paste and broth near the stove as well.

4. In a medium saucepan, warm the oil over medium heat until it's so hot that a sprinkle of the flour and spice mixture sizzles on contact (this will take a few minutes, so be patient). Pour in the flour and spice mixture. While stirring constantly with a whisk, cook until fragrant

(CONTINUED)

CHANGE IT UP

Feel free to substitute other roasted or sautéed vegetables for the sweet potato and peppers (you should have about the right amount if you start with $1\frac{1}{4}$ pounds vegetables). You can also replace the roasted vegetables with red onion and spinach sautéed in olive oil (plan on one small red onion and 10 to 12 ounces spinach).

(CONTINUED FROM PAGE 148)

ENCHILADAS

2 cans (15 ounces each) black beans, drained and rinsed, or 3 cups cooked black beans

$1/3$ cup sour cream, plus more for serving

$1/2$ teaspoon fine sea salt

Freshly ground black pepper

8 whole-grain tortillas (8-inch)

1 cup shredded Monterey Jack cheese (4 ounces)

$1/4$ cup raw pepitas (hulled pumpkin seeds)

1 avocado, sliced into long thin strips

Handful of chopped fresh cilantro, for garnish

TIP: *This enchilada sauce is completely worth the effort. As written, the recipe makes 2 cups of sauce, but you might as well double it and freeze the extras for your next batch of enchiladas.*

and slightly deepened in color, about 1 minute. Whisk the tomato paste into the mixture, then slowly pour in the broth while whisking constantly to remove any lumps.

5. Increase the heat to medium-high and bring the mixture to a simmer, then reduce the heat as necessary to maintain a gentle simmer. Cook, whisking often, until the sauce has thickened a bit and a spoon encounters some resistance as you stir, 5 to 7 minutes. (The sauce will further thicken as it cools.)

6. Remove from the heat, then whisk in the vinegar. Season to taste with a generous amount of black pepper and extra salt, if necessary. Set aside.

7. *To prepare the enchiladas:* In a medium bowl, combine the black beans, sour cream, and roasted vegetables. Season the filling with the salt and black pepper to taste.

8. Pour $1/4$ cup enchilada sauce into the prepared baking dish and tilt it from side to side until the bottom of the pan is evenly coated. To assemble your first enchilada, spread $1/2$ cup vegetable filling mixture down the middle of a tortilla, then snugly wrap the left side over and then the right, to make a wrap. Place it seam side down against the edge of your pan. Repeat with the remaining tortillas and filling.

9. Drizzle the remaining enchilada sauce evenly over the enchiladas, leaving the tips of the enchiladas bare. Sprinkle the Monterey Jack evenly over the enchiladas, followed by the pepitas.

10. Bake, uncovered, on the middle rack for 20 minutes. If the cheese on top isn't golden enough for your liking, carefully transfer the enchiladas to the upper rack of the oven and bake for an additional 3 to 6 minutes, until sufficiently golden and bubbling.

11. Remove from the oven and let the enchiladas cool for 10 minutes (they're super hot!). Before serving, arrange thin slices of avocado down the center of the enchiladas and sprinkle with chopped cilantro. Serve with sour cream on the side, if you'd like. Leftovers store well, chilled, for up to 4 days. Gently reheat in a microwave or oven before serving.

GLUTEN FREE: *Substitute certified gluten-free "flour" tortillas, or use corn tortillas (corn tortillas are smaller, so you will need 12 to 14 of them). If you use corn tortillas, you'll need to gently warm them before you try to roll them up, or they might break. To make the sauce gluten free, substitute gluten-free all-purpose flour for the whole wheat flour.* • **DAIRY FREE/VEGAN:** *Substitute Cashew Sour Cream (page 217) for the dairy sour cream. Omit the cheese on top.* • **EGG FREE** • **NUT FREE** • **SOY FREE**

Roasted Cauliflower and Kale Spaghetti with Toasted Almonds

Cauliflower haters, hear me out on this one. You know those bland cauliflower florets that you've been avoiding on veggie trays for all these years? If you toss them with olive oil and salt and give them a good, long roast in the oven, you end up with an entirely different animal. The insides of those florets get nice and tender, while the edges caramelize and develop a deep, nutty flavor. The little cauliflower crumbs in between turn into breadcrumb-like bits of pure goodness.

Still skeptical? Give this pasta dish a try. It reminds me of the plain buttered spaghetti of my youth, but without the blood sugar crash. Roasted cauliflower and kale, toasted almonds, and whole-grain spaghetti combine to create a surprising and sophisticated weeknight dinner. The method requires some coordination, but it all comes together while the cauliflower roasts in the oven.

MAKES 4 SERVINGS

1 large head cauliflower (about 2 pounds), florets cut into bite-size pieces

3 tablespoons extra-virgin olive oil, divided, or more if needed

Fine sea salt and freshly ground black pepper

$1/3$ cup sliced almonds

1 medium bunch Tuscan (lacinato) kale (about 8 ounces) or collard greens

8 ounces whole-grain spaghetti

1 tablespoon unsalted butter or extra-virgin olive oil

1 tablespoon lemon juice

1 to 2 cloves garlic, pressed or minced

$3/4$ cup grated Parmesan cheese (about $1 1/2$ ounces), plus more for garnish

Pinch of red pepper flakes (optional)

TIP: *If you're serving someone who is texturally averse, you can skip the kale altogether.*

1. Preheat the oven to 425°F with racks in the middle and upper third of the oven.

2. Pour the almonds onto a large rimmed baking sheet in a single layer. On another large rimmed baking sheet, drizzle the cauliflower with 2 tablespoons of the olive oil, followed by a sprinkle of salt and pepper. Toss until the cauliflower is lightly coated on all sides, and arrange the florets in a single layer.

3. Place the almonds on the top rack and the cauliflower on the middle rack. Toast the almonds until they are fragrant and golden, 4 to 5 minutes. Transfer the almonds to a bowl to cool, but keep the pan handy for the kale.

4. Bake the cauliflower until the cauliflower florets are deeply golden on the edges, 30 to 40 minutes, tossing halfway.

5. Meanwhile, to prepare the kale, slice off the tough bottom ends of the stalk. Then stack a few leaves at a time and roll them up toward the center ribs into a long, cigar-like shape. Slice across the roll as thinly as possible to yield kale ribbons about $1/4$ inch wide.

(CONTINUED)

(CONTINUED FROM PAGE 151)

6. On the same baking sheet that you used for the almonds, drizzle the kale ribbons with the remaining 1 tablespoon olive oil and toss until they are lightly coated on all sides (add another drizzle of olive oil if necessary). Arrange the kale in an even layer across the pan and sprinkle with salt. Place the pan on the top rack and roast the kale until the edges are turning darker and becoming crisp, about 10 minutes, tossing halfway.

7. Meanwhile, bring a large pot of salted water to boil. Cook the spaghetti until al dente, according to package directions. Before draining, reserve about 1 cup of the pasta cooking water; drain the pasta and return it to the pot.

8. Add the butter, lemon juice, and 1 clove minced garlic. Drizzle the pasta with $\frac{1}{4}$ cup of the reserved pasta cooking water and sprinkle the Parmesan on top. Toss to combine, adding more splashes of cooking water as necessary until the butter and Parmesan transform into a light sauce. Taste and add another clove of garlic if necessary (I like this pasta a little on the garlicky side).

9. Transfer the spaghetti to a large serving bowl. Once the cauliflower is done roasting, add it to the bowl, followed by the roasted kale and toasted almonds. Toss and season generously with salt (I usually add $\frac{1}{4}$ to $\frac{1}{2}$ teaspoon more) and pepper to taste. If you'd like a little extra kick, add the pepper flakes as well.

10. Portion the pasta into bowls and garnish each with a sprinkle of Parmesan. Serve immediately. This pasta keeps well, chilled, for 4 days. Gently reheat before serving.

GLUTEN FREE: *Use gluten-free spaghetti.* • **DAIRY FREE/VEGAN:** *Substitute olive oil for the butter and omit the Parmesan. You might want to stir in some nutritional yeast, to taste, for some cheese-like flavor.* • **EGG FREE** • **NUT FREE:** *Omit the almonds.* • **SOY FREE**

Sun-Dried Tomato Fettuccine Alfredo with Spinach

$\frac{1}{2}$ pound whole wheat fettuccine or linguine

2 tablespoons extra-virgin olive oil

4 cloves garlic, pressed or minced

Fine sea salt

5 to 6 ounces baby spinach (5 to 6 packed cups)

$\frac{2}{3}$ cup raw cashews (soaked for at least 4 hours if you do not have a high-powered blender)

2 tablespoons lemon juice

$\frac{1}{2}$ cup oil-packed sun-dried tomatoes, drained and chopped

$\frac{1}{3}$ cup grated Parmesan cheese (about $\frac{2}{3}$ ounce)

1 tablespoon chopped fresh basil

Pinch of red pepper flakes (optional)

TIME WARNING:
If you don't have a high-powered blender (like a Vitamix or Blendtec), you will need to soak the cashews for at least 4 hours.

I've always been a little wary of cashew-based sauces. Can they really replace those creamy dairy sauces that are so captivating, they hush a loud table on the first bite? This fettuccine "Alfredo" sauce proves that they can, at least sometimes. Cashews blended with reserved pasta cooking water and a squeeze of lemon juice make a rich, tangy sauce that clings to the pasta. Add some umami-rich sun-dried tomatoes, and I can't stop going back for more. This dish is just perfect for busy weeknights when you're craving comfort food, without the sleepy regret that follows.

Restaurant-style fettuccine Alfredo never fills me up, no matter how much I eat. This variation actually does, since it's made with whole-grain pasta, spinach, and cashews, which combined offer fiber, plant-based protein, and healthy fat. **MAKES 4 SERVINGS**

1. Bring a large pot of salted water to boil. Cook the pasta until al dente, according to package directions. Before draining the pasta, reserve about $1\frac{1}{3}$ cups of the pasta cooking water. Drain the pasta and return it to the pot.

2. Meanwhile, in a large skillet, warm the olive oil over medium heat until shimmering. Add the garlic and a pinch of salt and cook, stirring constantly, until fragrant but not browned, about 20 seconds. Add several handfuls of spinach and stir until wilted, then repeat with additional handfuls of spinach until all of the spinach has wilted. Remove the pan from the heat and set aside.

3. If you soaked the cashews, drain and rinse them. In a blender, combine the cashews with $\frac{2}{3}$ cup of the reserved pasta cooking water, the lemon juice, and $\frac{1}{2}$ teaspoon salt. Blend until the "Alfredo" sauce is completely smooth. If the mixture is too thick to blend, add up to $\frac{1}{3}$ cup more pasta cooking water to help.

4. In a large serving bowl, combine the cooked pasta, spinach mixture, sun-dried tomatoes, and Alfredo sauce. Gently toss until all of the pasta is lightly coated in sauce. Season to taste with additional salt, if necessary (I usually add another $\frac{1}{4}$ teaspoon). If the pasta seems dry, add another small splash of pasta cooking water and toss again.

(CONTINUED)

TIP: *Starchy, reserved pasta cooking water has a magical ability to bind ingredients together and make sauces nice and creamy, without the cream. While the pasta is cooking, place a heatproof liquid measuring cup in the sink to serve as a reminder. Then, just pour some of the hot pasta cooking water into the cup before draining off the rest. Be careful with that pasta cooking water, too—it's nearly boiling hot!*

(CONTINUED FROM PAGE 154)

5. Portion the pasta into bowls and top with a sprinkle of Parmesan and basil. Add a pinch of red pepper flakes if you'd like some heat. Serve immediately.

6. This pasta keeps well, chilled, for 4 days. Gently reheat before serving.

GLUTEN FREE: *Use gluten-free pasta.* • **DAIRY FREE/VEGAN:** *Use a sprinkle of nutritional yeast instead of the Parmesan.* • **EGG FREE** • **SOY FREE**

Chickpea Tikka Masala with Green Rice

Someday soon, I'd like to go to India and sample all of the authentic vegetable curries I can find. For now, I have this dish to tide me over. I modeled it after chicken tikka masala from stateside Indian restaurants, which may have actually originated in England. I took quite a few creative liberties, replacing the chicken, yogurt, and heavy cream with chickpeas and coconut milk. It's a comforting, hot meal with hearty chickpeas and my favorite Indian spices.

Tikka masala is usually served with plain basmati rice, but I kicked up the flavor a few notches by cooking it with a blend of spinach, jalapeño, onion, and garlic. It tastes more fresh than spicy, and counterbalances the rich tikka masala nicely. Everyone who tries it, loves it. You just wait! **MAKES 4 TO 6 SERVINGS**

1. *To prepare the green rice:* In a food processor or blender, combine the spinach, jalapeño, onion, garlic, olive oil, salt, and ¹/₂ cup of the water. Blend until smooth. Pour the mixture into a medium saucepan, reserving the food processor or blender bowl for later.

2. Add the remaining 1¹/₄ cups water to the pan and bring the mixture to a boil over high heat. Add the rice, reduce the heat to low, cover, and cook on a low simmer until the rice is tender and has absorbed all of the liquid, about 40 minutes. There will be a layer of green on top, so you'll need to take off the lid and check underneath with a fork to be sure it's done. (If the rice has absorbed all of the moisture but is still a little crunchy, add a couple more tablespoons of water and cook for a few minutes longer.) Once the rice is done, remove the pot from the heat and let the rice steam, covered, for 10 minutes.

3. *Meanwhile, to prepare the chickpea tikka masala:* The tikka masala comes together quickly, so before you get started, prepare the ginger and garlic and place in a small bowl. In another small bowl, combine all of the ground spices (coriander, cumin, turmeric, cardamom, cinnamon, and cayenne, if using). Place both bowls near the stove so they are handy.

4. Rinse out the food processor or blender bowl. Pour the tomatoes and their liquid into the food processor or blender and blend until smooth.

(CONTINUED)

GREEN RICE

2 cups packed baby spinach (about 2 ounces)

1 jalapeño or serrano pepper, seeded, deribbed, and roughly chopped

¹/₄ large yellow onion, roughly chopped

2 cloves garlic, roughly chopped

2 tablespoons extra-virgin olive oil

¹/₂ teaspoon fine sea salt

1³/₄ cups water, divided

1¹/₂ cups long-grain brown rice, preferably basmati, rinsed

CHICKPEA TIKKA MASALA

1 tablespoon grated or minced fresh ginger

3 cloves garlic, pressed or minced

1 tablespoon ground coriander

1¹/₂ teaspoons ground cumin

¹/₂ teaspoon ground turmeric

¹/₄ teaspoon ground cardamom

Pinch of ground cinnamon

Pinch of cayenne pepper (optional, if you like some heat)

1 can (28 ounces) whole tomatoes or diced tomatoes, with their liquid

(CONTINUED)

(CONTINUED FROM PAGE 157)

5. In a large, nonreactive skillet or Dutch oven, warm the olive oil over medium heat until shimmering. Add the onion and salt. Cook until the onions are soft and translucent, 5 to 7 minutes. Add the ginger and garlic and cook until fragrant, about 1 minute. Add the ground spice mixture and cook, stirring constantly, until fragrant, about 30 seconds. Add the puréed tomatoes, chickpeas, coconut milk, and cilantro. Increase the heat to medium-high and bring to a simmer, then reduce the heat to low to maintain a gentle simmer. Cook, stirring occasionally, until the sauce thickens, about 20 minutes.

6. Fluff the rice with a fork, stirring the green on top back into the rice, and season with additional salt if necessary (I always need at least $1/4$ teaspoon more). Season the tomato mixture with additional salt until the flavors really sing (again, I always need at least $1/4$ teaspoon more). If necessary, add another splash of coconut milk to mellow the spices.

7. To serve, spoon the rice into individual bowls and top with the chickpea masala. Finish the bowls with a light sprinkle of chopped cilantro. If you have leftovers, store the rice and masala separately. Leftover masala is also great with warm whole-grain naan.

TIP: *A "nonreactive" skillet is one that will not react with acid, such as stainless steel, enamel-coated (like Le Creuset), or one with a quality nonstick surface. Don't use your cast iron skillet, since the acidity in the tomatoes can eat away at the seasoned surface that you've worked so hard to maintain.*

1 tablespoon extra-virgin olive oil

$3/4$ large yellow onion, finely chopped

$1/2$ teaspoon fine sea salt

1 can (15 ounces) chickpeas, rinsed and drained, or $1^1/2$ cups cooked chickpeas

$3/4$ cup canned coconut milk, or more if needed

$1/2$ cup chopped fresh cilantro, plus more for garnish

GLUTEN FREE • DAIRY FREE • VEGAN • EGG FREE • NUT FREE • SOY FREE

Grilled Veggie Skewers with Cilantro-Lime Rice, Black Beans, and Avocado Chimichurri Sauce

RICE AND BEANS

1 cup long-grain brown rice or brown basmati rice, rinsed

1 bay leaf

2 tablespoons chopped fresh cilantro

2 tablespoons lime juice

1 tablespoon extra-virgin olive oil

$1/2$ teaspoon fine sea salt

1 can (15 ounces) black beans, rinsed and drained, or $1^{1}/_{2}$ cups cooked black beans

AVOCADO CHIMICHURRI SAUCE

2 avocados, halved and pitted

2 cups lightly packed fresh flat-leaf parsley (some stems are okay)

$1/2$ cup lightly packed fresh cilantro (some stems are okay)

2 cloves garlic

2 tablespoons sherry vinegar or lime juice

$1/2$ teaspoon red pepper flakes

$1/2$ teaspoon fine sea salt

Freshly ground black pepper

1 tablespoon extra-virgin olive oil

3 tablespoons water

(CONTINUED)

Chimichurri is as full of flavor as it is fun to say. It's a classic Argentinian parsley sauce that is typically served on grilled meat. It is fantastic on grilled vegetables as well, especially when you blend creamy avocado into it. Hearty mushrooms, toasted pepitas, and my favorite cilantro-lime rice make this dish a complete meal!

MAKES 4 SERVINGS

1. *To prepare the rice and beans:* Bring a large pot of water to boil over high heat. Pour in the rice and drop in the bay leaf. Give the mixture a brief stir and let it boil for 30 minutes, reducing the heat if necessary to prevent overflow. Drain the rice, return it to the pot, cover, and let it rest for 10 minutes off the heat. Discard the bay leaf and fluff the rice with a fork. Stir in the cilantro, lime juice, olive oil, and salt. Add the black beans and gently stir to combine. Cover until you're ready to serve.

2. *To make the chimichurri sauce:* Using a spoon, scoop the flesh of the avocados into a food processor. Add the parsley, cilantro, garlic, vinegar, pepper flakes, salt, and a few twists of black pepper. Process, stopping to scrape down the sides of the container once or twice. With the machine running, slowly stream in the olive oil and water. Add another tablespoon or so of water if you're having trouble blending the mixture. Taste and add more salt and pepper if necessary. Set aside.

3. *To grill the veggies:* Preheat your grill to medium heat. To prepare the mushrooms for grilling, slice them so they are evenly sized–use a sharp knife to quarter the large mushrooms, halve the medium mushrooms, and leave small mushrooms whole. Combine the prepared mushrooms, bell peppers, and onion in a medium bowl. Drizzle in the olive oil and sprinkle with salt and pepper. Toss until the pieces are lightly coated in oil, then thread the mushrooms, peppers, and chunks of onion onto skewers, alternating the vegetables as you go. You should have enough for 8 skewers.

4. Place each skewer on the grill. Turn the skewers by 90 degrees once the undersides have developed good grill lines. Continue cooking and turning until the vegetables are tender throughout, 10 to 15 minutes. Carefully transfer the skewers to a platter once they're done.

(CONTINUED)

(CONTINUED FROM PAGE 160)

GRILLED VEGGIES

8 ounces cremini (baby bella) mushrooms, washed and patted dry

2 red bell peppers, cut into 1-inch squares

1 red onion, cut into $1/2$-inch-wide wedges

2 tablespoons extra-virgin olive oil

Fine sea salt and freshly ground black pepper

GARNISH

$1/4$ cup raw pepitas (hulled pumpkin seeds)

5. Meanwhile, in a small skillet, toast the pepitas over medium heat, stirring often, until they turn golden on the edges and make little popping noises, about 5 minutes.

6. When you're ready to assemble, spoon the rice and beans onto 4 plates. Top each plate with 2 skewers, a generous drizzle of avocado chimichurri sauce, and a sprinkle of pepitas. Serve immediately.

7. If you intend to have leftovers, store the avocado chimichurri sauce separately from the rest, in a small bowl with plastic wrap pressed against the top to prevent browning. Reheat the rice and beans and veggies, then drizzle with sauce just before serving.

TIP: *If you don't have a grill (or it's too cold outside to fire it up), roast the prepared vegetables in a single layer on a large rimmed baking sheet at 400°F for 30 to 35 minutes, tossing halfway.*

GLUTEN FREE • DAIRY FREE • VEGAN • EGG FREE • NUT FREE • SOY FREE

Roasted Eggplant Lasagna

Eggplant Parmesan, meet spinach lasagna. This is Italian comfort food at its finest! Roasted slices of eggplant are sandwiched between layers of whole-grain noodles, simple homemade tomato sauce, and a creamy spinach and cottage cheese blend. I prefer to use cottage cheese instead of ricotta in my lasagnas, since it offers more flavor and a creamier texture than warm ricotta does. Make this lasagna for a fancy weekend dinner, and enjoy lasagna leftovers throughout the workweek. Leftovers taste even better the next day.

MAKES 9 TO 12 SERVINGS

1. *To roast the eggplant:* Preheat the oven to 425°F. Line a large rimmed baking sheet with parchment paper for easy cleanup.

2. Slice off both rounded ends of the eggplant, then stand the eggplant up on its widest flat side. Slice through the eggplant vertically to make long, even $1/4$- to $1/2$-inch-thick slabs. Discard both of the sides that are covered in eggplant skin.

3. Brush both sides of the eggplant slabs with olive oil, then arrange them in a single layer on the prepared baking sheet. Sprinkle with a few dashes of salt and pepper. Roast until golden and tender, about 20 minutes, turning halfway.

4. *To make the tomato sauce:* In a food processor, combine the tomatoes, basil, olive oil, garlic, salt, and pepper flakes. Pulse the mixture about 15 times, until the tomatoes have broken down to an easily spreadable consistency. Pour the sauce into a bowl and set aside.

5. *To make the spinach-cheese mixture:* Rinse out the food processor bowl and return it to the machine. Pour 1 cup of the cottage cheese into the processor and blend until smooth, about 1 minute. Set aside (we'll add more to the processor soon).

6. In a large skillet, warm the olive oil over medium heat until shimmering. Add the onion and $1/4$ teaspoon salt. Cook, stirring often, until the onion is tender and translucent, 4 to 5 minutes. Add the garlic and cook, stirring constantly, until fragrant, about 30 seconds.

7. Add a few large handfuls of spinach. Cook, stirring and tossing frequently, until the spinach has wilted. Repeat with the remaining spinach and cook until all of the spinach has wilted, about 3 minutes.

(CONTINUED)

ROASTED EGGPLANT

1 medium eggplant ($1^1/_2$ to 2 pounds)

2 to 3 tablespoons extra-virgin olive oil, for brushing

Fine sea salt and freshly ground black pepper

TOMATO SAUCE

1 can (28 ounces) diced tomatoes, drained

$1/_4$ cup roughly chopped fresh basil

2 tablespoons extra-virgin olive oil

2 cloves garlic, pressed or minced

$1/_2$ teaspoon fine sea salt

$1/_4$ teaspoon red pepper flakes

(CONTINUED)

⏱ TIME WARNING: *This lasagna requires about 1 hour of work, but it's worth it! If you're short on time, you can skip the eggplant altogether for a simpler spinach lasagna, and/or replace the home-made marinara with your favorite jarred marinara sauce (you'll need 16 ounces).*

(CONTINUED FROM PAGE 163)

SPINACH-CHEESE MIXTURE

2 cups (16 ounces) low-fat cottage cheese, divided

1 tablespoon extra-virgin olive oil

1 cup chopped red onion (about 1 small)

Fine sea salt

4 cloves garlic, pressed or minced

5 to 6 ounces baby spinach (5 to 6 packed cups)

Freshly ground black pepper

ASSEMBLY

9 no-boil (oven ready) lasagna noodles, preferably whole wheat*

2 cups freshly grated part-skim mozzarella cheese (about 8 ounces), divided

Chopped fresh basil, for garnish

Ingredient Note: My favorite brands of no-boil whole wheat lasagna noodles are DeLallo (available at Whole Foods) and Simply Balanced (available at Target). If you can't find no-boil noodles, you'll need to cook the noodles according to the package directions, which adds another step to the process.

8. Transfer the spinach mixture to the food processor and pulse until the spinach is chopped (but not puréed!), 5 to 7 times. Transfer the mixture to a medium bowl. Top with the remaining 1 cup cottage cheese and add a pinch of salt and lots of black pepper. Stir to combine. Now it's lasagna assembly time!

9. *To assemble the lasagna:* Spread $^1/_2$ cup tomato sauce evenly over the bottom of a 9 × 9-inch baking dish. Layer 3 lasagna noodles on top, overlapping their edges as necessary. Spread half of the cottage cheese mixture evenly over the noodles. Arrange half of the eggplant slices evenly over the cottage cheese mixture. Top with $^3/_4$ cup tomato sauce, then sprinkle $^1/_2$ cup mozzarella on top.

10. Top with 3 more noodles, followed by the remaining cottage cheese mixture. Arrange the remaining eggplant slices over the cottage cheese. (We're skipping the tomato sauce in this layer.) Sprinkle $^1/_2$ cup mozzarella on top.

11. Top with 3 more noodles, then spread $^3/_4$ cup tomato sauce over the top (you may have a little sauce left over) to evenly cover the noodles. Sprinkle evenly with the remaining 1 cup mozzarella.

12. Wrap a sheet of parchment paper around the top of the lasagna (or cover the lasagna with foil, but don't let the foil touch the cheese). Bake, covered, for 18 minutes, then uncover, rotate the pan by 180 degrees, and continue cooking until the top turns spotty brown, about 12 minutes more. Remove from the oven and let the lasagna cool for 15 to 20 minutes, so it has time to set and cool down to a reasonable temperature. Garnish with a sprinkling of basil, then slice and serve.

GLUTEN FREE: *Substitute gluten-free lasagna noodles. Choose no-boil (oven ready) noodles if possible; if not, cook them according to package directions.* • **DAIRY FREE/VEGAN:** *Double the recipe for Cashew Sour Cream (page 217) and use 2 cups instead of the cottage cheese. Skip the step where you would blend the cottage cheese and just stir cooked, chopped spinach into the sour cream. Omit the mozzarella and use all of the tomato sauce for the final layer. Serve the lasagna with a dollop of additional Cashew Sour Cream or, better yet, Basic Pesto (page 216).* • **EGG FREE** • **NUT FREE** • **SOY FREE**

CHANGE IT UP
You can replace the eggplant
with any variety of roasted or
sautéed veggies. Just try to
prepare them so they layer
easily (for example, you might
slice cauliflower into thin slabs
rather than standard florets).

CHANGE IT UP

Feel free to play around with the toppings on this one. If heirloom tomatoes aren't available, use 1 cup cherry tomatoes, halved lengthwise. Thin slices of roasted red peppers and mushrooms are great options as well.

Heirloom Tomato Pesto Pizza

While I adore cheesy, traditional pizzas, I tend to make lighter pizzas with pesto sauce at home. Here is one of my favorite combinations yet, which has far more flavor than delivery. Modest amounts of mozzarella accented with tangy goat cheese create one epic pizza! (Or in this case, two.)

Both the whole wheat pizza dough and pesto come together very quickly in the food processor, so this pizza is a fun weeknight option. I love basil pesto but opted for arugula here, which is less expensive and available in sufficient quantities year-round. Almonds are a complementary stand-in for pine nuts and are more cost-effective as well. **MAKES 2 PIZZAS (ABOUT 6 SERVINGS TOTAL)**

Easiest Honey Whole Wheat Pizza Dough (page 171)

PESTO

3 cups packed baby arugula and/or basil leaves (about 3 ounces)

$1/2$ cup raw almonds

1 tablespoon lemon juice

2 cloves garlic, roughly chopped

$1/2$ teaspoon fine sea salt

$1/2$ cup extra-virgin olive oil

Freshly ground black pepper

REMAINING TOPPINGS

$1^{1}/_{2}$ cups shredded part-skim mozzarella cheese (about 6 ounces)

$1/4$ cup crumbled goat cheese (about $1^{1}/_{2}$ ounces)

1 pound heirloom tomatoes, sliced into $1/4$-inch-thick rounds

Red pepper flakes (optional), for garnish

1. Preheat the oven to 500°F with a rack in the upper third of the oven. (Or, if you're using a pizza stone, make sure it's in the oven on the appropriate rack. Consult the manufacturer's directions.) Prepare the pizza dough.

2. *To make the pesto:* In a food processor, combine the arugula, almonds, lemon juice, garlic, and salt. With the machine running, drizzle in the olive oil. Continue processing until the mixture is well blended, pausing to scrape down the sides as necessary. Season to taste with black pepper.

3. *To top the pizzas:* Spread each pizza with half of the pesto. Evenly distribute half of the mozzarella, goat cheese, and sliced tomatoes over each pizza (you might not use all of the tomatoes–leftovers are great as a tomato salad with a light drizzle of olive oil and a sprinkle of flaky salt).

4. Transfer one pizza (parchment paper and all) onto a baking sheet and into the oven. Bake until the crust is golden and the cheese on top is bubbling, 9 to 12 minutes (or as few as 5 minutes if using a pizza stone).

5. Repeat with the remaining pizza. Top each pizza with a light sprinkle of pepper flakes, if desired. Slice and serve.

EGG FREE • NUT FREE: *Substitute pepitas (hulled pumpkin seeds) for the almonds.* **• SOY FREE**

Crispy Kale Pizza with Marinara Sauce

MARINATED KALE

1½ teaspoons extra-virgin olive oil

3 cups packed chopped curly kale leaves, tough ribs removed (about ½ medium bunch)

Fine sea salt

RED SAUCE

3 tablespoons tomato paste

1 can (14.5 ounces) crushed tomatoes

1 tablespoon extra-virgin olive oil

3 cloves garlic, pressed or minced

1 teaspoon balsamic vinegar

½ teaspoon dried oregano

½ teaspoon fine sea salt

Freshly ground black pepper

Up to 1 teaspoon coconut sugar or brown sugar (optional)

DOUGH AND TOPPINGS

Easiest Honey Whole Wheat Pizza Dough (page 171)

2 cups shredded part-skim mozzarella cheese (about 8 ounces)

Red pepper flakes, for garnish

Have you tried kale chips? This pizza is like a classic American cheese pizza with kale chips on top. All of the bitterness in the kale bakes away as it gets a little crispy and crackly. It's so good!

I designed this recipe to be a classic red sauce pizza that you might order for delivery from your favorite pizza place. It's made with whole wheat dough that bubbles up in the oven, a quick tomato sauce that tastes like it's been simmering on the stove for hours (thanks to some tomato paste), and a hefty sprinkle of mozzarella cheese that gets nice and golden in the oven. Crumbled feta is a nice addition here, if you have any in your fridge.

MAKES 2 PIZZAS (ABOUT 6 SERVINGS TOTAL)

1. Preheat the oven to 500°F with a rack in the upper third of the oven. (Or, if you're using a pizza stone, make sure it's in the oven on the appropriate rack. Consult the manufacturer's directions.) Prepare the pizza dough.

2. *To prepare the kale:* On a cutting board, or in a medium bowl, drizzle the olive oil over the chopped kale, then add a dash of salt. Lightly massage the oil into the kale so the pieces are lightly coated all over, then set it aside to marinate.

3. *To make the red sauce:* Measure the tomato paste into a small bowl. Add a big splash of crushed tomatoes and whisk until the tomato paste is fully incorporated. Pour in the rest of the tomatoes, then add the olive oil, garlic, vinegar, oregano, salt, and black pepper to taste. Whisk to blend. Taste, and if the mixture is too acidic, add a little sugar to balance it out. Set aside.

4. Spread each pizza with about half of the sauce (you might have a little sauce left over, depending on how saucy you like your pizza). Top each pizza with half of the mozzarella. Now, we're going to bake the pizza as is for a few minutes before adding the kale, to make sure the kale doesn't burn.

5. Transfer one cheese pizza (parchment paper and all) onto a baking sheet and into the oven. Bake until the cheese has melted and the edges of the crust are turning golden brown, 4 to 6 minutes. Remove the pizza from the oven and sprinkle half of the marinated

CHANGE IT UP
You can replace the marinated kale with your favorite pizza toppings, or skip the kale for an awesome homemade cheese pizza. Either way, just bake each pizza until the crust is golden and the cheese on top is bubbling, for a total of 8 to 12 minutes on a baking sheet or as few as 5 minutes on a pizza stone.

kale evenly over the top. Return the pizza to the oven and bake until the cheese on top is bubbling and the kale is crispy in parts, 5 to 8 minutes more (or as few as 2 minutes more on a pizza stone).

6. Repeat with the remaining pizza. Top each pizza with a light sprinkle of pepper flakes. Slice and serve.

TIP: *If you only have canned diced tomatoes, you can pulse them in the food processor just until they are more smooth than chunky. Fire-roasted crushed tomatoes are fine here.*

EGG FREE • NUT FREE • SOY FREE

Easiest Honey Whole Wheat Pizza Dough

This whole wheat dough is the easiest dough ever—no waiting required. It's actually best when baked immediately after making, so whip it up when you're ready for pizza. The Parmesan lends some richness and flavor that you wouldn't normally find in no-rise pizza doughs. I can't take credit for that trick. This recipe is an adaptation of *Cook's Illustrated*'s grilled pizza dough, so you can use this dough to make grilled pizzas, too! **MAKES 1 POUND (ENOUGH FOR TWO 11-INCH PIZZAS)**

1 cup very warm water (110°F, almost too hot for comfort)

1 tablespoon extra-virgin olive oil, plus more for brushing

1 tablespoon honey

1 envelope (2$\frac{1}{4}$ teaspoons) rapid-rise or instant yeast

2$\frac{3}{4}$ cups white whole wheat flour or regular whole wheat flour, or more as needed

$\frac{1}{4}$ cup grated Parmesan cheese (about $\frac{1}{2}$ ounce)

1 teaspoon fine sea salt

1. Preheat the oven to 500°F with a rack in the upper third of the oven. (Or, if you're using a pizza stone, make sure it's in the oven on the appropriate rack. Consult the manufacturer's directions.)

2. In a liquid measuring cup or small bowl, combine the warm water, oil, honey, and yeast. Whisk to combine and let the mixture rest for 5 minutes. It should puff up some by then.

3. In a food processor (see Tip), combine the flour, Parmesan, and salt. Process the mixture until combined. While running the food processor, slowly pour in the yeast mixture and process until a shaggy ball forms and pulls away from the sides of the bowl, about 1 minute.

4. Touch the dough, and if it clings to your fingers and doesn't hold its shape, add more flour, just 1 tablespoon at a time. Process briefly to blend again (or stir again, if making by hand).

5. Lightly flour a work surface, then dump the dough onto it. Quickly knead the dough a few times until it comes together. Use a sharp knife to slice the dough in half, then pick up each half and gently tuck the sides of the dough under to round out the edges.

6. Use a rolling pin to roll each piece of dough into a round about 11 inches in diameter. For best results, roll the dough out about as thin as reasonably possible (aim for even thickness rather than a perfectly round shape).

7. Carefully lift and transfer each round of dough onto individual pieces of parchment paper. Brush the outer 1 inch of dough with a light coating of olive oil, then proceed with your pizza recipe as directed.

TIP: *If you don't have a food processor, you can combine the flour, Parmesan, and salt in a large bowl. Whisk to combine, then drizzle the yeast and water mixture into the bowl while stirring with a large spoon. Stir until all of the flour has been incorporated and the dough comes together, then proceed with the next step.*

DAIRY FREE/VEGAN: *Substitute maple syrup or sugar for the honey, and omit the Parmesan. Your dough won't have quite the same depth of flavor, but it will still be good! You'll need to top the pizza with vegan ingredients, of course.* •
EGG FREE • NUT FREE • SOY FREE

Roasted Cherry Tomato and Brown Rice Risotto

2 tablespoons extra-virgin olive oil, divided

1 small yellow onion, chopped

Fine sea salt

2 cloves garlic, pressed or minced

4 cups (32 ounces) vegetable broth, divided

1 cup water

1½ cups brown Arborio (short-grain) rice

2 pints (4 cups) cherry or grape tomatoes

Freshly ground black pepper

1 cup grated Parmesan cheese (about 2 ounces)

½ cup dry white wine

3 tablespoons unsalted butter, cut into ½-inch cubes

RICE TIP: *It's important to use short-grain rice for risotto, because it contains the starch responsible for making risotto so creamy. Look for brown Arborio or other short-grain brown rice at well-stocked grocery stores or health food stores. Check the rice aisle, health section, or bulk bin section. This recipe is designed for short-grain brown rice; white Arborio rice would only need to be baked for 40 to 45 minutes.*

This luscious risotto is the grown-up love child of grandma's mac and cheese and spaghetti with marinara sauce. It's rich and comforting, like curling up under a warm blanket after a long day. Roasted cherry tomatoes and nutty brown rice keep it fresh and interesting. It pairs marvelously with a simple green salad–just toss fresh greens with my Liquid Gold Salad Dressing (page 52) and some grated Parmesan–and a chilled glass of white wine (you'll have most of the bottle left for sipping).

The only downside to using brown rice in risotto is that it takes longer to cook, but I've developed a minimal-stirring, baked rice technique. **MAKES 6 SERVINGS**

1. Preheat the oven to 375°F with one rack in the highest position and the other rack a little below center (low enough that you have enough clearance for your Dutch oven to fit between them).

2. In a medium Dutch oven, warm 1 tablespoon of the olive oil over medium heat until shimmering. Add the onion and a pinch of salt. Cook until the onions are golden on the edges, about 8 to 10 minutes, stirring occasionally. Add the garlic and continue cooking, stirring frequently, until the onions are well-browned, 2 to 4 minutes longer.

3. Add 3 cups of the broth and the water, cover, and increase the heat to medium-high. Once the mixture comes to a boil, remove it from the heat and stir in the rice. Cover the pot and bake on the lower rack until the rice is tender and cooked through, 1 hour 5 minutes to 1 hour 10 minutes. The rice will look awfully dry at this point, but don't worry.

4. During the last 20 minutes of baking time, prepare the tomatoes. On a small rimmed baking sheet, toss the cherry tomatoes with the remaining 1 tablespoon olive oil. Sprinkle them with salt and pepper. Roast on the top rack until most of the tomatoes have burst open, about 20 minutes.

5. Remove the pot from the oven. Pour in the remaining 1 cup broth, the Parmesan, wine, butter, 1 teaspoon salt, and a generous amount of pepper. Stir vigorously until the rice is thick and creamy, 2 to 3 minutes. Gently stir in the tomatoes and their liquid.

CHANGE IT UP

You can use this baked risotto technique to make all kinds of risotto. Just prepare the rice mixture as directed. Cook seasonal veggies until they're tender using your preferred method, and stir them into the rice instead of the burst cherry tomatoes.

6. Season to taste with additional salt (I usually add another ¼ teaspoon) and pepper, then serve immediately. This risotto makes for great leftovers–just wait until it cools before covering and storing in the refrigerator. It keeps well for up to 4 days. Gently reheat on the stove or in the microwave before serving.

TIP: *If you don't have a Dutch oven, you can prepare this risotto in a large saucepan on the stove, then carefully pour the boiling broth and rice mixture into a casserole dish. If the casserole dish has an oven-safe lid, use that; if not, cover it tightly with foil. Bake as directed.*

WINE TIP: *By dry white wine, I mean a relatively inexpensive Sauvignon Blanc, Pinot Grigio, or unoaked Chardonnay–just pick the variety you'll want to pour into a glass later! The wine adds a lovely depth of flavor, but you can omit it if you don't drink (no substitutions necessary).*

GLUTEN FREE • DAIRY FREE/VEGAN: *Skip the Parmesan or season with nutritional yeast, to taste. Replace the butter with olive oil, to taste.* **• EGG FREE • NUT FREE • SOY FREE**

TIP: *To save time, bake the tofu while you roast the veggies. Just place the tofu on the middle rack and the veggies on the upper rack. They'll be done at about the same time.*

Roasted Broccoli, Bell Pepper, and Tofu Bowl with Peanut Sauce

Where to begin? This abstractly Asian dish features tender, caramelized roasted veggies, crispy pillows of cubed tofu, and an insanely tasty peanut sauce, which I want to slather on just about everything. I could probably eat this meal for dinner every night (Cookie wouldn't mind).

This recipe requires some prep work, but once you're ready to go, you can cook the rice, veggies, and tofu in about 30 minutes. You'll have plenty of downtime to whisk together the peanut sauce and do a little dance (or flip through Instagram, or clean up the kitchen) while they cook. **MAKES 4 SERVINGS**

1. Preheat the oven to 400°F with a rack in the upper third of the oven.

2. Bring a large pot of water to boil. Add the rice and boil for 30 minutes. Drain the rice, return to the pot, cover, and let it rest for 5 minutes off the heat.

3. Meanwhile, on a large rimmed baking sheet, combine the broccoli florets and bell pepper and drizzle them with the olive oil. Toss until they're lightly and evenly coated in oil. Arrange the broccoli and bell pepper in an even layer, with the flat sides lying against the pan for maximum caramelization. Sprinkle lightly with salt.

4. Bake the veggies on the upper rack until the broccoli is deeply golden on the edges, 25 to 30 minutes, tossing halfway through.

5. *To make the sauce:* In a small bowl, combine the peanut butter, tamari, vinegar, honey, sesame oil, garlic, and pepper flakes. Whisk until blended, then whisk in 1 to 2 tablespoons water, or as much as necessary to reach a thick but drizzly consistency.

6. Before assembling, uncover the rice, add $1/4$ teaspoon salt, and use a fork to fluff the rice. Spoon the rice into individual bowls and top with plenty of roasted veggies and tofu. Drizzle the peanut sauce on top. Finish each bowl with a sprinkle of chopped peanuts and cilantro. Serve with Sriracha on the side.

7. Store leftover peanut sauce separately from any remaining rice, veggies, or tofu. Extra sauce makes a great dip for raw vegetables. Leftovers will keep well, chilled, for up to 4 days.

(CONTINUED)

PEANUT ALLERGY NOTE: *If you're allergic to peanuts, substitute almond butter or sunflower butter for the peanut butter and skip the peanut garnish.*

$1^{1}/_{4}$ cups brown rice, preferably Arborio (short-grain), rinsed

Fine sea salt

16 ounces broccoli florets (from about 2 medium bunches), cut into bite-size pieces

1 red bell pepper, cut into 1-inch squares

2 tablespoons extra-virgin olive oil

Extra-Crispy Baked Tofu (page 176)

PEANUT SAUCE

$1/_{4}$ cup creamy peanut butter

2 tablespoons reduced-sodium tamari or soy sauce

1 tablespoon rice vinegar

1 tablespoon honey

2 teaspoons toasted sesame oil

1 clove garlic, pressed or minced

Pinch of red pepper flakes

1 to 2 tablespoons water, or more as needed

GARNISHES

2 tablespoons chopped roasted peanuts

2 tablespoons chopped fresh cilantro

Sriracha or other chili-garlic sauce, for the spice lovers

(CONTINUED FROM PAGE 175)

EXTRA-CRISPY BAKED TOFU

You can use this crispy baked tofu to add to any of my salads or entrees for extra protein. The soy sauce adds some subtle saltiness and complex flavor, so I'd probably include it even when making recipes that don't include other Asian flavors. If you're concerned about gluten, be sure to use a certified gluten-free tamari instead of soy sauce. **MAKES 4 TO 5 SERVINGS**

- 1 block (12 to 15 ounces) organic extra-firm tofu
- 1 tablespoon extra-virgin olive oil
- 1 tablespoon reduced-sodium tamari or soy sauce
- 1 tablespoon arrowroot starch or cornstarch

1. Preheat the oven to 400°F. Line a large rimmed baking sheet with parchment paper.

2. Drain the tofu and use your palms to gently squeeze out some of the water. Slice the tofu into thirds lengthwise so you have 3 even slabs.

Stack the slabs on top of each other and slice through them vertically to make 3 even columns, then slice across to make 5 even rows.

3. Place a lint-free tea towel or paper towels over a cutting board and arrange the tofu in a single layer on top. Fold the towel(s) over the cubed tofu, then place something heavy on top (like another cutting board, topped with a cast iron pan or large cans of tomatoes) to help drain the tofu. Set aside.

4. Transfer the pressed tofu to a medium bowl. Drizzle the olive oil and tamari on top and toss to combine. Sprinkle the arrowroot starch over the tofu and toss until the tofu is evenly coated, and there are no powdery spots remaining. Tip the bowl of tofu over onto a large rimmed baking sheet and arrange the tofu in an even layer.

5. Bake the tofu until deeply golden on the edges, 25 to 30 minutes, tossing halfway. Tofu is best served promptly. Leftovers will keep well, chilled, for up to 4 days.

GLUTEN FREE: *Substitute certified gluten-free tamari for the soy sauce in the peanut sauce and baked tofu.* • **DAIRY FREE** • **VEGAN:** *Use maple syrup instead of honey.* • **EGG FREE**

Sweet Potato–Black Bean Veggie Burgers with Cabbage-Pepita Slaw

I take my veggie burgers seriously. My ideal veggie burger is crisp on the outside, and tender but cooked through on the inside. It is neither bland, nor too salty, and the patty retains its shape both before and after cooking. It's full of fresh flavor, which needn't be reminiscent of ground beef.

These veggie burgers satisfy all of my requirements, and taste incredible. They're a sublime combination of sweet and spicy, thanks to the roasted sweet potatoes and spicy adobo sauce, which comes from a can of chipotle peppers. The sauce lends a hint of smoky grilled flavor, even though these burgers are baked in the oven. You can cook them on the grill during the summer, too.

These burgers are fantastic when served with the regular fixings. They're also great on salads. My favorite way to eat them, though, is by sandwiching them between buns or butter lettuce leaves with guacamole and a crisp, colorful slaw. The slaw can also be a lovely, light side dish for burgers and more. **MAKES 8 VEGGIE BURGERS**

1. To make the burgers: Preheat the oven to 400°F. Line a large rimmed baking sheet with parchment paper.

2. Place the sweet potatoes cut side down on the baking sheet. Roast until they yield to a gentle squeeze, 30 to 40 minutes. Set them aside and leave the oven on for the burgers. (Save the lined baking sheet for the burgers, too.)

3. Meanwhile, in a small saucepan, combine the quinoa and water. Bring the mixture to a boil over medium-high heat, then reduce the heat as necessary to maintain a gentle simmer. Simmer, uncovered, until all of the water is absorbed, 11 to 14 minutes. Remove the pan from the heat, cover, and let the quinoa steam for 10 minutes.

4. Once the sweet potatoes are cool enough to handle, remove the skin (it should pull off easily) and discard. Roughly chop the sweet potatoes and transfer them to a large bowl. Add the cooked quinoa, black beans, onion, cilantro, garlic, adobo sauce, cumin, chili powder, and salt. Use a potato masher or big spoon to mix really well. It's okay if the black beans get smashed in the process. Sprinkle the oats over the mixture

(CONTINUED)

VEGGIE BURGERS

1½ pounds sweet potatoes (2 medium–large), halved lengthwise

½ cup quinoa, rinsed

1 cup water

1 can (15 ounces) black beans, rinsed and drained, or 1½ cups cooked black beans

½ cup chopped red onion (about ½ small onion)

⅓ cup chopped fresh cilantro

2 cloves garlic, pressed or minced

2 tablespoons adobo sauce, from a can of chipotle peppers in adobo*

2 teaspoons ground cumin

1 teaspoon chili powder

½ teaspoon fine sea salt

1¼ cups quick–cooking oats*

Extra-virgin olive oil, for brushing

CABBAGE-PEPITA SLAW

⅓ cup raw pepitas (hulled pumpkin seeds)

6 cups shredded cabbage (1¼ pounds)–red, green, or a combination

⅓ cup chopped fresh cilantro

1 clove garlic, pressed or minced

(CONTINUED)

(CONTINUED FROM PAGE 177)

and mix well with a big spoon until the mixture holds together when you shape a portion into a patty.

5. Make 8 patties, using about $^1/_2$ cup of the mixture per burger, and gently shape each into a patty about $3^1/_2$ inches in diameter. Use your hands to gently flatten the burgers and smooth out any jagged edges. Brush both sides of each patty generously with olive oil and place them on the lined baking sheet, leaving a few inches of space around each one. Bake until the patties are deeply golden on the outside, about 35 minutes, flipping halfway.

6. *Meanwhile, to prepare the slaw:* In a small skillet, toast the pepitas over medium heat, stirring often, until they turn golden on the edges and make little popping noises, about 5 minutes. Pour the pepitas into a large bowl, then add the cabbage, cilantro, garlic, lime juice, olive oil, cumin, and salt. Toss well, then set the bowl aside to marinate.

7. Serve the burgers on hamburger buns or lettuce leaves with a thick spread of guacamole and a generous helping of slaw on top. Serve immediately.

8. Leftovers are best stored individually. Press plastic wrap against the top surface of the guacamole to help prevent browning. Leftover burgers and slaw will last for up to 4 days, chilled. For more long-term storage, you can freeze leftover cooked burgers in a freezer bag for up to 3 months (just thaw in the microwave for about 1 minute or in a 400°F oven for 12 to 15 minutes).

3 tablespoons lime juice (from about $1^1/_2$ limes)

2 tablespoons extra-virgin olive oil

$^1/_2$ teaspoon ground cumin

$^1/_4$ teaspoon fine sea salt

8 hamburger buns, toasted, or 2 heads butter lettuce

Quick Guacamole (page 225)

Ingredient Notes: Check the international/Hispanic aisle of your grocery store for chipotle peppers in adobo sauce. Or, replace them with 2 teaspoons smoked paprika.

If you only have old-fashioned oats, process them briefly in a food processor or blender until they are broken up but not yet flour.

GLUTEN FREE: *Be sure to use certified gluten-free oats and gluten-free hamburger buns, if using.* • **DAIRY FREE** • **VEGAN** • **EGG FREE** • **NUT FREE** • **SOY FREE**

Mexican Roasted Veggie Bowl with Beer Beans

ROASTED POTATOES AND RED BELL PEPPERS

1 pound sweet potatoes, peeled and cut into $3/4$-inch chunks

$3/4$ pound Yukon Gold or russet (baking) potatoes, scrubbed clean and cut into $3/4$-inch chunks

2 tablespoons extra-virgin olive oil, divided, or more if needed

1 teaspoon ground cumin

$1/2$ teaspoon chili powder

$1/4$ teaspoon cayenne pepper

Fine sea salt

2 red bell peppers, sliced lengthwise into $1/2$-inch-wide strips

$1/2$ medium white onion, cut into $1/2$-inch-thick wedges

BEER BEANS

1 tablespoon extra-virgin olive oil

$1/2$ cup finely chopped yellow or white onion (about $1/2$ small onion)

$1/4$ teaspoon fine sea salt

2 cloves garlic, pressed or minced

$1/2$ teaspoon chili powder

$1/4$ teaspoon ground cumin

2 cans (15 ounces each) pinto beans, rinsed and drained, or 3 cups cooked pinto beans

$3/4$ cup Mexican beer* or water

When you're craving a hearty but fresh dinner (which is me, every night), make this one! This Mexican(ish) recipe starts with a base of pinto beer beans, which are so good on their own, you might want to turn them into a regular side dish. Then, pile on some roasted potatoes (both sweet and regular), fajita-like bell peppers and onion, followed by crisp romaine lettuce and avocado. Serve with tortilla chips or warmed tortillas and dig in! This is a meal you can enjoy in sweatpants on the couch, or serve for a casual get-together with chips and guacamole. **MAKES 4 SERVINGS**

1. *To roast the veggies:* Preheat the oven to 425°F with racks in the middle and upper third of the oven. Line two large rimmed baking sheets with parchment paper.

2. On one baking sheet, combine the sweet potatoes and potatoes. Drizzle 1 tablespoon of the olive oil over the potatoes, followed by the cumin, chili powder, cayenne, and a sprinkle of salt. Toss until they are lightly and evenly coated, adding extra olive oil if necessary. Arrange the potatoes in a single layer and bake on the middle rack until they are tender and caramelizing on the edges, 30 to 40 minutes, tossing halfway.

3. Meanwhile, on the second baking sheet, combine the bell pepper strips and onion wedges. Drizzle with the remaining 1 tablespoon olive oil, sprinkle with salt, and gently toss until evenly coated, leaving the onion wedges intact if possible. Arrange the veggies in a single layer and bake on the top rack until they are tender and caramelizing on the edges, 20 to 25 minutes, tossing halfway.

4. *To prepare the beans:* In a medium saucepan, warm the olive oil over medium heat until shimmering. Add the onion and salt and cook, stirring occasionally, until the onion is tender and turning translucent, 4 to 6 minutes. Add the garlic, chili powder, and cumin and cook, stirring constantly, until fragrant, about 30 seconds.

5. Add the beans and the beer. Increase the heat to medium-high and bring the mixture to a simmer, then reduce the heat as necessary to maintain a gentle simmer. Cook, stirring occasionally, until the beans are very tender and the liquid has condensed somewhat, 15 to 18 minutes. Remove the pot from the heat and stir in the cilantro and

lime juice. Season to taste with additional salt (I usually add up to ¼ teaspoon more, which helps counteract any remaining bitterness in the beer), and a little more lime juice, if necessary.

6. Portion the beans into bowls, followed by the roasted veggies and your choice of garnishes. Serve with your favorite red salsa on the side.

Ingredient Note: These beans are extra tasty when cooked with beer. My personal favorite is Negra Modelo, but if you're sensitive to bitterness in beer, choose a lighter beer, such as Corona. Don't worry—these beans are still great with water if you're avoiding alcohol (I can't promise that all of the alcohol evaporates during cooking).

2 tablespoons chopped fresh cilantro

1 tablespoon lime juice, or more if needed

GARNISHES (THE MORE, THE BETTER)

Chopped romaine lettuce

Sliced avocado or Quick Guacamole (page 225)

Crumbled feta cheese

Tortilla chips and/or warmed corn tortillas

Red salsa, homemade (pages 101–102) or store-bought, for serving

GLUTEN FREE: *Use gluten-free beer or water instead, and make sure your chips and/or tortillas are also gluten-free.* •
DAIRY FREE/VEGAN: *Skip the feta cheese.* • **EGG FREE** • **NUT FREE** • **SOY FREE**

Coconut Fried Rice with Edamame

1½ cups frozen shelled edamame, thawed and drained

2 tablespoons melted coconut oil or avocado oil, divided

1 cup finely chopped carrots (3 to 4 medium)

1 red bell pepper, finely chopped

1 cup thinly sliced green onions (about 1 medium bunch)

3 large cloves garlic, pressed or minced

1 cup unsweetened coconut flakes*

3 cups cold cooked brown rice, preferably jasmine

2 tablespoons reduced-sodium tamari or soy sauce, plus more for serving

2 teaspoons Sriracha or other chili-garlic sauce, plus more for serving

1 tablespoon lime juice

¼ cup chopped fresh cilantro, for garnish

1 lime, cut into wedges, for serving

*Ingredient Note: Look for unsweetened coconut flakes in the baking section at health food stores or well-stocked grocery stores (sometimes you will find them in the health food section). The brands I see most often are Let's Do Organic and Bob's Red Mill, which is labeled "flaked coconut."

This untraditional, vaguely Thai fried rice dish transforms leftover rice, tender edamame, and basic veggies into a weeknight dinner that I crave constantly. While coconut in fried rice might seem surprising, the large coconut flakes turn savory and lightly crisp once golden. It makes this dish even more fun and satisfying.

Fried rice is typically cooked with refined vegetable oil at a high heat, but I opted for coconut oil and medium heat, so it doesn't start smoking. Make this when you have leftover rice, since cold rice is less clumpy. Leftovers are great for lunch the next day. **MAKES 4 SERVINGS**

1. Before you get started, be sure all of your ingredients are prepared and ready to go near the stove. Put the edamame in a medium bowl and keep it near the stove.

2. Warm a large skillet, preferably cast iron, over medium heat. Once the pan is hot enough that a drop of water sizzles on contact, add 1 tablespoon of the oil and swirl the pan to coat. Add the carrots and bell pepper. Cook, stirring often, until they are tender, 5 to 8 minutes.

3. Add the green onions and garlic and cook, stirring constantly, until fragrant, about 30 seconds. Carefully transfer the contents of the pan to the bowl of edamame.

4. Add the remaining 1 tablespoon oil to the pan. Pour in the coconut flakes and cook, stirring frequently, until the flakes are lightly golden, about 30 seconds. Add the rice to the pan and cook, stirring occasionally, until the rice is hot, about 3 minutes.

5. Pour the contents of the bowl back into the pan. Add the tamari and Sriracha. Stir to combine and cook just until all of the ingredients are warmed through.

6. Remove the pan from the heat and drizzle the lime juice over the dish. Promptly spoon the fried rice into individual bowls, garnishing each one with a generous sprinkle of chopped cilantro and a lime wedge. Serve with bottles of Sriracha or chili-garlic sauce (for the spice lovers) and tamari on the side.

GLUTEN FREE: Use certified gluten-free tamari instead of standard soy sauce. • **DAIRY FREE** • **VEGAN** • **EGG FREE** • **NUT FREE**

CHANGE IT UP

This recipe is a great way to use up leftover vegetables in your crisper drawer, as long as you slice them very small. Toss in some very thinly sliced broccoli, chopped zucchini or yellow squash, shredded Brussels sprouts, or cabbage instead of the carrots and bell pepper.

TIP: *To chill freshly cooked rice quickly, spread it onto a large rimmed baking sheet and place it in the refrigerator. You'll need to cook 1 cup raw rice to yield the 3 cups cooked called for in this recipe. See my favorite cooking method on page 224.*

CHANGE IT UP

These pita sandwiches are also great with a store-bought roasted garlic hummus, or with Tzatziki Sauce (page 219) instead of hummus.

Simple Roasted Veggie, Arugula, and Hummus Pita Sandwiches

Imagine we're wandering through a cute seaside Mediterranean town. It's warm and sunny, and pomegranates grow like rubies from the trees. Hunger strikes, and we order the best pita sandwich of our lives from a street vendor. It's slathered with hummus and stuffed with roasted vegetables and fresh greens–so simple, and so good. These pita sandwiches are a perfect weekend lunch or weeknight dinner option. **MAKES 4 SANDWICHES**

1. *To roast the veggies:* Preheat the oven to 425°F with racks in the middle and upper third of the oven.

2. On a large rimmed baking sheet, drizzle the cauliflower with 1 tablespoon of the olive oil, just enough to lightly coat the cauliflower once tossed (add more if needed). Toss well and sprinkle with salt. On a second large rimmed baking sheet, combine the eggplant and bell pepper. Drizzle those veggies with the remaining 1 tablespoon olive oil, just enough to lightly coat them once tossed (add more if needed). Toss well and sprinkle with salt.

3. Transfer the pan of cauliflower to the top rack, and the pan of eggplant and bell pepper to the middle rack. Bake until the veggies are tender and caramelizing on the edges, 30 to 35 minutes, tossing halfway. Leave the oven on for warming the pitas later.

4. Once the veggies are done roasting, scoot the cauliflower onto the eggplant and bell pepper pan (keep the former cauliflower pan handy for the pitas). Drizzle the lemon juice on top and toss to combine. Taste and season with additional salt, if necessary.

5. *To make the pita sandwiches:* Brush both sides of each pita lightly with olive oil and arrange them across the used cauliflower pan. Bake on the top rack just until warmed through, 2 to 4 minutes.

6. Spread a generous layer of hummus over each pita. Top half of each pita with roasted veggies, then top the veggies with a handful of arugula. Fold the other half of the pita over the veggies to form a sandwich. Serve immediately. Leftover sandwiches keep well for up to 3 days in the refrigerator, and are best served chilled.

ROASTED VEGGIES

1 small head cauliflower (about 1½ pounds), florets cut into bite-size pieces

2 tablespoons extra-virgin olive oil, divided, or more if needed

Fine sea salt

1 small eggplant (½ to ¾ pound), cut into bite-size pieces

1 red bell pepper, cut into bite-size pieces

1 tablespoon lemon juice

PITA SANDWICHES

4 whole-grain pitas (7-inch)

Extra-virgin olive oil, for brushing

1 cup Green Goddess Hummus (page 120)

2 to 3 cups lightly packed baby arugula, as needed (about 2 to 3 ounces)

GLUTEN FREE: *Substitute gluten-free "flour" tortillas for the pitas (you might want to stack 2 tortillas per sandwich for a similar effect).* • **DAIRY FREE** • **VEGAN** • **EGG FREE** • **NUT FREE** • **SOY FREE**

Roasted Carrots with Farro, Chickpeas, and Herbed Tahini Sauce

1 cup farro, rinsed

1¼ teaspoons plus
1 tablespoon extra-virgin
olive oil, divided

1 teaspoon lemon juice

1 clove garlic, pressed
or minced

Fine sea salt

Pinch of red pepper
flakes

1 can (15 ounces)
chickpeas, rinsed and
drained, or 1½ cups
cooked chickpeas

1 pound slender heirloom
carrots, scrubbed clean
and patted dry (no need
to peel)

¼ teaspoon ground
cumin

Freshly ground black
pepper

3 tablespoons raw pepitas
(hulled pumpkin seeds)

HERBED TAHINI SAUCE
⅓ cup tahini

2 tablespoons lemon juice

2 tablespoons chopped
fresh flat-leaf parsley,
divided

¼ teaspoon fine sea salt

Freshly ground black
pepper

3 to 4 tablespoons water,
as needed

She's a beauty, isn't she? This showstopper is actually pretty simple to make, which makes it a great weeknight dinner. It's also a holiday-worthy vegan dish–just be prepared to fend off the carnivores. It's a riff on a popular blog recipe, but with tangy, herbed tahini sauce instead of crème fraîche. Combined with earthy and sweet caramelized carrots, nutty farro, and toasted pepitas, it makes one stellar main dish or side. **MAKES 4 ENTREE OR 8 SIDE SERVINGS**

1. In a medium saucepan, combine the farro with enough water to cover by a couple of inches (at least 3 cups water). Bring the water to a boil, then reduce the heat to a gentle simmer. Cook, stirring occasionally, until the farro is tender to the bite but still pleasantly chewy (pearled farro will take around 15 minutes; unprocessed farro will take 25 to 40 minutes). Drain off the excess water and return the farro to the pot. Add 1 teaspoon of the olive oil, the lemon juice, garlic, ½ teaspoon salt, and the pepper flakes. Mix well, then add the chickpeas and stir to combine. Cover and set aside.

2. Meanwhile, preheat the oven to 425°F. Line a large rimmed baking sheet with parchment paper for easy clean-up.

3. Place the carrots on the baking sheet and drizzle with 1 tablespoon of the olive oil. Sprinkle the cumin on top, followed by a few dashes of salt and black pepper. Rub the oil and spices over the carrots so they are all evenly coated. Roast until the carrots are easily pierced by a fork near the top of their stems, 20 to 35 minutes. (Roasting time will depend entirely on the size of your carrots. I removed some of the more slender carrots at 20 minutes and checked them in 5-minute intervals thereafter, removing individual carrots as they were done.)

4. In a small skillet, combine the pepitas, the remaining ¼ teaspoon olive oil, and a pinch of salt. Cook over medium heat, stirring frequently, until the pepitas turn golden on the edges and start making little popping noises, about 5 minutes. Set aside.

5. *To make the herbed tahini sauce:* In a liquid measuring cup or small bowl, combine the tahini, lemon juice, 1 tablespoon of the chopped parsley (reserve the rest for garnishing), salt, and several twists of black pepper. Whisk to combine, then whisk in 3 to 4 tablespoons water, or as much as necessary to reach a thick but drizzly consistency.

Stir to combine, then taste and season with additional salt and pepper if necessary. Set aside.

6. To assemble the dish, pour the farro and chickpea mixture evenly across a large serving platter. Arrange the carrots in a single layer over the mixture. Drizzle the herbed tahini sauce generously over the carrots, then sprinkle them with pepitas and the remaining 1 tablespoon parsley. Serve with any extra tahini sauce on the side.

7. This dish is great warm, or cooled to room temperature. Leftovers keep well, chilled, for 3 to 4 days.

TIP: *You can substitute wheat berries or spelt berries for the farro, but they will take longer to cook (likely 45 to 60 minutes). Cook as directed for the farro, but check the pot occasionally and add more water if necessary.*

GLUTEN FREE: *Substitute wild rice or long-grain brown rice for the farro (see page 224 for cooking instructions).* •
DAIRY FREE • **VEGAN** • **EGG FREE** • **NUT FREE** • **SOY FREE**

Taco Party!

Who doesn't love tacos? No one! Taco parties are my favorite, since (a) they include both friends and tacos, and (b) they're suitable for friends with a variety of dietary restrictions (vegan, gluten free, nut free, etc.), so everyone can enjoy them.

I dreamed up a menu for my next taco party, which includes refried black beans, meaty roasted mushrooms, and a kale slaw with feta and toasted pepitas that doubles as a side salad. If you're in the mood for a lighter taco, skip the roasted veggies, but be sure to add guacamole on top. **MAKES 8 HEARTY TACOS**

1. Preheat the oven to 425°F. Line a large rimmed baking sheet with parchment paper for easy cleanup.

2. *To make the kale slaw:* Make the slaw first so it has ample time to marinate. In a small skillet, toast the pepitas over medium heat, stirring frequently, until they turn golden on the edges and make little popping noises, 4 to 5 minutes. Set aside to cool.

3. Place the chopped kale in a large serving bowl. Sprinkle lightly with salt and massage the kale until it's fragrant, darker in color, and reduced in volume by about one-third. Add the feta and the toasted pepitas.

4. In a small bowl, combine the olive oil, lime juice, jalapeño, garlic, cumin, and 1/4 teaspoon salt. Whisk until blended. Pour the dressing over the kale mixture and toss until the kale is lightly coated in dressing. Set aside.

5. *To prepare the roasted veggies:* Quarter the large mushrooms, halve the medium mushrooms, and leave small mushrooms whole. Transfer the mushrooms and pepper pieces to the prepared baking sheet. Drizzle the olive oil over the veggies and sprinkle them with the chili powder and salt. Toss until they are lightly coated in oil and spices. Roast until the mushrooms and peppers are tender and starting to brown, about 20 minutes, tossing halfway. Transfer the roasted veggies to a bowl. Keep the baking sheet handy and leave the oven on, as we'll use them to warm the tortillas just before serving.

(CONTINUED)

KALE SLAW
1/3 cup raw pepitas (hulled pumpkin seeds)

1 medium bunch curly kale (about 8 ounces), tough ribs removed and leaves chopped into bite-size pieces

Fine sea salt

1/2 cup crumbled feta cheese (about 2 1/2 ounces)

3 tablespoons extra-virgin olive oil

2 tablespoons lime juice

1 medium jalapeño, seeded, deribbed, and finely chopped

1 clove garlic, pressed or minced

1/2 teaspoon ground cumin

ROASTED VEGGIES
16 ounces cremini (baby bella) mushrooms, cleaned and stems trimmed

2 poblano peppers or red bell peppers, cut into 1-inch squares

2 tablespoons extra-virgin olive oil

1 teaspoon chili powder

1/4 teaspoon fine sea salt

REFRIED BLACK BEANS
1 tablespoon extra-virgin olive oil

1/2 cup finely chopped yellow or white onion (about 1/2 small)

Fine sea salt

(CONTINUED)

(CONTINUED FROM PAGE 189)

2 cloves garlic, pressed or minced

2 teaspoons ground cumin

2 cans (15 ounces each) black beans, rinsed and drained, or 3 cups cooked black beans

$1/2$ cup water

$1/2$ teaspoon fine sea salt

Freshly ground black pepper

$1/4$ teaspoon sherry vinegar or 1 teaspoon lime juice

ASSEMBLY
8 corn tortillas

Salsa verde, homemade (page 105) or store-bought

Quick-Pickled Red Onions (page 222) or pickled jalapeños

Guacamole (pages 111 or 225) or sliced avocado

Hot sauce

6. *To cook the refried black beans:* In a medium saucepan, warm the olive oil over medium heat until shimmering. Add the onion and a sprinkle of salt. Cook, stirring occasionally, until the onions have softened and are turning translucent, 5 to 8 minutes.

7. Add the garlic and cumin. Cook, stirring constantly, until fragrant, about 30 seconds. Pour in the beans and water. Stir, cover, and cook for 5 minutes. Reduce the heat to low, uncover, and use a potato masher or the back of a fork to mash up at least half of the beans. Continue to cook the beans, uncovered, stirring often, for 3 minutes more.

8. Remove the saucepan from the heat and stir in $1/2$ teaspoon salt, black pepper to taste, and the vinegar. Taste and add more salt, pepper, or vinegar if necessary. If the beans seem dry, add a very small splash of water and stir to combine. Cover until you're ready to serve.

9. Arrange the tortillas in a single layer on an unlined baking sheet (some overlap is okay). Bake just until warmed through, about 3 minutes.

10. *To assemble the tacos:* Spread a couple spoonfuls of refried beans down the middle of the tortillas. Top with the roasted veggies and marinated kale. Serve with garnishes of your choice: salsa verde, pickled onions or jalapeños, guacamole or avocado, and hot sauce. If you have any leftover kale slaw and/or black beans, serve them as sides.

GLUTEN FREE: *Use certified gluten-free tortillas.* • **DAIRY FREE/VEGAN:** *Omit the feta cheese and serve the tacos with Cashew Sour Cream (page 217) on the side.* • **EGG FREE** • **NUT FREE** • **SOY FREE**

Alternative Taco Party Menus

Craving variety? Mix and match from the following columns. Choose one option from the substance column, one from the veggies column, and as many final touches as you'd like. My only recommendation is that the tacos contain something crisp for textural interest, which could be one of the slaws, pickled onions or jalapeños, or chopped romaine lettuce.

SUBSTANCE

Refried Black Beans (page 189)

Taco Filling (page 56)

Beer Beans (page 180)

VEGGIES

Fajita Veggies (page 32)

Cabbage-Pepita Slaw (page 177)

Roasted Potatoes and Red Bell Peppers (page 180)

Zesty Black Bean and Corn Salad (page 123)

Kale Slaw (page 189)

FINAL TOUCHES

Creamy Avocado-Cilantro Sauce (page 219), Guacamole (small batch, page 225, or big batch, page 111), or sliced avocado

Cashew Sour Cream (page 217) or dairy sour cream

Crumbled feta cheese

Your favorite salsa (pages 101–105)

Quick-Pickled Red Onions (page 222)

Pickled jalapeños

Chopped romaine lettuce

6 *Sweet Treats*

CELEBRATIONS ARE THE SPICE OF LIFE, AND NO OCCASION IS TOO SMALL TO COMMEMORATE. Surviving a long day, receiving good news from a friend, finishing a big project, turning one year wiser? Let's celebrate! I insist.

Celebrations almost inevitably involve a sweet treat, and I've included 10 of my favorites in this chapter. Each of the following desserts offers some redeeming qualities, including fruit, heart-healthy nuts and whole grains, and/or dark chocolate. I used natural sweeteners whenever possible, too.

If you're consuming mostly whole foods elsewhere, you've already significantly reduced your sugar intake. So go ahead! Treat yourself.

Pomegranate Ambrosia

2 pounds mandarins or clementines (8 to 12), as needed to yield 2 cups segments and $\frac{1}{2}$ cup juice

2 cups small bite-size fresh pineapple chunks (1 small pineapple will be plenty)

Arils (seeds) from 1 medium-large pomegranate (about $1\frac{1}{2}$ cups)

$\frac{3}{4}$ cup unsweetened shredded coconut

1 tablespoon honey

1 cup vanilla or coconut yogurt (optional),* for serving

*Ingredient Note:
My favorite brand of lightly sweetened yogurt is Siggi's, which is technically skyr, a very thick, traditional Icelandic yogurt.

My sweet grandmother Mimi used to make ambrosia, a Southern fruit salad that typically includes canned mandarins, pineapple, and maraschino cherries mixed with sweetened shredded coconut and miniature marshmallows. Mimi isn't here anymore, so it pains me that I used to crinkle my little nose at her fruit salad. I didn't like coconut back then.

This fresh ambrosia is a nod to Mimi's ambrosia, featuring equal parts fresh pineapple and mandarin segments and tossed with pomegranate arils, unsweetened shredded coconut, and a touch of honey-sweetened fresh mandarin juice. Top it with a dollop of your favorite vanilla or coconut yogurt for a simple, fresh dessert that really tastes like it could be "food of the gods." Or, skip the creamy stuff and you'll be left with the best fruit salad you have ever tasted.

MAKES 4 TO 6 SERVINGS

1. Peel the mandarins and pull apart the individual segments. Use your fingers to remove as much pith from the segments as you reasonably can. Repeat until you have 2 cups segments and transfer them to a medium bowl. Add the pineapple, pomegranate arils, and shredded coconut.

2. To get $\frac{1}{2}$ cup mandarin juice, cut a few mandarins in half crosswise and use a handheld citrus juicer to squeeze the juice into a liquid measuring cup. Or just hand-squeeze the halved fruit over the liquid measuring cup, repeating until you have $\frac{1}{2}$ cup.

3. Whisk the honey into the juice until well combined (if the honey refuses to blend, briefly warm the juice in the microwave, or in a small saucepan on the stove, and try again).

4. Pour the mixture over the fruit and toss until well combined. For best flavor, cover and chill the mixture for at least 1 hour or up to 1 day.

5. To serve, spoon the ambrosia into bowls. Serve as is, or top with a dollop of your yogurt of choice.

TIP: *Preparing fresh pineapple and pomegranate is a time-consuming task, so feel free to buy pre-cut fresh pineapple and pomegranate arils if you're in a hurry. Just avoid canned mandarin segments, because they aren't nearly as tasty as fresh fruit.*

GLUTEN FREE • DAIRY FREE/VEGAN: *Use vegan coconut yogurt, if desired. For vegan ambrosia, also use maple syrup instead of honey.* **• EGG FREE • NUT FREE • SOY FREE**

CHANGE IT UP
Substitute raspberries for the pomegranate arils, and orange segments for the mandarins or clementines. Any member of the orange family will do, really.

CHANGE IT UP
Substitute other fresh fruits
for the blueberries, such
as chopped cherries,
strawberries, peaches,
or nectarines.

Lemony Almond-Blueberry Cake

This almond-blueberry cake is lightly sweet and possesses an almost graham crackery flavor and lemony tang. Plus, it's studded with gorgeous, jammy blueberries. It would be a great treat to serve as dessert for any occasion, but it's wholesome enough to pass for breakfast or a midafternoon snack. It's also easy to make and gluten free, which means that I can share it with more of my friends!

MAKES 1 LOAF CAKE (ABOUT 8 SLICES)

1. Preheat the oven to 325°F. Generously grease a 9 × 5-inch loaf pan and dust it with almond meal to prevent sticking.

2. In a large bowl, combine 2 cups of the almond meal, the baking powder, baking soda, salt, and cinnamon. Whisk to blend.

3. Crack the eggs into a medium bowl and beat with a whisk until the yolks and egg whites have blended together. Add the maple syrup, olive oil, and lemon zest and whisk to blend. Pour the wet ingredients into the almond meal mixture and stir until there are just a few clumps remaining.

4. In a small bowl, toss the blueberries with the remaining 1 tablespoon almond meal (this helps prevent the blueberries from sinking to the bottom of the cake). Gently fold the blueberries into the batter.

5. Scrape the batter into the prepared pan. Bake until the cake is deeply golden brown, the center is firm to the touch, and a toothpick inserted in the center comes out clean, 1 hour 10 minutes to 1 hour 15 minutes.

6. *Meanwhile, to make the lemon-maple glaze:* In a small bowl, whisk together the lemon juice and maple syrup until blended. (If you're using honey and having a hard time blending it into the lemon juice, place the bowl on top of your stove to warm it up while the cake bakes, or warm it briefly in the microwave until you can whisk them together.)

7. Once the cake is out of the oven, place the cake, pan and all, on a cooling rack. While the cake is warm, use a pastry brush to brush the glaze over the top of the cake. It should soak right in. Let the cake cool for at least 30 minutes before carefully inverting it onto a serving plate or cutting board. Carefully flip it back over, then use a bread knife to cut it into 1-inch-thick slices.

8. Store any remaining cake in the refrigerator, covered, for up to 4 days.

GLUTEN FREE • DAIRY FREE • SOY FREE

2 cups (8 ounces) plus 1 tablespoon packed almond meal

1 teaspoon baking powder

1/2 teaspoon baking soda

1/2 teaspoon fine sea salt

1/4 teaspoon ground cinnamon

4 eggs

2/3 cup maple syrup or honey

1/4 cup extra-virgin olive oil

1 1/2 teaspoons grated lemon zest (from 2 medium lemons, preferably organic)

1 cup blueberries (6 ounces), fresh or frozen

LEMON-MAPLE GLAZE

2 tablespoons lemon juice

2 teaspoons maple syrup or honey

🕐 **TIME WARNING:** *This cake is very simple to make, but requires about 1 hour 45 minutes combined baking and cooling time.*

Dark Cherry Almond Crisp

CHERRY FILLING

2 pounds dark sweet cherries, frozen (thawed)* or fresh (pitted and halved)

1/3 cup maple syrup

2 tablespoons arrowroot starch or cornstarch

1 teaspoon vanilla extract

TOPPING

1 cup old-fashioned rolled oats

1/2 cup packed almond meal (2 ounces)

1/3 cup packed coconut sugar or brown sugar

1/3 cup sliced almonds

1/4 teaspoon fine sea salt

1/4 teaspoon ground cinnamon

1/4 cup plain yogurt

1/4 cup melted unsalted butter

Vanilla ice cream or plain or vanilla yogurt, for serving

TIP: *Don't try to substitute honey for the maple syrup, as it will stick to cold thawed cherries.*

Ingredient Note: *If you're using frozen cherries, you can defrost them in the microwave, at room temperature for at least 2 hours, or overnight in the refrigerator. Before adding them to the filling, drain off most of the excess juices.*

This dessert reminds me of classic cherry pie, but in simplified crisp form. That makes it my ideal fruity dessert, since I just don't have the patience for pie crust, and all the rolling and crimping that goes along with it. Fortunately, this crisp is just as satisfying and stunning in its own right. Unlike typical cherry pies made with canned tart cherry pie filling, this crisp is made with fresh or frozen dark sweet cherries. As a result, it tastes super fresh, and it's free of artificial coloring and high-fructose corn syrup. I actually recommend using thawed frozen cherries here, since they're less expensive and already pitted (see note).

I opted for almond meal instead of flour because almonds and cherries play so well together. That means this hearty crisp is also gluten free. Leftovers make a great breakfast the next morning.

MAKES 8 SERVINGS

1. Preheat the oven to 350°F.

2. *To prepare the cherry filling:* In a 9 × 9-inch baking dish, combine the cherries, maple syrup, starch, and vanilla. Stir until the mixture is evenly blended and no powdery spots remain. Set aside.

3. *To make the topping:* In a medium bowl, combine the oats, almond meal, coconut sugar, sliced almonds, salt, and cinnamon. Stir to combine, then add the yogurt and melted butter. Stir until all of the almond meal is incorporated and the mixture is moistened throughout.

4. To assemble, stir the filling one last time, then evenly distribute the topping over the filling (don't pack it down). Bake until the filling is bubbling around the edges and the top is turning lightly golden, about 40 minutes.

5. Let the crisp cool for 10 minutes before serving. Serve with vanilla ice cream, I insist! This crisp keeps well in the refrigerator, covered, for up to 5 days. Leftovers are great for breakfast with yogurt.

GLUTEN FREE: *Use certified gluten-free oats.* • **DAIRY FREE/VEGAN:** *Use nondairy yogurt and coconut oil instead of butter.* • **EGG FREE** • **NUT FREE:** *Substitute your flour of choice for the almond meal, and skip the sliced almonds.* • **SOY FREE**

CHANGE IT UP
Feel free to substitute almost any other fruit for the cherries—chopped apples, pears, peaches, plums, strawberries, or whole blueberries would all be great.

Strawberry Balsamic Ice Cream Sundaes

1 quart vanilla ice cream

Strawberry Balsamic Sauce

OPTIONAL TOPPINGS
Freshly toasted nuts, chopped

Finely chopped dark chocolate or mini chocolate chips

My Favorite Granola (page 5)

Here is a sophisticated strawberry dessert for your next get-together. I can't wait to serve it at girls' night, to go with our glasses of red wine. You can keep it simple with the strawberry balsamic sauce over ice cream, or offer a variety of toppings for a sweet crunch. **MAKES 4 TO 8 SERVINGS**

Scoop ice cream into individual bowls and top with strawberry sauce. Enjoy as is, or sprinkle with additional toppings of your choice. Serve at once!

STRAWBERRY BALSAMIC SAUCE

A touch of balsamic vinegar brings this strawberry sauce to life, and contrasts deliciously with sweet vanilla ice cream. You can use more or less vinegar to suit your preferences, or skip it for pure strawberry flavor. I added the strawberries in two stages for textural interest, which sends this sauce over the top.

This sauce goes great with all kinds of sweets, not just ice cream. Swirl it into yogurt for breakfast, or treat it like jam and dollop it onto scones and muffins, toast, waffles, and cheesecake, of course. **MAKES 1½ CUPS**

> 1 pound strawberries, hulled and sliced into ¼-inch-thick pieces
>
> 2 tablespoons honey, or more if needed
>
> Fine sea salt
>
> 2 teaspoons balsamic vinegar, or more if needed

1. Measure out half of the strawberries and set aside. Place the remaining berries in a medium saucepan and use a potato masher to mash them until they are mostly smashed and juicy, about 1 minute.

2. Add the honey and a dash of salt, stir to combine, and bring the mixture to a boil over medium-high heat. Reduce the heat to medium and let the mixture continue simmering, stirring often, until the sauce has reduced in volume by nearly one-half, about 5 minutes. Add the remaining strawberries, stir to combine, and cook for just 30 seconds to soften them slightly. They will continue to soften as they cool.

3. Remove the pot from the heat and stir in the balsamic vinegar. Taste, and if you would like a more pronounced balsamic flavor, add another teaspoon or so. If the sauce isn't sweet enough for your liking, stir in a little more honey, keeping in mind the sweetness level of what you're serving this with. Let the sauce cool for 10 minutes.

4. Leftover sauce keeps well in the refrigerator, covered, for up to 2 weeks.

GLUTEN FREE: *Assuming your toppings are gluten free.* • **DAIRY FREE/VEGAN:** *Make the sundaes with your favorite vegan vanilla ice cream. For vegan sundaes, also use maple syrup instead of honey in the sauce.* • **EGG FREE:** *Choose an egg-free ice cream.* • **NUT FREE:** *Depending on your choice of toppings.* • **SOY FREE**

Peanut Butter Chocolate Chip Cookies

complicated

These heavenly little mounds are peanut butter cups in cookie form. They're a little doughy and tender on the inside (more or less, depending on how long you bake them), which I love. The hard part is waiting until they've cooled, so you can enjoy the contrast between the lightly crisp exterior and soft interior.

I've been disappointed by dry peanut butter cookies at coffee shops, but these are winners, every time. They're easy to make with one standard (16-ounce) jar of peanut butter, and they are conveniently gluten free, too. **MAKES 42 SMALL COOKIES**

2 cups lightly packed coconut sugar

2 eggs

$^1/_2$ teaspoon vanilla extract

$^1/_4$ teaspoon fine sea salt

1 jar (16 ounces) creamy peanut butter ($1^3/_4$ cups)*

1 cup bittersweet chocolate chips, preferably 60% cacao

*Ingredient Note: Natural peanut butter works well here. I used salted peanut butter, which is standard. If you are using unsalted peanut butter, add an additional $^1/_4$ teaspoon salt to the recipe. Almond butter and sunflower butter work too, although I am partial to the peanut version.

1. Preheat the oven to 350°F. Line a large rimmed baking sheet with parchment paper.

2. In a medium bowl, combine the coconut sugar and eggs and whisk until smooth (the eggs might resist incorporating into the sugar at first, but keep whisking!). Whisk in the vanilla and salt until blended.

3. Add the peanut butter and whisk until the dough is smooth and the peanut butter has completely blended into the batter (you might need to switch to a big spoon toward the end, which you'll need for mixing in the chocolate chips, anyway). Add the chocolate chips and stir until the chocolate chips are evenly incorporated.

4. For cookies that stay perfectly mounded, chill the dough for 15 minutes before proceeding (if you're in a hurry, skip the chilling step). Use a 1-tablespoon cookie dough scoop or two spoons to scoop heaping tablespoons of dough onto the prepared baking sheet, leaving 1 to 2 inches of space around each one. Chill any remaining dough while you bake the first batch.

5. Bake until the cookies are golden at the edges but still just a little underdone in the center, 11 to 13 minutes. Let the cookies rest on the hot baking sheet for 2 minutes before transferring them with a metal spatula to a cooling rack to cool completely. Repeat with the remaining dough. (If your first round was a little too doughy, bake this round for 1 minute longer, or if they were done past your liking, bake for 1 minute less–make note of this time, because you'll probably want to make these cookies again!)

6. These cookies keep well at room temperature for about 4 days, and freeze well for up to 3 months.

GLUTEN FREE • DAIRY FREE/VEGAN: *Use nondairy chocolate chips. For vegan cookies, omit the eggs.* **• EGG FREE:** *For cookies with a lighter, more meringue-like texture, omit the eggs. They will be slightly gritty, but I love them nonetheless.* **•**
SOY FREE

Chocolate Oatmeal Cookies

¾ cup chocolate chips
(I prefer 60% cacao
bittersweet)

¾ cup creamy almond
butter or peanut butter

2 to 4 tablespoons maple
syrup

2 tablespoons melted
coconut oil

¼ teaspoon fine sea salt

¼ teaspoon ground
cinnamon

1 teaspoon vanilla extract

1 cup quick-cooking oats

¾ cup sliced almonds

Flaky sea salt (optional),
for sprinkling

These little chocolate treats remind me so much of the no-bake
cookies my mom made when we were little. She isn't much of
a baker, but she does love chocolate, so my younger brothers and I
occasionally joined forces to beg for no-bake cookies. Lucky for us,
she usually obliged.

These cookies are somewhat more redeeming than my mom's
no-bake cookies, which call for a lot of sugar, butter, and milk. These
require just a few minutes on the stove, and a 30-minute chill to bring
them together. I used quick-cooking oats, which are less chewy than
rolled oats, and sliced almonds for texture. Combined, they lend a
light crispness to the interior that reminds me of a Nestlé Crunch bar.

MAKES 2 DOZEN COOKIES

1. Line a large rimmed baking sheet with parchment paper. In a heavy-
bottomed medium saucepan, combine the chocolate chips, almond
butter, 2 tablespoons of the maple syrup, the coconut oil, salt, and
cinnamon. Warm over medium heat, stirring often, just until the
mixture is melted throughout. Remove from the heat and immediately
stir in the vanilla. Then stir in the oats and almonds. Taste and add up
to 2 more tablespoons maple syrup if your cookies need a little more
sweetness.

2. Using a 1-tablespoon cookie dough scoop or two spoons, scoop out
about 1 tablespoon of the mixture at a time, placing it in a rounded
mound shape on the prepared baking sheet. Repeat until you have no
more of the mixture left. You might need to use your fingers to press
any loose pieces together to form a more cohesive cookie. Sprinkle the
cookies lightly with flaky sea salt, if desired.

3. Place the baking sheet in the refrigerator to chill for at least
30 minutes. Then, they are ready to eat!

4. Cookies are best stored in the refrigerator for up to 1 week, or for up
to 3 months in the freezer, sealed in a freezer bag. Let frozen cookies
come to room temperature before serving.

GLUTEN FREE: *Use certified gluten-free oats.* • **DAIRY FREE/VEGAN:** *Use nondairy chocolate chips.* • **EGG FREE** • **SOY FREE**

CHANGE IT UP

Feel free to substitute
additional oats for the
almonds. You can also replace
the almonds with your
favorite chopped nuts,
toasted for extra flavor.

Banana Pecan Shakes

These shakes taste like banana pecan ice cream crossed with a banana smoothie, and you can't go wrong with that. Freshly toasted pecans and caramel-like dates make them naturally decadent. You can easily double the recipe if you're serving 4. Pay attention to the blending method, which will produce a super creamy shake with delicious little bits of dates and pecans. **MAKES 2 SMALL SHAKES**

1/2 cup chopped raw pecans

1/2 cup almond milk or milk of choice, plus more if needed

2 large just-ripe bananas, frozen in chunks

1/2 teaspoon vanilla extract

Fine sea salt

Scant 3/4 cup ice cubes

4 Medjool dates, pitted*

Coconut Whipped Cream (optional; page 220), for garnish

1. In a small skillet, toast the pecans over medium heat, stirring frequently, just until fragrant, about 4 minutes.

2. In a blender, combine the milk, bananas, vanilla, and a dash of salt. Add half of the toasted pecans (set the remainder aside for later).

3. Blend until the mixture is smooth using your blender's smoothie function, if it has one. If it doesn't, start blending on low speed until the mixture gains traction, then switch to high speed until fully blended. (If the mixture is too thick to blend, add a bit more milk, as necessary.)

4. Add the ice and blend until smooth. Then, add the pitted dates and blend until they have broken into very small pieces, stopping before they have completely blended into the shake for a slight caramel effect (that's my favorite part!). Add half of the remaining pecans and pulse the blender a few times to break them up.

5. Pour the shakes into 2 small glasses. Top with Coconut Whipped Cream, if desired, and divide the remaining pecans over the 2 shakes. Serve immediately, with straws or spoons, whichever you prefer.

Ingredient Note: *If your dates are not ultra plump and juicy, soften them first before pitting. Soak them in a bowl of hot water for 10 minutes, then drain. If you don't have dates, you can substitute maple syrup (around 1 tablespoon, or to taste).*

GLUTEN FREE • DAIRY FREE • VEGAN • EGG FREE • SOY FREE

Easy Carrot Cake with Cream Cheese Frosting

CAKE

1³/₄ cups whole wheat pastry flour*

2 teaspoons ground cinnamon

1¹/₂ teaspoons baking powder

¹/₂ teaspoon baking soda

¹/₂ teaspoon fine sea salt

1 pound carrots, peeled and grated (about 3 cups)

¹/₂ cup chopped raw pecans or walnuts

¹/₃ cup melted coconut oil or extra-virgin olive oil

¹/₂ cup maple syrup

2 eggs, preferably at room temperature

1 cup plain Greek yogurt

1 teaspoon vanilla extract

CREAM CHEESE FROSTING

8 ounces cream cheese, at room temperature

2 tablespoons unsalted butter, at room temperature

1¹/₄ cups powdered sugar

1 teaspoon vanilla extract

Ingredient Note: If you can't find whole wheat pastry flour, use half all-purpose flour and half whole wheat flour. (I tried using all white whole wheat flour, but it produced a disappointingly dense cake.)

Finally, classic carrot cake made easy. I skipped the layers, and the stand mixer, and ended up with a small, square cake. It's simple enough for casual get-togethers but decadent enough for celebratory occasions. The cake is made with whole wheat pastry flour, which keeps it light and fluffy while still being made with 100 percent whole grains, and sweetened with maple syrup. Heaven is lined with cream cheese frosting, so I couldn't resist topping the cake with classic cream cheese frosting. Did I mention that there's a whole pound of carrots in the cake? **MAKES ONE 9-INCH SQUARE CAKE (12 SLICES)**

1. To make the cake: Preheat the oven to 425°F. Grease a 9 × 9-inch baking dish. (Don't forget to pull the cream cheese and butter for the frosting out of the fridge so they can come to room temperature.)

2. In a large bowl, combine the flour, cinnamon, baking powder, baking soda, and salt. Stir to blend. Add the grated carrots and chopped pecans and stir to combine.

3. In a medium bowl, whisk together the oil and maple syrup until blended. Add the eggs and beat until smooth, then whisk in the yogurt and vanilla. (If the coconut oil solidifies on contact with the cold ingredients, gently warm the mixture in the microwave in 30-second intervals until it melts again, or let the bowl rest in a warm place for a few minutes.)

4. Pour the wet ingredients into the flour mixture and mix with a big spoon, just until combined (a few lumps are okay). Pour the batter into the prepared baking dish. Bake until the center of the cake is springy to the touch and a toothpick inserted into the center comes out clean, 26 to 28 minutes. Place the baking dish on a cooling rack to cool completely.

5. To make the cream cheese frosting: When you're ready to frost the cooled cake, combine the cream cheese and butter in a medium bowl. Using a hand mixer (or your own strength), beat the cream cheese and butter together until they are fully blended. Add the powdered sugar and vanilla, then stir the mixture with a spoon until the powdered sugar is incorporated (or else powdered sugar will fly everywhere!). Finally, whip the frosting until it's nice and fluffy.

CHANGE IT UP

For an untraditional yet refined sugar-free carrot cake frosting, use my German Chocolate Cake frosting (page 212). It's made with dates, coconut, and pecans.

6. Spread the frosting evenly over the top of the cake, then slice and serve. This cake is very moist, so it is best stored in the refrigerator, where it will keep for up to 5 days.

TIP: *The easiest way to grate lots of carrots is to use the grating attachment on your food processor. If you don't have a food processor, a sturdy box grater is your best bet.*

GLUTEN FREE: *Substitute all-purpose gluten-free flour for the wheat flour.* • **NUT FREE:** *Skip the walnuts or pecans.* • **SOY FREE**

Bourbon Maple Candied Pecans

My grandmother Mimi's family grew pecans on their farm in southern Oklahoma. I'll never forget the way she talked about them–like sweet little nuggets of gold that grew from trees. I inherited her love for pecans, so I just had to include a candied pecan recipe in my cookbook. Instead of baking them with lots of refined sugar and egg whites, mine are sweetened with maple syrup. At first, the maple syrup just pools on the bottom of the pan, but over the course of about 25 minutes, it transforms into a glossy, maple shell coating.

I couldn't help but include a little bit of warming bourbon (another nod to the South), cinnamon, and a pinch of cayenne pepper. These pecans make a great party snack, after-dinner treat, or holiday gift!

MAKES 3 CUPS

1/4 cup maple syrup

1 tablespoon unsalted butter, melted

1 tablespoon bourbon or 1 teaspoon vanilla extract

1 1/2 teaspoons kosher salt

1/4 teaspoon ground cinnamon

Scant 1/4 teaspoon cayenne pepper (optional)

3 cups raw pecan halves

TIP: *If necessary, you can substitute honey for the maple syrup. The nuts will need a little longer in the oven, about 30 minutes.*

1. Preheat the oven to 325°F. Line a large rimmed baking sheet with parchment paper.

2. In a medium bowl, combine the maple syrup, melted butter, bourbon, salt, cinnamon, and cayenne (if you like your pecans to have a spicy kick) and whisk until blended. Add the pecans and stir to coat. Dump the contents of the bowl onto the prepared baking sheet and spread out in a single layer (the maple syrup will pool on the bottom of the pan, but that's okay).

3. Bake, stirring after the first 10 minutes and then every 5 minutes thereafter, until almost no maple syrup remains on the parchment paper and the nuts are deeply golden, 23 to 26 minutes. (The maple syrup coating will be a little sticky right out of the oven, but will harden as the pecans cool.)

4. Remove from the oven and stir the pecans one more time, spreading them into an even layer across the pan. Let them cool down for about 10 minutes, then, while the nuts are still warm, carefully separate any large clumps. Let the pecans cool completely on the pan.

5. Candied pecans will keep for up to 2 months in a sealed bag at room temperature.

GLUTEN FREE • DAIRY FREE/VEGAN: *Use olive oil instead of butter.* **• EGG FREE • SOY FREE**

Use Carrot Cake Frosting (Pg. 208)

German Chocolate Cake

CAKE

1$\frac{1}{2}$ cups whole wheat flour

1 cup sugar (I use organic cane sugar)

$\frac{2}{3}$ cup unsweetened cocoa powder

1 teaspoon baking powder

$\frac{1}{2}$ teaspoon baking soda

$\frac{1}{2}$ teaspoon fine sea salt

$\frac{1}{2}$ cup melted coconut oil

1 tablespoon apple cider vinegar

2 teaspoons vanilla extract

1 cup warm water

FROSTING

12 large Medjool dates (about 1 cup firmly packed)

$\frac{1}{2}$ cup water

1 tablespoon maple syrup

1 teaspoon vanilla extract

1 teaspoon coconut oil

Pinch of fine sea salt

$\frac{1}{2}$ cup unsweetened shredded coconut

$\frac{1}{2}$ cup pecan pieces

German chocolate cake is my dad's favorite cake. If you haven't had it before, it's a rich chocolate cake with a decadent coconut-pecan frosting. The frosting typically includes egg yolks, evaporated milk, butter, and sugar, so it's not exactly the kind of treat I want to serve to my dear dad. I came up with a more nutritious topping made with caramel-like dates instead, and it tastes strikingly similar.

The chocolate cake itself is based on Depression-era "crazy" cakes, which are so easy to make–no butter, eggs, or electric mixers required. The ingredients list might look a little crazy at first glance, but I promise, you will end up with one tasty chocolate cake.

MAKES ONE 9-INCH SQUARE CAKE (12 SLICES)

1. *To make the cake:* Preheat the oven to 350°F. Grease a 9 × 9-inch baking dish.

2. In a medium bowl, combine the flour, sugar, cocoa powder, baking powder, baking soda, and salt. Stir to blend. Pour in the coconut oil, vinegar, and vanilla. Pour the warm water over all of the ingredients and stir until well blended.

3. Pour the batter into the prepared baking dish and bake until the edges of the cake are starting to pull away from the sides and a toothpick inserted in the center comes out clean, 32 to 34 minutes. Set the cake aside to cool for at least 30 minutes, or preferably until it reaches room temperature.

4. *Meanwhile, to make the frosting:* Place the dates in a heatproof bowl and pour hot water over them until they are covered (this ensures that the dates are hydrated and soft enough to blend–don't skip this step!). Let them soak for 10 minutes, then drain. Once the dates are cool enough to handle, remove the pits and discard them.

5. In a food processor, combine the pitted dates, water, maple syrup, vanilla, coconut oil, and salt. Process until smooth, pausing to scrape down the sides as necessary. Add the shredded coconut and pecans and pulse a few times, just until they are evenly distributed. Set aside.

6. Once the cake has cooled, spread the frosting over the cake in an even layer. Slice and serve. This cake keeps well, refrigerated, for up to 5 days.

GLUTEN FREE: *Substitute all-purpose gluten-free flour for the wheat flour.* • **DAIRY FREE** • **VEGAN** • **EGG FREE** • **SOY FREE**

CHANGE IT UP

If you serve this chocolate cake with the cream cheese frosting from the carrot cake (page 208) instead of the German chocolate frosting, you will end up with *my* favorite kind of cake!

7 *Extras*

EVERY CUISINE HAS ITS OWN GO-TO SAUCES. I've picked and borrowed from them to develop my own repertoire of sauces that liven up meatless meals. With leftover prepared ingredients (such as roasted veggies, washed greens, beans, and rice or pasta) and a complementary sauce, spread, or dressing, you can easily improvise a delicious meal.

In this chapter, you'll find pesto with several variations, tzatziki (an herbed cucumber yogurt sauce), a creamy avocado-cilantro sauce, and a tangy, dairy-free "sour cream," which is also a remarkably good stand-in for or alternative to goat cheese and ricotta.

If none of those will do, consider my peanut dipping sauce (page 98), which is fantastic with Asian ingredients, and all of the salsas (pages 101–105) in the happy hour chapter. There's also the herbed tahini sauce (page 186) that I drizzle over my favorite Mediterranean ingredients, as well as the four salad dressings provided on pages 52–53. Take one, and run with it!

I've also included a few helpful recipes that are referenced elsewhere in the book, including tangy and crisp Quick-Pickled Red Onions (page 222), Coconut Whipped Cream (page 220), and Flax "Eggs" (page 221).

Basic Pesto

1/2 cup raw almonds, walnuts, pecans, or pepitas (hulled pumpkin seeds)

2 cups packed fresh leafy herbs (basil, cilantro, or parsley) and/or bold greens (arugula or kale)

1/4 cup grated Parmesan cheese (optional)

1 tablespoon lemon juice

2 cloves garlic, roughly chopped

1/2 teaspoon fine sea salt

1/2 cup extra-virgin olive oil

Freshly ground black pepper

A FEW OF MY FAVORITE PESTO COMBINATIONS:

Basil and almonds

Kale and pecans

Arugula and walnuts

Cilantro, parsley, and pepitas (you can add a small jalapeño—seeded, deribbed, and roughly chopped–to the mix for some kick)

I love pesto on pasta and zucchini noodles, pizza, sandwiches, and dolloped onto savory dishes that could use an extra dose of complementary flavor. For example, a spoonful of pesto takes leftover Roasted Eggplant Lasagna (page 163) and Quinoa-Stuffed Sweet Potatoes (page 144) up a few notches.

Traditional pesto calls for pine nuts and lots of basil, but their price tags often make me balk. Fortunately, pesto is fantastic with almonds, walnuts, pecans, or pepitas instead. You can also deviate from traditional basil by using arugula, kale, cilantro, parsley, or any combination thereof. You really can't go wrong. **MAKES 1 CUP**

1. In a medium skillet, toast the nuts or pepitas over medium heat, stirring frequently, until nice and fragrant, 4 to 5 minutes. Pour them into a bowl to cool for a few minutes.

2. In a food processor or blender, combine the basil or greens, cooled nuts or pepitas, Parmesan (if using), lemon juice, garlic, and salt. With the machine running, slowly drizzle in the olive oil. Continue processing until the mixture is well blended but still has some texture, pausing to scrape down the sides as necessary. Season to taste with black pepper.

3. If necessary, you can thin the mixture with additional olive oil, or if you're using the pesto on pasta, toss the pesto and pasta together with small splashes of reserved pasta cooking water.

4. Store leftover pesto in the refrigerator, covered, for up to 1 week.

GLUTEN FREE • DAIRY FREE/VEGAN: *Omit the Parmesan or replace with 1 tablespoon nutritional yeast.* **• EGG FREE • NUT FREE:** *Use pepitas instead of nuts.* **• SOY FREE**

Cashew Sour Cream

I was surprised by how much I enjoyed this dairy-free sour cream option. It's creamy, rich, and tangy, just like sour cream. Use it in place of sour cream in my enchiladas (page 148), in place of the goat cheese in my stuffed sweet potatoes (page 144), or swirl it into marinara sauce to make it creamy. Dollop a spoonful on any other savory recipes that could benefit from it! **MAKES 1 CUP**

1 cup raw cashews, soaked for at least 4 hours if you do not have a high-powered blender

1/2 cup water

1 tablespoon lemon juice, or more if needed

1 teaspoon apple cider vinegar

Heaping 1/4 teaspoon fine sea salt

1/4 teaspoon Dijon mustard

1. If you soaked your cashews, drain and rinse them until the water runs clear.

2. In a blender, combine the cashews, water, lemon juice, vinegar, salt, and mustard. Blend until the mixture is smooth and creamy, stopping to scrape down the sides as necessary. If you're having trouble blending the mixture, or would prefer a thinner consistency, slowly blend in up to 1/2 cup additional water, as needed.

3. Taste and add an additional teaspoon of lemon juice if you would like more tang, or additional salt if a more intense flavor is desired. Serve immediately or chill for later. The sour cream will thicken up a bit more as it rests; you can thin it by whisking in a small amount of water later, if necessary. Leftovers keep well, chilled, for about 5 days.

CHEESY CASHEW CREAM

▸ Add 1 tablespoon nutritional yeast to give the cashew cream a more cheese-like flavor.

🕐 **TIME WARNING:** *If you don't have a high-powered blender (like a Vitamix or Blendtec), you will need to soak the cashews for at least 4 hours.*

GLUTEN FREE • DAIRY FREE • VEGAN • EGG FREE • SOY FREE

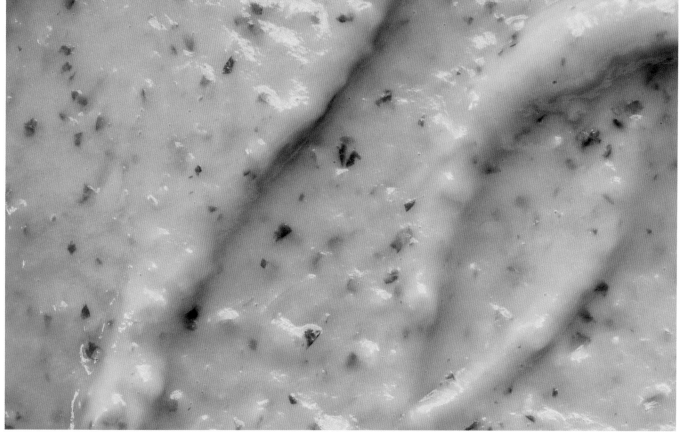

Tzatziki Sauce/Dip

You might know tzatziki as the refreshing Greek cucumber-yogurt sauce that is often served on falafel. I love it as a dip for veggies and toasted pita wedges as well! If you're making the dip for a party, you might want to double or triple this recipe. **MAKES 1 CUP**

1 cup grated cucumber (no need to peel–grate on the large holes of a box grater)

$1/2$ cup plain Greek yogurt

1 tablespoon extra-virgin olive oil

2 teaspoons chopped fresh mint and/or dill

$1^{1}/_{2}$ teaspoons lemon juice, or more if needed

1 clove garlic, pressed or minced

$1/4$ teaspoon fine sea salt

1. Working with one big handful at a time, squeeze the grated cucumber between your palms over the sink to remove excess moisture. Transfer the cucumber to a small serving bowl. Repeat with the remaining cucumber.

2. Add the yogurt, olive oil, herbs, lemon juice, garlic, and salt to the bowl, and stir to blend. Taste and add additional chopped fresh mint or dill, lemon juice, and/or salt, if necessary. Leftover tzatziki keeps well, chilled, for about 4 days.

GLUTEN FREE • EGG FREE • NUT FREE • SOY FREE

Creamy Avocado-Cilantro Sauce

Like guacamole, I can't think of a single Mexican entree that wouldn't benefit from this zippy avocado sauce. It's an epic dip for quesadillas (see page 147) and goes great with roasted sweet potatoes, eggs, and black beans. It's also fantastic drizzled over tacos (see page 189) and burritos, served as a dip with sliced veggies or chips, and even makes a good salad dressing. **MAKES 1½ CUPS**

2 large avocados, halved and pitted

$1/2$ cup lightly packed fresh cilantro (some stems are okay)

$1/3$ cup lime juice (from about $2^{1}/_{2}$ limes)

1 small jalapeño, seeded, deribbed, and roughly chopped

2 tablespoons water

$1/2$ teaspoon fine sea salt

1. Using a spoon, scoop the flesh of the avocados into a food processor or blender. Add the cilantro, lime juice, jalapeño, water, and salt. Process, stopping to scrape down the sides as necessary, until the sauce is smooth and creamy. (If the mixture refuses to blend, add additional water in 1-tablespoon increments, as necessary.)

2. Taste and add more salt if it's not quite flavorful enough. Transfer the avocado sauce to a small serving bowl. This sauce keeps well in the refrigerator, covered, for about 4 days.

GLUTEN FREE • DAIRY FREE • VEGAN • EGG FREE • NUT FREE • SOY FREE

Coconut Whipped Cream

1 can (14 ounces) coconut cream or regular coconut milk, well chilled

1 tablespoon honey or maple syrup

½ teaspoon vanilla extract

Have you discovered coconut whipped cream yet? Just like dairy whipped cream, it's rich, luxurious, and the perfect decadent topping for ice cream and milkshakes, cakes, and pies. I can't resist adding a dollop to my coffee in the morning when I have leftovers in the fridge.

To make coconut whipped cream, you need to use full-fat coconut milk, or better yet, coconut cream, which is available at Trader Joe's. I generally have better luck with coconut cream (sometimes, I open a can of coconut milk that hasn't separated or doesn't whip well, and have to start over). Both come in cans, and both need to be chilled in the refrigerator overnight or longer. I keep cans in the refrigerator at all times for this purpose, so they are ready when I need them.

MAKES 1⅓ CUPS

1. Before you get started, place a medium bowl in the freezer to chill for at least 10 minutes. This step helps prevent your whipped cream from separating into a gloppy mess.

2. Remove the can of coconut cream or coconut milk from the refrigerator (don't shake it up!). Use a can opener to remove the lid, then use a spoon to scoop the thick cream into your chilled bowl, leaving the clear, watery liquid behind (you can use it in smoothies, if you'd like).

3. Using a handheld mixer, start mixing the cream on low speed, and slowly increase to high. Beat the coconut cream until it's smooth and fluffy (note that coconut whipped cream won't get quite as fluffy as regular whipped cream). Add the honey and vanilla and blend to combine.

4. Use the coconut whipped cream immediately, or cover and refrigerate for up to 1 week. It is soft at room temperature, but becomes firmer after several hours in the refrigerator.

GLUTEN FREE • DAIRY FREE • VEGAN: *Use maple syrup instead of honey.* **• EGG FREE • NUT FREE • SOY FREE**

Flax "Eggs"

Flax "eggs" are a popular replacement for regular chicken eggs in baked goods. They are a great option for vegans, those with egg allergies, and me, since I'm constantly running out of eggs while I'm baking.

Like real eggs, flax eggs help bind ingredients together. However, they don't provide loft and structure to baked goods like real eggs do, so they don't work well in all recipes. I find that flax eggs work best in recipes that call for regular (not gluten-free) flours, because gluten offers structure of its own. I tried using flax eggs in my Lemony Almond-Blueberry Cake (page 197), which is gluten free, and I ended up with a pudding-like concoction.

You can use store-bought ground flaxseeds, which is what I do, or grind whole flaxseeds into meal in a clean spice/coffee grinder. I use Bob's Red Mill brand of ground flaxseed and store it in a mason jar in the refrigerator, since flaxseed can go rancid fairly quickly (just give it a sniff to make sure it doesn't smell funny before using).

MAKES 1 FLAX "EGG"

1 tablespoon flaxseed meal or freshly ground flaxseeds

3 tablespoons water

In a bowl, combine the flaxseed meal and water (multiplying as necessary for more than 1 egg). Stir to combine, and let it rest for 5 minutes to thicken.

GLUTEN FREE • DAIRY FREE • VEGAN • EGG FREE • NUT FREE • SOY FREE

Quick-Pickled Red Onions

1 medium red onion, very thinly sliced

$1/2$ cup water

$1/4$ cup apple cider vinegar

$1/4$ cup distilled white vinegar

$1^1/2$ tablespoons maple syrup or honey

$1^1/2$ teaspoons fine sea salt

$1/4$ teaspoon red pepper flakes (optional)

Pickled red onions, unlike their pungent raw state, are tangy and a little sweet. They are fantastic on tacos, sandwiches, salads, and more. The thinner you slice your onions, the quicker they will soften up and become infused with pickled flavor. I use a mandoline to slice mine evenly, but you can use a sharp chef's knife if you don't have a mandoline. Fair warning: This recipe will make your kitchen smell strongly of vinegar. **MAKES 2 CUPS**

1. Pack the onions into a 1-pint mason jar or similar heatproof vessel. Place the jar in the sink, to catch any splashes of hot vinegar later.

2. In a small saucepan, combine the water, both vinegars, maple syrup, salt, and pepper flakes (if you would like a spicy kick). Bring the mixture to a gentle simmer over medium heat, then carefully pour the mixture into the jar over the onions. Use a chopstick or butter knife to pop any air bubbles in the jar.

3. Let the pickled onions cool to room temperature, at which point they should be sufficiently pickled for serving. Leftover pickled onions keep well, chilled, for 2 to 3 weeks in the refrigerator. Please note that this recipe is not designed for canning, so do not can these pickled onions.

GLUTEN FREE • DAIRY FREE • VEGAN: *Use maple syrup instead of honey.* **• EGG FREE • NUT FREE • SOY FREE**

CHANGE IT UP
You can also pickle cleaned and thinly sliced radishes, carrot ribbons, and cabbage using this recipe. White wine vinegar is a good substitute for the vinegars used here.

Ta-da! Here is a collection of my go-to recipe components. For several years I've kept a handwritten cheat sheet like this taped inside my kitchen cabinet for easy reference. Now you have one, too!

COOKING GRAINS

Brown Rice (any variety) and Wild Rice

1 CUP DRY RICE YIELDS 3 CUPS COOKED

Bring a large pot of water to boil, using at least 6 cups water per 1 cup rice. Add the rice and boil, uncovered, until tender but pleasantly chewy, 30 minutes for brown rice or 40 to 55 minutes for wild rice. Drain off the remaining cooking water and return the rice to the pot. Cover the pot and let the rice steam, off the heat, for 10 minutes. Fluff, season, and serve.

Farro, Wheat Berries, and Spelt Berries

1 CUP DRY GRAIN YIELDS 3 CUPS COOKED

In a saucepan, combine the grain of choice with enough water to cover by several inches. Bring the water to a boil, then reduce the heat to a gentle simmer. Cook, stirring occasionally, until the grains are tender to the bite but still pleasantly chewy, 15 to 25 minutes for pearled farro; 25 to 40 minutes for unprocessed farro; and about 1 hour for wheat berries and spelt berries. Drain off the excess water. Extra cooked grains can be frozen and thawed later.

Quinoa

1 CUP DRY QUINOA YIELDS 3 CUPS COOKED

In a medium saucepan, combine 1 cup rinsed quinoa and 2 cups water. Bring to a boil over medium-high heat, then reduce the heat as necessary to maintain a gentle simmer. Simmer, uncovered, until all of the water is absorbed, 15 to 20 minutes. Remove the pot from the heat, cover the pot, and let the quinoa steam for 5 minutes. Remove the lid and fluff the quinoa with a fork.

Steel-Cut Oats

1 CUP DRY OATS YIELDS 3 CUPS COOKED

In a medium saucepan over medium heat, combine 1 tablespoon butter or coconut oil and 1 cup steel-cut oats. Cook until fragrant, stirring occasionally, about 2 minutes. Add 4 cups water and 1/4 teaspoon salt. Bring the mixture to a boil, then reduce the heat to medium-low. Gently simmer until the mixture is very thick and creamy, about 35 minutes, stirring more frequently as time goes on and reducing the heat as necessary to prevent scorching. Let the oats rest for 5 minutes before serving.

HELPFUL CONVERSIONS

These conversions come in handy when you are dividing or multiplying a recipe, and when you're making cocktails with measuring spoons.

1 tablespoon	=	3 teaspoons	=	½ fluid ounce
2 tablespoons	=			1 fluid ounce
¼ cup	=	4 tablespoons	=	2 fluid ounces
⅓ cup	=	5 tablespoons + 1 teaspoon		
½ cup	=	8 tablespoons	=	4 fluid ounces
⅔ cup	=	½ cup + 2 tablespoons + 2 teaspoons		
1 cup	=			8 fluid ounces
2 cups	=	1 pint	=	16 fluid ounces
4 cups	=	1 quart	=	32 fluid ounces

BAKING TIPS

HOW TO MAKE BUTTERMILK:
1 tablespoon vinegar + 1 scant cup milk of choice = 1 cup buttermilk (let rest for 5 minutes before using)

HOW TO MAKE LIGHT COCONUT MILK: One can (14 ounces) regular coconut milk + 2½ cups water = 4¼ cups light coconut milk (extra milk can be frozen and thawed later)

HOW TO MAKE FLAX "EGGS":
1 tablespoon flaxseed meal or freshly ground flaxseeds +

3 tablespoons water = 1 flax "egg" (let rest for 5 minutes before using)

HOW TO MAKE BROWN SUGAR:
1 cup granulated sugar + 1 tablespoon molasses = 1 cup brown sugar (whisk together in a bowl, then use your fingers to squish out any lumps)

HOW TO MAKE POWDERED SUGAR: Blend granulated sugar in a blender or food processor until it's fine and fluffy. Best used promptly, as it hardens over time.

HOW TO MAKE OAT FLOUR: Blend old-fashioned or quick-cooking oats (certified gluten-free if necessary) in your blender or food processor until they turn into a fine, even flour. Leftover flour stores well for later.

HOW TO MAKE ALMOND MEAL: (Warning, this is loud.) Blend whole almonds in your food processor or blender until they are broken into a very fine flour, but stop before they turn into almond butter. 1 cup whole almonds = 1 cup packed almond meal

GO-TO RECIPES

Liquid Gold Salad Dressing

MAKES 1 SCANT CUP

⅓ cup extra-virgin olive oil

⅓ cup lemon juice (from about 2 lemons)

2 tablespoons Dijon mustard

2 tablespoons honey or maple syrup

3 cloves garlic, pressed or minced

¼ teaspoon fine sea salt

Generous amount of freshly ground black pepper

Pinch of red pepper flakes (optional)

Combine all the ingredients and whisk to blend. Adjust to taste.

Cashew Sour Cream

MAKES 1 CUP

1 cup raw cashews, soaked and drained if necessary

½ cup water

1 tablespoon lemon juice

1 teaspoon apple cider vinegar

Heaping ¼ teaspoon fine sea salt

¼ teaspoon Dijon mustard

In a blender, combine all the ingredients. Blend until smooth and creamy, adding more water if necessary. Taste and add additional lemon juice and/or salt, if desired.

Quick Guacamole

MAKES ABOUT 1¼ CUPS

2 avocados, halved and pitted

1 tablespoon lime juice

¼ teaspoon kosher salt

Scoop the flesh of the avocados into a small bowl. Add the lime juice and salt and mash until the mixture is no longer chunky. Taste and add additional lime juice and/or salt, if necessary.

Pesto

MAKES 1 CUP

2 cups packed fresh herbs or bold greens

½ cup toasted nuts or seeds

¼ cup grated Parmesan cheese or 1 tablespoon nutritional yeast (both optional)

1 tablespoon lemon juice

2 medium cloves garlic, roughly chopped

½ teaspoon fine sea salt

Freshly ground black pepper, to taste

½ cup extra-virgin olive oil

In a food processor or blender, combine everything but the olive oil. With the machine running, slowly drizzle in the olive oil and process until the mixture is well blended.

Menus and Helpful Recipe Lists

PICNIC IN THE PARK
▸ Outrageous Herbaceous Chickpea Salad *(page 71)*

▸ Creamy Arugula, Goat Cheese, and Tomato Pasta Salad *(page 75)*

▸ Green Goddess Hummus *(page 120)* or Avocado, Spinach, and Artichoke Dip with Toasted Pita Wedges *(page 124)*

▸ Peanut Butter Chocolate Chip Cookies *(page 203)*

SUMMER GRILL-OUT
▸ Green Goddess Kale Salad *(page 67)*

▸ Outrageous Herbaceous Chickpea Salad *(page 71)*

▸ Pineapple Pico de Gallo *(page 106)*

▸ Salsa *(pages 101–105)*

▸ Pitcher of Margaritas *(page 131)*

▸ Hibiscus Pink Lemonade *(page 138)*

▸ Grilled Veggie Skewers with Cilantro-Lime Rice, Black Beans, and Avocado Chimichurri Sauce *(page 160)*

▸ Sweet Potato–Black Bean Veggie Burgers with Cabbage-Pepita Slaw *(page 177)*

▸ Lemony Almond-Blueberry Cake *(page 197)*

IMPROMPTU CELEBRATION
▸ Olive Oil and Black Pepper Popcorn *(page 119)*

▸ Green Goddess Hummus *(page 120)* or a variation, with crackers or raw veggies for dipping

▸ Elderflower Champagne Cocktail *(page 127)*

▸ Dark Cherry Almond Crisp *(page 198)* and vanilla ice cream

▸ Peanut Butter Chocolate Chip Cookies *(page 203)*

▸ Chocolate Oatmeal Cookies *(page 204)*

FALL GAME DAYS
▸ Thai-Style Mango Slaw *(page 55)*

▸ Kale and Quinoa Salad with Crisp Celery, Plumped Cranberries, and Lemon Dressing *(page 59)*

▸ Colorful Kale, Apple, and Fennel Slaw with Tart Cherries *(page 68)*

▸ Outrageous Herbaceous Chickpea Salad *(page 71)*

▸ Butternut Squash Chipotle Chili *(page 83)*

▸ Salsa *(pages 101–105)*

▸ Pineapple Pico de Gallo *(page 106)*

▸ Best-Ever Guacamole with Toasted Pepitas and Chipotle Sauce *(page 111)*

▸ Pitcher of Margaritas *(page 131)*

▸ Colorful Weeknight Burrito Bowls *(page 142)*

▸ Sweet Potato–Black Bean Veggie Burgers with Cabbage-Pepita Slaw *(page 177)*

▸ Peanut Butter Chocolate Chip Cookies *(page 203)*

▸ Chocolate Oatmeal Cookies *(page 204)*

THANKSGIVING OR CHRISTMAS
▸ Banana Nut Bread *(page 22)*

▸ Simple, Seasonal Side Salads *(page 49:* fall or winter variation)

▸ Kale and Quinoa Salad with Crisp Celery, Plumped Cranberries, and Lemon Dressing *(page 59)*

▸ Outrageous Herbaceous Chickpea Salad *(page 71)*

▸ Tahini Kale Caesar Salad with Whole-Grain Croutons *(page 72)*

▸ Elderflower Champagne Cocktail *(page 127)*

▸ Brown Derby Cocktail *(page 132)*

▸ Quinoa-Stuffed Sweet Potatoes *(page 144)*

- Roasted Carrots with Farro, Chickpeas, and Herbed Tahini Sauce (*page 186*)
- Pomegranate Ambrosia (*page 194*)
- Peanut Butter Chocolate Chip Cookies (*page 203*)
- Chocolate Oatmeal Cookies (*page 204*)
- Easy Carrot Cake with Cream Cheese Frosting (*page 208*)
- Bourbon Maple Candied Pecans (*page 211*)

GREAT FOR LEFTOVERS
- Spinach-Artichoke Quiche (*page 38*)
- Thai-Style Mango Slaw (*page 55*)
- Kale and Quinoa Salad with Crisp Celery, Plumped Cranberries, and Lemon Dressing (*page 59*)
- Green Goddess Kale Salad (*page 67*)
- Colorful Kale, Apple, and Fennel Slaw with Tart Cherries (*page 68*)
- Outrageous Herbaceous Chickpea Salad (*page 71*)
- Creamy Arugula, Goat Cheese, and Tomato Pasta Salad (*page 75*)
- Roasted Cauliflower, Farro, and Arugula Salad with Lemony Tahini Dressing (*page 76*)
- Any of the hearty soups (*pages 80–94*)
- Colorful Weeknight Burrito Bowls (*page 142*)
- Quinoa-Stuffed Sweet Potatoes (*page 144*)
- Roasted Cauliflower and Kale Spaghetti with Toasted Almonds (*page 151*)
- Chickpea Tikka Masala with Green Rice (*page 157*)
- Roasted Eggplant Lasagna (*page 163*)
- Pizza (*page 167 or 168*)
- Roasted Cherry Tomato and Brown Rice Risotto (*page 172*)
- Roasted Broccoli, Bell Pepper, and Tofu Bowl with Peanut Sauce (*page 175*)

- Coconut Fried Rice with Edamame (*page 182*)
- Roasted Carrots with Farro, Chickpeas, and Herbed Tahini Sauce (*page 186*)

PREP-AHEAD PARTY OPTIONS
- Thai-Style Mango Slaw (*page 55*)
- Outrageous Herbaceous Chickpea Salad (*page 71*)
- Fresh Sesame Soba Spring Rolls with Peanut Dipping Sauce (*page 98*)
- Salsas (*pages 101–105*)
- Pineapple Pico de Gallo (*page 106*)
- Green Goddess Hummus (*page 120*)
- Avocado, Spinach, and Artichoke Dip with Toasted Pita Wedges (*page 124*)
- Tzatziki Sauce/Dip (*page 219*)
- Pitcher of Margaritas (*page 131*)
- Hibiscus Pink Lemonade (*page 138*)
- Pomegranate Ambrosia (*page 194*)
- Lemony Almond-Blueberry Cake (*page 197*)
- Strawberry Balsamic Ice Cream Sundaes (*page 200*)
- Peanut Butter Chocolate Chip Cookies (*page 203*)
- Chocolate Oatmeal Cookies (*page 204*)
- Easy Carrot Cake with Cream Cheese Frosting (*page 208*)
- German Chocolate Cake (*page 212*)

SIDES
- Fajita Veggies (*page 32*)
- Simple, Seasonal Side Salads (*page 49*)
- Taco Filling (*page 56*)
- Kale and Quinoa Salad with Crisp Celery, Plumped Cranberries, and Lemon Dressing (*page 59*)
- Southwestern Roasted Veggies (*page 64*)

- Green Goddess Kale Salad *(page 67)*
- Colorful Kale, Cabbage, and Apple Slaw with Tart Cherries *(page 68)*
- Outrageous Herbaceous Chickpea Salad *(page 71)*
- Tahini Kale Caesar Salad with Whole-Grain Croutons *(page 72)*
- Classic Tomato Soup *(page 93)*
- Creamy Roasted Cauliflower Soup *(page 94)*
- Zesty Black Bean and Corn Salad *(page 123)*
- Cabbage and Black Bean Slaw *(page 142)*
- Cilantro-Lime Rice *(page 142)*
- Quinoa-Stuffed Sweet Potatoes *(page 144)*
- Green Rice *(page 157)*
- Cabbage-Pepita Slaw *(page 177)*
- Beer Beans *(page 180)*
- Refried Black Beans *(page 189)*

Butternut Squash Chipotle Chili *(page 83)*

Acknowledgments

This book was a long time coming, and I couldn't have done it alone.

To my parents, thank you for always encouraging me to dream big and for not treating me like a crazy person when I quit my job to work on a food blog. Mom, thank you for proofreading all 272 pages of this book. That is love.

To Steve Troha, my agent, thank you for reaching out to me and helping me find a great home for this book. This book wouldn't have happened without you.

To Mara Culbertson, we need to come up with a new title for you. "Kitchen assistant" doesn't begin to cover it. You are my number one recipe tester, my therapist, my friend, and a delightful human being.

To my recipe testers, I wanted to think my recipes were perfect when we sent them to you, but your questions and feedback made them immeasurably better. Thank you to Abby Bayatpour, Alanna Taylor-Tobin, Amy Cook, Angela Muir, Caterina Snyder, Colleen Flynn, Courtney Gill, Danette Davis, Deborah LeMoine, Deepthi Gorapalli, Emily Leung, Grace Heymsfield, Jennifer Schmidt-McCormack, Jessica Grosman, MS, RD, Mandy McComas, Nella Sammartino, Nicole Flanagan, Renae Lightcap, Sara Cornelius, Sara Kelly Harris, Sarah Clifford, Stephanie Davis, and Toby Trachy.

To Sarah Sweeney, my lifestyle photographer, your photos brought this book to life. Thank you for inviting Cookie and me into your home and letting us play pretend in your beautiful kitchen.

To Dervla Kelly, my editor, thank you for reading my blog for so many years and believing in my vision for this book. It's even more than I'd hoped it would be, thanks to your help.

To Rae Ann Spitzenberger, my book designer, thank you for putting these words and photos into such a gorgeous format. I love it.

To the rest of the Rodale team–Aly Mostel, Anna Cooperberg, Andrea Modica, Angie Giammarino, Gail Gonzales, Jennifer Levesque, and Kate Slate–thank you for helping to make this book a reality. I hope to meet you all someday.

To my girls Alissa Sutter, Jordan Morris, Margaret Kinkeade, and Tessa Fisher, thank you for drinking wine with me throughout this process (I needed it) and for showing up to say, "Cheers" for the happy hour photos. I'm so thankful for you.

To my friends and fellow food bloggers Ali Ebright, Angela Liddon, Dana Shultz, Erin Alderson, and Jeanine Donofrio, thank you for your support and advice throughout this project.

To Cookie, my best friend of eight years, I am never alone when you're around. Thanks for all the laughs and for dragging me outside for breaks. We have a million more miles to walk together, my girl.

Last, but certainly not least, to my blog readers, thank you for letting me do what I love for a living. I never would have gathered up the guts to write another cookbook proposal without your support and enthusiasm.

Index

Underscored page references indicate sidebars and tables. **Boldface** references indicate photographs.

A

Adobo sauce
  Best-Ever Guacamole with Toasted Pepitas and Chipotle Sauce, **110**, 111
  Butternut Squash Chipotle Chili, **82**, 83
  Southwestern Roasted Veggie Salad with Chipotle-Balsamic Dressing, 64–65, **65**
Agave nectar, substitute for, 130
Almond butter
  Cinnamon-Almond Green Smoothie, **12**, 13
Almond meal
  Dark Cherry Almond Crisp, 198, **199**
  how to make, 225
  Lemony Almond-Blueberry Cake, **196**, 197
  Spinach-Artichoke Quiche, 38, **39**
Almonds
  Dark Cherry Almond Crisp, 198, **199**
  Heirloom Tomato Pesto Pizza, **166**, 167
  Make-Your-Own Instant Oatmeal Mix, **10**, 11
  Roasted Cauliflower and Kale Spaghetti with Toasted Almonds, 151, **152**, 153
  Trail Mix Granola Bites, 14, **15**
Ambrosia
  Pomegranate Ambrosia, 194, **195**
Animal Poison Hotline, xvi
Anxiety, managing, x
Appetizers and snacks, 97
  Avocado, Spinach, and Artichoke Dip with Toasted Pita Wedges, 124, **125**
  Best-Ever Guacamole with Toasted Pepitas and Chipotle Sauce, **110**, 111
  Everyday Red Salsa, **100**, 101
  Fresh Greek Nachos with Herbed Tahini Sauce, 116, **117**
  Fresh Sesame Soba Spring Rolls with Peanut Dipping Sauce, 98–99, **99**
  Green Goddess Hummus, 120, **121**
  Olive Oil and Black Pepper Popcorn, **118**, 119
  Pineapple Pico de Gallo, 106, **107**
  Roasted Cherry Tomato Crostini with White Bean Pesto, 112, **113**
  Roasted Salsa Verde, **104**, 105
  Roasted Strawberry, Basil, and Goat Cheese Crostini, **114**, 115
  Roasted Summertime Salsa, 102
  Zesty Black Bean and Corn Salad in Lettuce Cups, **122**, 123
Apples
  Apple Crisp Breakfast Parfaits, **6**, 7
  Apple-Ginger Green Smoothie, **12**, 13
  Colorful Kale, Apple, and Fennel Slaw with Tart Cherries, **xxi**, 68, **69**
  Strawberry Rosé Sangria, **136**, 137
Artichokes
  Avocado, Spinach, and Artichoke Dip with Toasted Pita Wedges, 124, **125**
  Spinach-Artichoke Quiche, 38, **39**
Arugula
  Basic Pesto, 216
  Creamy Arugula, Goat Cheese, and Tomato Pasta Salad, 74, 75

  Fresh Taco Salad with Creamy Avocado-Lime Dressing, 56, **57**, 58
  Heirloom Tomato Pesto Pizza, **166**, 167
  Moroccan Roasted Carrot, Arugula, and Wild Rice Salad, **xi**, 62, **63**
  Roasted Cauliflower, Farro, and Arugula Salad with Lemony Tahini Dressing, 76–77, **77**
  in salads, 48
  Simple Roasted Veggie, Arugula, and Hummus Pita Sandwiches, **184**, 185
Atwater, Wilbur Olin, xiii
Avocados
  Avocado, Spinach, and Artichoke Dip with Toasted Pita Wedges, 124, **125**
  Best-Ever Guacamole with Toasted Pepitas and Chipotle Sauce, **110**, 111
  Creamy Avocado-Cilantro Sauce, **218**, 219
  Everything Avocado Toast, **30**, 31
  Fresh Taco Salad with Creamy Avocado-Lime Dressing, 56, **57**, 58
  Green Goddess Kale Salad, **66**, 67
  Grilled Veggie Skewers with Cilantro-Lime Rice, Black Beans, and Avocado Chimichurri Sauce, 160, **161**, 162
  Quick Guacamole, 34, 225
  Spicy Breakfast Fajitas with Fried Eggs and Guacamole, 32, **33**, 34
  Zesty Black Bean and Corn Salad in Lettuce Cups, **122**, 123

B

Baking tips, 225
Balsamic vinegar
  Southwestern Roasted Veggie Salad with Chipotle-Balsamic Dressing, 64–65, **65**
  Strawberry Balsamic Ice Cream Sundaes, 200, **201**
  Strawberry Balsamic Sauce, 200, **201**
Bananas
  Banana-Coconut Pancakes, **16**, 17
  Banana Nut Bread, 22, **23**
  Banana Pecan Shakes, **206**, 207
  measuring, for recipes, xxii
Basil
  Basic Pesto, 216
  Burst Cherry Tomato, Basil, and Goat Cheese Scrambled Egg Toasts, **40**, 41
  Green Goddess Hummus, 120, **121**
  Heirloom Tomato Pesto Pizza, **166**, 167
  Roasted Cherry Tomato Crostini with White Bean Pesto, 112, **113**
  Roasted Strawberry, Basil, and Goat Cheese Crostini, **114**, 115
Beans
  Beans and Greens Quesadillas, **146**, 147
  Black Bean Tortilla Soup with Sweet Potatoes, 80–81, **81**
  Cabbage and Black Bean Slaw, **vi**, 142, **143**
  chickpeas (see Chickpeas)
  Classic Tomato Soup, **92**, 93
  Coconut Fried Rice with Edamame, 182, **183**

Colorful Weeknight Burrito Bowls, **vi**, 142, **143**
Fresh Taco Salad with Creamy Avocado-Lime
    Dressing, 56, **57**, 58
Grilled Veggie Skewers with Cilantro-Lime Rice,
    Black Beans, and Avocado Chimichurri Sauce,
    160, **161**, 162
Hearty Lentil Minestrone, 90, **91**
Mexican Roasted Veggie Bowl with Beer Beans,
    180–81, **181**
Refried Black Beans, for Taco Party!, **188**, 189–90
Roasted Cherry Tomato Crostini with White Bean
    Pesto, 112, **113**
in salads, 48
Sweet Potato, Poblano, and Black Bean Enchiladas,
    148, **149**, 150
Sweet Potato-Black Bean Veggie Burgers with
    Cabbage-Pepita Slaw, 177, **178**, 179
Tuscan White Bean, Kale, and Farro Stew, **86**, 87
Zesty Black Bean and Corn Salad in Lettuce Cups,
    122, 123
Beer
    Mexican Roasted Veggie Bowl with Beer Beans,
        180–81, **181**
Bell peppers. *See* Peppers, bell
Beverages
    alcoholic (*see* Cocktails)
    nonalcoholic
        Banana Pecan Shakes, **206**, 207
        Creamy Cashew Chai Lattes, 28–29, **29**
        Hibiscus Pink Lemonade, 138, **139**
        Make-Ahead Green Smoothies, 12–13, **12**
Binge eating, x
Black pepper
    Olive Oil and Black Pepper Popcorn, **118**, 119
Blueberries
    Blueberry Maple Muffins, **24**, 25
    Lemony Almond-Blueberry Cake, **196**, 197
Bourbon
    Bourbon Maple Candied Pecans, **210**, 211
BPA-free cans, xxvi
Bread. *See also* Pitas
    Banana Nut Bread, 22, **23**
    Burst Cherry Tomato, Basil, and Goat Cheese
        Scrambled Egg Toasts, **40**, 41
    Everything Avocado Toast, **30**, 31
    ingredients list on, xiv
    Roasted Cherry Tomato Crostini with White Bean
        Pesto, 112, **113**
    Roasted Strawberry, Basil, and Goat Cheese
        Crostini, **114**, 115
    Tahini Kale Caesar Salad with Whole-Grain
        Croutons, 72–73, **73**
Breakfasts, 1
    Apple Crisp Breakfast Parfaits, **6**, 7
    Banana-Coconut Pancakes, **16**, 17
    Banana Nut Bread, 22, **23**
    Best Waffles Ever, **20**, 21
    Blueberry Maple Muffins, **24**, 25
    Burst Cherry Tomato, Basil, and Goat Cheese
        Scrambled Egg Toasts, **40**, 41
    Carrot Cake Breakfast Cookies, 26, **27**
    Creamy Cashew Chai Lattes, 28–29, **29**
    Everything Avocado Toast, **30**, 31
    Fluffy Cinnamon Oat Pancakes, 18–19, **19**
    healthy choices for, ix, 1
    Kale, Sweet Potato, and Feta Scramble, 42, **43**
    Make-Ahead Green Smoothies, 12–13, **12**

Make-Your-Own Instant Oatmeal Mix, **10**, 11
Mango Lassi Smoothie Bowl with Toasted Coconut
    Muesli, 2, **3**
My Favorite Granola, **xxiv**, 4, 5
Quick Guacamole, 34
Quinoa Piña Colada Granola, 8, **9**
Shredded Brussels and Kale Hash with Crispy
    Parmesan, **44**, 45
Simple Honey Scones, 35, **36–37**
Spicy Breakfast Fajitas with Fried Eggs and
    Guacamole, 32, **33**, 34
Spinach-Artichoke Quiche, 38, **39**
Trail Mix Granola Bites, 14, **15**
Broccoli
    Roasted Broccoli, Bell Pepper, and Tofu Bowl with
        Peanut Sauce, **174**, 175–76
    Southwestern Roasted Veggie Salad with Chipotle-
        Balsamic Dressing, 64–65, **65**
Brown rice. *See* Rice, brown
Brown sugar, how to make, 225
Brussels sprouts
    Colorful Kale, Apple, and Fennel Slaw with Tart
        Cherries, **xxi**, 68, **69**
    Shredded Brussels and Kale Hash with Crispy
        Parmesan, **44**, 45
    shredding, 68
Burgers
    Sweet Potato-Black Bean Veggie Burgers with
        Cabbage-Pepita Slaw, 177, **178**, 179
Burrito bowls
    alternative menus for, 143
    Colorful Weeknight Burrito Bowls, **vi**, 142, **143**
Buttermilk, how to make, 225
Butternut squash
    Butternut Squash Chipotle Chili, **82**, 83
    Moroccan Butternut, Chickpea, and Couscous Stew,
        88, **89**

Cabbage
    Cabbage and Black Bean Slaw, **vi**, 142, **143**
    Colorful Kale, Apple, and Fennel Slaw with Tart
        Cherries, **xxi**, 68, **69**
    Colorful Weeknight Burrito Bowls, **vi**, 142, **143**
    measuring, for recipes, xxii
    shredding, 68
    Sweet Potato-Black Bean Veggie Burgers with
        Cabbage-Pepita Slaw, 177, **178**, 179
    Thai-Style Mango Slaw, **54**, 55
Cakes
    Easy Carrot Cake with Cream Cheese Frosting,
        208–9, **209**
    German Chocolate Cake, 212, **213**
    Lemony Almond-Blueberry Cake, **196**, 197
Calories, xiii
Caramelizing vegetables, xxiv
Carrots
    Carrot Cake Breakfast Cookies, 26, **27**
    Easy Carrot Cake with Cream Cheese Frosting,
        208–9, **209**
    grating, 209
    Green Goddess Kale Salad, **66**, 67
    heirloom, 63
    Moroccan Roasted Carrot, Arugula, and Wild Rice
        Salad, **xi**, 62, **63**
    Roasted Carrots with Farro, Chickpeas, and Herbed
        Tahini Sauce, 186–87, **187**

Cashews
    Cashew Sour Cream, 217, 225
    Creamy Cashew Chai Lattes, 28–29, **29**
    Quinoa Piña Colada Granola, 8, **9**
    Sun-Dried Tomato Fettuccine Alfredo with Spinach, 154, **155**, 156
Cauliflower
    Creamy Roasted Cauliflower Soup, 94–95, **95**
    Roasted Cauliflower, Farro, and Arugula Salad with Lemony Tahini Dressing, 76–77, **77**
    Roasted Cauliflower and Kale Spaghetti with Toasted Almonds, 151, **152**, 153
    Simple Roasted Veggie, Arugula, and Hummus Pita Sandwiches, **184**, 185
Celery
    Kale and Quinoa Salad with Crisp Celery, Plumped Cranberries, and Lemon Dressing, 59, **60**, **61**
    Outrageous Herbaceous Chickpea Salad, **70**, 71, **71**
Chai tea
    Creamy Cashew Chai Lattes, 28–29, **29**
    recommended brands of, 29
Champagne
    Elderflower Champagne Cocktail, **126**, 127
"Change It Up" labels, xix
Cheat Sheet, for cooking, 224–25
Cheese
    Beans and Greens Quesadillas, **146**, 147
    Burst Cherry Tomato, Basil, and Goat Cheese Scrambled Egg Toasts, **40**, 41
    Creamy Arugula, Goat Cheese, and Tomato Pasta Salad, **74**, 75
    Easy Carrot Cake with Cream Cheese Frosting, 208–9, **209**
    Kale, Sweet Potato, and Feta Scramble, 42, **43**
    Parmesan cheese, xxvii
    Roasted Eggplant Lasagna, 163–64, **165**
    Roasted Strawberry, Basil, and Goat Cheese Crostini, **114**, 115
    in salads, 48
    Shredded Brussels and Kale Hash with Crispy Parmesan, **44**, 45
    volume of, in recipes, xxii
Cherries
    Colorful Kale, Apple, and Fennel Slaw with Tart Cherries, **xxi**, 68, **69**
    Dark Cherry Almond Crisp, 198, **199**
Chickpeas
    Chickpea Tikka Masala with Green Rice, 157, **158**, 159
    Fresh Greek Nachos with Herbed Tahini Sauce, 116, **117**
    Green Goddess Hummus, 120, **121**
    Moroccan Butternut, Chickpea, and Couscous Stew, 88, **89**
    Outrageous Herbaceous Chickpea Salad, **70**, 71, **71**
    Quinoa-Stuffed Sweet Potatoes, 144–45, **145**
    Roasted Carrots with Farro, Chickpeas, and Herbed Tahini Sauce, 186–87, **187**
    Roasted Cauliflower, Farro, and Arugula Salad with Lemony Tahini Dressing, 76–77, **77**
    West African Peanut Soup, 84, **85**
Chili
    Butternut Squash Chipotle Chili, **82**, 83
Chimichurri sauce
    Grilled Veggie Skewers with Cilantro-Lime Rice, Black Beans, and Avocado Chimichurri Sauce, 160, **161**, 162

Chipotle peppers in adobo sauce, xxvi. *See also* Adobo sauce
    where to find, 65, 82, 111, 179
Chives
    Green Goddess Hummus, 120, **121**
Chocolate
    Chocolate Oatmeal Cookies, 204, **205**
    German Chocolate Cake, 212, **213**
    Peanut Butter Chocolate Chip Cookies, **202**, 203
Christmas menu, 229–30
Chronic diseases, prevalence of, xiii
Cilantro
    Basic Pesto, 216
    Cilantro-Lime Rice, **vi**, 142, **143**
    Creamy Avocado-Cilantro Sauce, **218**, 219
    Green Goddess Hummus, 120, **121**
    Grilled Veggie Skewers with Cilantro-Lime Rice, Black Beans, and Avocado Chimichurri Sauce, 160, **161**, 162
    Pineapple Pico de Gallo, 106, **107**
Cinnamon
    Cinnamon-Almond Green Smoothie, **12**, 13
    Fluffy Cinnamon Oat Pancakes, 18–19, **19**
Clementines
    Pomegranate Ambrosia, 194, **195**
Cocktails
    Brown Derby Cocktail, 132, **133**
    Elderflower Champagne Cocktail, **126**, 127
    Honey Simple Syrup for, 133
    Pineapple-Infused Vodka for, 134
    Pineapple-Tini, 134, **135**
    Pitcher of Margaritas, **130**, 131
    Simple Syrup for, 131
    Spicy Cucumber Margarita, 128, **129**
    Strawberry Rosé Sangria, **136**, 137
Coconut
    Banana-Coconut Pancakes, **16**, 17
    Coconut Fried Rice with Edamame, 182, **183**
    Mango Lassi Smoothie Bowl with Toasted Coconut Muesli, 2, **3**
    Pineapple-Coconut Green Smoothie, **12**, 13
    Pomegranate Ambrosia, 194, **195**
    Quinoa Piña Colada Granola, 8, **9**
    Trail Mix Granola Bites, 14, **15**
Coconut cream
    Coconut Whipped Cream, 220
Coconut flakes, where to find, 182
Coconut milk, xxvi
    Banana-Coconut Pancakes, **16**, 17
    Coconut Whipped Cream, 220
    light, how to make, 225
    separated, remixing, 35
Coconut oil, xxvi
Coconut sugar, xxvi
Collard greens
    Beans and Greens Quesadillas, **146**, 147
    Moroccan Butternut, Chickpea, and Couscous Stew, 88, **89**
    West African Peanut Soup, 84, **85**
Conversions, 224
Cookies
    Carrot Cake Breakfast Cookies, 26, **27**
    Chocolate Oatmeal Cookies, 204, **205**
    Peanut Butter Chocolate Chip Cookies, **202**, 203
Cooking Cheat Sheet, 224–25
Cooking tips, xxiii–xxv

Corn
    Zesty Black Bean and Corn Salad in Lettuce Cups,
        122, 123
Cottage cheese
    Roasted Eggplant Lasagna, 163–64, **165**
Couscous
    Moroccan Butternut, Chickpea, and Couscous Stew,
        88, **89**
    whole wheat, where to find, <u>89</u>
Cranberries
    Kale and Quinoa Salad with Crisp Celery, Plumped
        Cranberries, and Lemon Dressing, 59,
        60, **61**
    My Favorite Granola, **xxiv**, 4, 5
Cravings, indicating nutrient needs, xiv
Cream cheese
    Easy Carrot Cake with Cream Cheese Frosting,
        208–9, **209**
Crisp
    Dark Cherry Almond Crisp, 198, **199**
Crostini
    Roasted Cherry Tomato Crostini with White Bean
        Pesto, 112, **113**
    Roasted Strawberry, Basil, and Goat Cheese
        Crostini, **114**, 115
Croutons
    Tahini Kale Caesar Salad with Whole-Grain
        Croutons, 72–73, **73**
Cruciferous vegetables, in salads, <u>48</u>
Cucumbers
    Fresh Greek Nachos with Herbed Tahini Sauce, 116,
        117
    Green Goddess Kale Salad, **66**, 67
    Spicy Cucumber Margarita, 128, **129**
    Tzatziki Sauce/Dip, **218**, 219

Dates, Medjool, xxvii
Desserts, 193
    Banana Pecan Shakes, **206**, 207
    Bourbon Maple Candied Pecans, **210**, 211
    Chocolate Oatmeal Cookies, 204, **205**
    Dark Cherry Almond Crisp, 198, **199**
    Easy Carrot Cake with Cream Cheese Frosting,
        208–9, **209**
    German Chocolate Cake, 212, **213**
    Lemony Almond-Blueberry Cake, **196**, 197
    Peanut Butter Chocolate Chip Cookies, **202**, 203
    Pomegranate Ambrosia, 194, **195**
    Strawberry Balsamic Ice Cream Sundaes, 200, **201**
    Strawberry Balsamic Sauce, 200, **201**
Dijon mustard
    Honey-Mustard Dressing, **50**, 53
Dinners, ix. *See also* Main dishes
Dipping sauce
    Fresh Sesame Soba Spring Rolls with Peanut
        Dipping Sauce, 98–99, **99**
Dips
    Avocado, Spinach, and Artichoke Dip with Toasted
        Pita Wedges, 124, **125**
    Best-Ever Guacamole with Toasted Pepitas and
        Chipotle Sauce, **110**, 111
    Everyday Red Salsa, **100**, 101
    Green Goddess Hummus, 120, **121**
    Pineapple Pico de Gallo, 106, **107**
    Quick Guacamole, 34, 225
    Roasted Salsa Verde, **104**, 105
    Roasted Summertime Salsa, 102
    Tzatziki Sauce/Dip, **218**, 219
Dogs, dietary cautions for, <u>xvi</u>
Doughnuts, 1

Edamame
    Coconut Fried Rice with Edamame, 182, **183**
Eggplant
    Roasted Eggplant Lasagna, 163–64, **165**
    Simple Roasted Veggie, Arugula, and Hummus Pita
        Sandwiches, **184**, 185
Eggs
    Flax "Eggs" as replacement for, 221, 225
    Kale, Sweet Potato, and Feta Scramble, 42, **43**
    Spicy Breakfast Fajitas with Fried Eggs and
        Guacamole, 32, **33**, 34
Elderflower liqueur. *See* St-Germain elderflower
        liqueur
Enchiladas
    Sweet Potato, Poblano, and Black Bean Enchiladas,
        148, **149**, 150
Extra-virgin olive oil, xxvi
    Honey-Mustard Dressing, **50**, 53
    Jalapeño-Lime Dressing, **51**, 53
    Liquid Gold Salad Dressing, **51**, 52, 225
    Tangy Red Bell Pepper Dressing, **50**, 52

Fajitas
    Spicy Breakfast Fajitas with Fried Eggs and
        Guacamole, 32, **33**, 34
Fall Game Days menu, 229
Farro, xxvi
    cooking, 224
    Roasted Carrots with Farro, Chickpeas, and Herbed
        Tahini Sauce, 186–87, **187**
    Roasted Cauliflower, Farro, and Arugula Salad
        with Lemony Tahini Dressing, 76–77, **77**
    Tuscan White Bean, Kale, and Farro Stew,
        86, 87
Fennel
    Colorful Kale, Apple, and Fennel Slaw with Tart
        Cherries, **xxi**, 68, **69**
    slicing, 68
Feta cheese
    Kale, Sweet Potato, and Feta Scramble, 42, **43**
Fettuccine
    Sun-Dried Tomato Fettuccine Alfredo with Spinach,
        154, **155**, 156
Fine sea salt, xxvii
Fire safety tip, 119
Flavor boosters, xxiv–xxv
Flaxseeds
    Flax "Eggs," 221, 225
Food advice, conflicting, xiii
Food allergies and sensitivities, xix
Food pyramid, x
Freezing
    chipotle peppers in adobo sauce, xxvi
    granola, 8
    muesli, <u>3</u>
    rosemary, 87
    soups, 79
Frosting
    Easy Carrot Cake with Cream Cheese Frosting,
        208–9, **209**

Fruits. *See also specific fruits*
  dried
    Make-Your-Own Instant Oatmeal Mix, **10**, 11
    in recipes, xxii
    in salads, <u>48</u>

Garlic cloves, size to use, xxii
Ginger
  Apple-Ginger Green Smoothie, **12**, 13
Goat cheese, xxii
  Burst Cherry Tomato, Basil, and Goat Cheese
      Scrambled Egg Toasts, **40**, 41
  Creamy Arugula, Goat Cheese, and Tomato Pasta
      Salad, **74**, 75
  Roasted Strawberry, Basil, and Goat Cheese
      Crostini, **114**, 115
Grains
  cooking, 224
  in salads, <u>48</u>
Granola
  Apple Crisp Breakfast Parfaits, **6**, 7
  freezing, 8
  homemade, ix
  My Favorite Granola, **xxiv**, **4**, 5
  Quinoa Piña Colada Granola, 8, **9**
  Trail Mix Granola Bites, 14, **15**
Grapefruit juice
  Brown Derby Cocktail, 132, **133**
Greens. *See also specific greens*
  Basic Pesto, 216, 225
  Beans and Greens Quesadillas, **146**, 147
  salad, choosing, <u>48</u>
Guacamole
  Best-Ever Guacamole with Toasted Pepitas and
      Chipotle Sauce, **110**, 111
  Quick Guacamole, 34, 225
  Spicy Breakfast Fajitas with Fried Eggs and
      Guacamole, 32, **33**, 34

Hash
  Shredded Brussels and Kale Hash with Crispy
      Parmesan, **44**, 45
Helpful recipe lists, 230–31
Herbs. *See also specific herbs*
  Basic Pesto, 216, 225
  fresh, xxiv–xxv
  Roasted Carrots with Farro, Chickpeas, and Herbed
      Tahini Sauce, 186–87, **187**
Hibiscus tea
  Hibiscus Pink Lemonade, 138, **139**
Honey
  Easiest Honey Whole Wheat Pizza Dough, **170**, 171
  Honey-Mustard Dressing, **50**, 53
  Honey Simple Syrup, 133
  Simple Honey Scones, 35, **36–37**
Hummus
  Green Goddess Hummus, 120, **121**
  Simple Roasted Veggie, Arugula, and Hummus Pita
      Sandwiches, **184**, 185
Hypoglycemia, ix

Ice cream
  Strawberry Balsamic Ice Cream Sundaes, 200, **201**
Impromptu Celebration menu, 229

Ingredients
  author's favorite, xxvi–xxvii
  recipe descriptions of, xxii
Ingredients list
  as buying guide, xiv
  on nutrition label, x, <u>x</u>

Jalapeño peppers. *See* Peppers, jalapeño

Kalamata olives
  Fresh Greek Nachos with Herbed Tahini Sauce, 116, **117**
Kale
  Apple-Ginger Green Smoothie, **12**, 13
  Basic Pesto, 216
  Colorful Kale, Apple, and Fennel Slaw with Tart
      Cherries, **xxi**, 68, **69**
  Crispy Kale Pizza with Marinara Sauce, 168–69, **169**
  Green Goddess Kale Salad, **66**, 67
  Hearty Lentil Minestrone, 90, **91**
  Kale, Sweet Potato, and Feta Scramble, 42, **43**
  Kale and Quinoa Salad with Crisp Celery, Plumped
      Cranberries, and Lemon Dressing, 59, **60**, 61
  Kale Slaw, for Taco Party!, **188**, 189–90
  Moroccan Butternut, Chickpea, and Couscous Stew,
      88, **89**
  Roasted Cauliflower and Kale Spaghetti with
      Toasted Almonds, 151, **152**, 153
  in salads, <u>48</u>
  Shredded Brussels and Kale Hash with Crispy
      Parmesan, **44**, 45
  shredding, 68
  Tahini Kale Caesar Salad with Whole-Grain
      Croutons, 72–73, **73**
  Tuscan White Bean, Kale, and Farro Stew, **86**, 87
  West African Peanut Soup, 84, **85**
Katz, David, xiii

Lasagna
  no-boil noodles for, 164
  Roasted Eggplant Lasagna, 163–64, **165**
Lassi
  Mango Lassi Smoothie Bowl with Toasted Coconut
      Muesli, 2, **3**
Lattes
  Creamy Cashew Chai Lattes, 28–29, **29**
Leftovers, suggested recipes for, 230
Lemons
  Hibiscus Pink Lemonade, 138, **139**
  Kale and Quinoa Salad with Crisp Celery, Plumped
      Cranberries, and Lemon Dressing, 59, **60**, 61
  Lemony Almond-Blueberry Cake, **196**, 197
  Liquid Gold Salad Dressing, **51**, 52, 225
  Roasted Cauliflower, Farro, and Arugula Salad with
      Lemony Tahini Dressing, 76–77, **77**
Lentils
  Hearty Lentil Minestrone, 90, **91**
Lettuce
  Fresh Taco Salad with Creamy Avocado-Lime
      Dressing, 56, **57**, 58
  for salads, <u>48</u>
  Tahini Kale Caesar Salad with Whole-Grain
      Croutons, 72–73, **73**
  Zesty Black Bean and Corn Salad in Lettuce Cups,
      122, 123

Lime juice
  Cilantro-Lime Rice, **vi**, 142, **143**
  Fresh Taco Salad with Creamy Avocado-Lime
    Dressing, 56, **57**, 58
  Grilled Veggie Skewers with Cilantro-Lime Rice,
    Black Beans, and Avocado Chimichurri Sauce,
    160, **161**, 162
  Jalapeño-Lime Dressing, **51**, 53
  Pineapple-Tini, 134, **135**
  Pitcher of Margaritas, **130**, 131
  Spicy Cucumber Margarita, 128, **129**
Local foods, xiv
Lunches, ix

Main dishes, 141
  Beans and Greens Quesadillas, **146**, 147
  Chickpea Tikka Masala with Green Rice, 157, **158**,
    159
  Coconut Fried Rice with Edamame, 182, **183**
  Colorful Weeknight Burrito Bowls, **vi**, 142, **143**
    alternative menus for, 143
  Crispy Kale Pizza with Marinara Sauce, 168–69, **169**
  Easiest Honey Whole Wheat Pizza Dough, **170**, 171
  Extra-Crispy Baked Tofu, 176, **176**
  Grilled Veggie Skewers with Cilantro-Lime Rice,
    Black Beans, and Avocado Chimichurri Sauce,
    160, **161**, 162
  Heirloom Tomato Pesto Pizza, **166**, 167
  Mexican Roasted Veggie Bowl with Beer Beans, 180–
    81, **181**
  Quinoa-Stuffed Sweet Potatoes, 144–45, **145**
  Roasted Broccoli, Bell Pepper, and Tofu Bowl with
    Peanut Sauce, **174**, 175–76
  Roasted Carrots with Farro, Chickpeas, and Herbed
    Tahini Sauce, 186–87, **187**
  Roasted Cauliflower and Kale Spaghetti with
    Toasted Almonds, 151, **152**, 153
  Roasted Cherry Tomato and Brown Rice Risotto,
    172–73, **173**
  Roasted Eggplant Lasagna, 163–64, **165**
  Simple Roasted Veggie, Arugula, and Hummus Pita
    Sandwiches, **184**, 185
  Sun-Dried Tomato Fettuccine Alfredo with Spinach,
    154, **155**, 156
  Sweet Potato, Poblano, and Black Bean Enchiladas,
    148, **149**, 150
  Sweet Potato–Black Bean Veggie Burgers with
    Cabbage-Pepita Slaw, 177, **178**, 179
  Taco Party!, **188**, 189–90
    alternative menus for, 191
Mandarins
  Pomegranate Ambrosia, 194, **195**
Mangoes
  Mango Lassi Smoothie Bowl with Toasted Coconut
    Muesli, 2, **3**
  Thai-Style Mango Slaw, **54**, 55
Maple syrup, xxvii
  Blueberry Maple Muffins, **24**, 25
  Bourbon Maple Candied Pecans, **210**, 211
Margaritas
  best ingredients for, 130
  Pitcher of Margaritas, **130**, 131
  Spicy Cucumber Margarita, 128, **129**
Marinara sauce
  Crispy Kale Pizza with Marinara Sauce, 168–69, **169**

Measurements notes, about recipes, xxii
Meat, giving up, xviii
Medjool dates, xxvii
Menus
  alternative
    for burrito bowls, 143
    for taco party, 191
  special-occasion, 229–30
Minestrone
  Hearty Lentil Minestrone, 90, **91**
Moderation in eating, xiv
Muesli, 3
  Mango Lassi Smoothie Bowl with Toasted Coconut
    Muesli, 2, **3**
Muffins
  Blueberry Maple Muffins, **24**, 25
  testing doneness of, xix
Muir Glen tomatoes, xxvi
Mushrooms
  Grilled Veggie Skewers with Cilantro-Lime Rice,
    Black Beans, and Avocado Chimichurri Sauce,
    160, **161**, 162
  Roasted Veggies, for Taco Party!, **188**, 189–90

Nachos
  Fresh Greek Nachos with Herbed Tahini Sauce, 116, **117**
Nestle, Marion, x
Nonreactive skillet, examples of, 159
Nut butters. *See* Almond butter; Peanut butter
Nutrition label, how to read, x
Nuts. *See also* Almond meal
  Banana Nut Bread, 22, **23**
  Banana Pecan Shakes, **206**, 207
  Basic Pesto, 216
  Bourbon Maple Candied Pecans, **210**, 211
  Carrot Cake Breakfast Cookies, 26, **27**
  Cashew Sour Cream, 217, 225
  Creamy Cashew Chai Lattes, 28–29, **29**
  Dark Cherry Almond Crisp, 198, **199**
  Heirloom Tomato Pesto Pizza, **166**, 167
  Make-Your-Own Instant Oatmeal Mix, **10**, 11
  My Favorite Granola, **xxiv**, 4, 5
  Quinoa Piña Colada Granola, 8, **9**
  Roasted Cauliflower and Kale Spaghetti with
    Toasted Almonds, 151, **152**, 153
  in salads, 48
  Sun-Dried Tomato Fettuccine Alfredo with Spinach,
    154, **155**, 156
  toasting, xxiv
  Trail Mix Granola Bites, 14, **15**

Oat flour
  how to make, 21, 225
Oats
  Chocolate Oatmeal Cookies, 204, **205**
  Fluffy Cinnamon Oat Pancakes, 18–19, **19**
  Make-Your-Own Instant Oatmeal Mix, **10**, 11
  My Favorite Granola, **xxiv**, 4, 5
  Quinoa Piña Colada Granola, 8, **9**
  steel-cut, cooking, 224
  Trail Mix Granola Bites, 14, **15**
Obesity epidemic, ix
Oils
  hot, safety with, 119
  storing, xxiii

Olive oil
    Olive Oil and Black Pepper Popcorn, **118**, 119
Olives, Kalamata
    Fresh Greek Nachos with Herbed Tahini Sauce, 116, **117**
Onions
    Grilled Veggie Skewers with Cilantro-Lime Rice, Black Beans, and Avocado Chimichurri Sauce, 160, **161**, 162
    Quick-Pickled Red Onions, 222, **223**
    Spicy Breakfast Fajitas with Fried Eggs and Guacamole, 32, **33**, 34
Oranges or orange juice
    Pitcher of Margaritas, **130**, 131
    Spicy Cucumber Margarita, 128, **129**
    Strawberry Rosé Sangria, **136**, 137
Organic foods, xiv, xviii
Oven notes, about recipes, xxii

Pancakes, ix
    Banana-Coconut Pancakes, **16**, 17
    Fluffy Cinnamon Oat Pancakes, 18–19, **19**
    frozen, thawing, 19
Parfaits
    Apple Crisp Breakfast Parfaits, **6**, 7
Parmesan cheese, xxvii
    Shredded Brussels and Kale Hash with Crispy Parmesan, **44**, 45
Parsley
    Basic Pesto, 216
    Green Goddess Hummus, 120, **121**
    Green Goddess Kale Salad, **66**, 67
    Grilled Veggie Skewers with Cilantro-Lime Rice, Black Beans, and Avocado Chimichurri Sauce, 160, **161**, 162
    Outrageous Herbaceous Chickpea Salad, **70**, 71, **71**
    Roasted Carrots with Farro, Chickpeas, and Herbed Tahini Sauce, 186–87, **187**
Pasta
    Creamy Arugula, Goat Cheese, and Tomato Pasta Salad, **74**, 75
    Hearty Lentil Minestrone, 90, **91**
    Roasted Cauliflower and Kale Spaghetti with Toasted Almonds, 151, **152**, 153
    Roasted Eggplant Lasagna, 163–64, **165**
    Sun-Dried Tomato Fettuccine Alfredo with Spinach, 154, **155**, 156
Pasta cooking water, 155
Peanut butter
    Fresh Sesame Soba Spring Rolls with Peanut Dipping Sauce, 98–99, **99**
    Peanut Butter Chocolate Chip Cookies, **202**, 203
    Roasted Broccoli, Bell Pepper, and Tofu Bowl with Peanut Sauce, **174**, 175–76
    West African Peanut Soup, 84, **85**
Pecans
    Banana Nut Bread, 22, **23**
    Banana Pecan Shakes, **206**, 207
    Bourbon Maple Candied Pecans, **210**, 211
    Carrot Cake Breakfast Cookies, 26, **27**
    My Favorite Granola, **xxiv**, **4**, 5
    Trail Mix Granola Bites, 14, **15**
Pepitas, xxvii
    Basic Pesto, 216
    Best-Ever Guacamole with Toasted Pepitas and Chipotle Sauce, **110**, 111

My Favorite Granola, **xxiv**, **4**, 5
Quinoa-Stuffed Sweet Potatoes, 144–45, **145**
Sweet Potato–Black Bean Veggie Burgers with Cabbage-Pepita Slaw, 177, **178**, 179
Trail Mix Granola Bites, 14, **15**
Peppers, bell
    Grilled Veggie Skewers with Cilantro-Lime Rice, Black Beans, and Avocado Chimichurri Sauce, 160, **161**, 162
    Outrageous Herbaceous Chickpea Salad, **70**, 71, **71**
    Pineapple Pico de Gallo, 106, **107**
    Roasted Broccoli, Bell Pepper, and Tofu Bowl with Peanut Sauce, **174**, 175–76
    Roasted Cauliflower, Farro, and Arugula Salad with Lemony Tahini Dressing, 76–77, **77**
    Roasted Veggies, for Taco Party!, **188**, 189–90
    Simple Roasted Veggie, Arugula, and Hummus Pita Sandwiches, **184**, 185
    Southwestern Roasted Veggie Salad with Chipotle-Balsamic Dressing, 64–65, **65**
    Spicy Breakfast Fajitas with Fried Eggs and Guacamole, 32, **33**, 34
    Tangy Red Bell Pepper Dressing, **50**, 52
Peppers, jalapeño
    Chickpea Tikka Masala with Green Rice, 157, **158**, 159
    Everyday Red Salsa, **100**, 101
    Jalapeño-Lime Dressing, **51**, 53
    Pineapple Pico de Gallo, 106, **107**
    Roasted Salsa Verde, **104**, 105
    Roasted Summertime Salsa, 102
    Spicy Cucumber Margarita, 128, **129**
    West African Peanut Soup, 84, **85**
    Zesty Black Bean and Corn Salad in Lettuce Cups, **122**, 123
Peppers, poblano
    Roasted Veggies, for Taco Party!, **188**, 189–90
    Sweet Potato, Poblano, and Black Bean Enchiladas, 148, **149**, 150
Pesto
    Basic Pesto, 216, 225
    Heirloom Tomato Pesto Pizza, **166**, 167
    Roasted Cherry Tomato Crostini with White Bean Pesto, 112, **113**
Picnic in the Park menu, 229
Pico de gallo
    Pineapple Pico de Gallo, 106, **107**
Pineapple
    Pineapple-Coconut Green Smoothie, **12**, 13
    Pineapple-Infused Vodka, 134
    Pineapple Pico de Gallo, 106, **107**
    Pineapple-Tini, 134, **135**
    Pomegranate Ambrosia, 194, **195**
    Quinoa Piña Colada Granola, 8, **9**
Pitas
    Avocado, Spinach, and Artichoke Dip with Toasted Pita Wedges, 124, **125**
    Fresh Greek Nachos with Herbed Tahini Sauce, 116, **117**
    Simple Roasted Veggie, Arugula, and Hummus Pita Sandwiches, **184**, 185
Pizza
    Crispy Kale Pizza with Marinara Sauce, 168–69, **169**
    Easiest Honey Whole Wheat Pizza Dough, **170**, 171
    Heirloom Tomato Pesto Pizza, **166**, 167
Poblano peppers. *See* Peppers, poblano
Pollan, Michael, x, xiii, xviii, xviii

Pomegranate
    Pomegranate Ambrosia, 194, **195**
Popcorn
    Olive Oil and Black Pepper Popcorn, **118**, 119
Potatoes
    Mexican Roasted Veggie Bowl with Beer Beans, 180–81, **181**
Powdered sugar, how to make, 225
Prep-Ahead Party Options, 230
Processed foods
    negative reactions to, ix, xiii–xiv
    sodium in, xxv
Protein sources, x, xviii
Pumpkin seeds. *See* Pepitas

Quesadillas
    Beans and Greens Quesadillas, **146**, 147
Quiche
    Spinach-Artichoke Quiche, 38, **39**
Quinoa, xxvii
    Fresh Taco Salad with Creamy Avocado-Lime Dressing, 56, **57**, 58
    Kale and Quinoa Salad with Crisp Celery, Plumped Cranberries, and Lemon Dressing, 59, **60**, **61**
    Quinoa Piña Colada Granola, 8, **9**
    Quinoa-Stuffed Sweet Potatoes, 144–45, **145**
    Sweet Potato–Black Bean Veggie Burgers with Cabbage-Pepita Slaw, 177, **178**, 179

Radishes
    Green Goddess Kale Salad, **66**, 67
    Zesty Black Bean and Corn Salad in Lettuce Cups, **122**, 123
Raisins
    Carrot Cake Breakfast Cookies, 26, **27**
Reactions to food, ix, xiii–xiv
Recipes, overview of, xix, xxii
Relationship with food, author's, ix–x
Rice
    brown
        Chickpea Tikka Masala with Green Rice, 157, **158**, 159
        Cilantro-Lime Rice, **vi**, 142, **143**
        Coconut Fried Rice with Edamame, 182, **183**
        Colorful Weeknight Burrito Bowls, **vi**, 142, **143**
        cooking, 224
        Grilled Veggie Skewers with Cilantro-Lime Rice, Black Beans, and Avocado Chimichurri Sauce, 160, **161**, 162
        for risotto, choosing, 172
        Roasted Cherry Tomato and Brown Rice Risotto, 172–73, **173**
        chilling freshly cooked, 183
Rice, wild. *See* Wild rice
Rice papers
    Fresh Sesame Soba Spring Rolls with Peanut Dipping Sauce, 98–99, **99**
    where to find, 99
Risotto
    choosing rice for, 172
    Roasted Cherry Tomato and Brown Rice Risotto, 172–73, **173**
Rosemary, freezing, 87
Rosé wine
    Strawberry Rosé Sangria, **136**, 137

Salad dressings, 48
    Honey-Mustard Dressing, **50**, 53
    Jalapeño-Lime Dressing, **51**, 53
    Liquid Gold Salad Dressing, **51**, 52, 225
    Tangy Red Bell Pepper Dressing, **50**, 52
Salads, 47
    Colorful Kale, Apple, and Fennel Slaw with Tart Cherries, **xxi**, 68, **69**
    Creamy Arugula, Goat Cheese, and Tomato Pasta Salad, **74**, 75
    Fresh Taco Salad with Creamy Avocado-Lime Dressing, 56, **57**, 58
    Green Goddess Kale Salad, **66**, 67
    Kale and Quinoa Salad with Crisp Celery, Plumped Cranberries, and Lemon Dressing, 59, **60**, **61**
    lunch, ix
    Moroccan Roasted Carrot, Arugula, and Wild Rice Salad, **xi**, 62, **63**
    Outrageous Herbaceous Chickpea Salad, 70, 71, **71**
    Roasted Cauliflower, Farro, and Arugula Salad with Lemony Tahini Dressing, 76–77, **77**
    seasonal side, 49, **49**
    Southwestern Roasted Veggie Salad with Chipotle-Balsamic Dressing, 64–65, **65**
    steps for making, 48
    Tahini Kale Caesar Salad with Whole-Grain Croutons, 72–73, **73**
    Thai-Style Mango Slaw, **54**, 55
    Zesty Black Bean and Corn Salad in Lettuce Cups, **122**, 123
Salsas
    Everyday Red Salsa, **100**, 101
    Roasted Salsa Verde, **104**, 105
    Roasted Summertime Salsa, 102
Salt
    fine sea salt vs. table salt, xxvii
    in recipes, xxv
Sandwiches
    Simple Roasted Veggie, Arugula, and Hummus Pita Sandwiches, **184**, 185
    Sweet Potato–Black Bean Veggie Burgers with Cabbage-Pepita Slaw, 177, **178**, 179
Sangria
    Strawberry Rosé Sangria, **136**, 137
Sauces, 214, 215
    Basic Pesto, 216, 225
    Cashew Sour Cream, 217, 225
    Creamy Avocado-Cilantro Sauce, **218**, 219
    Crispy Kale Pizza with Marinara Sauce, 168–69, **169**
    Fresh Sesame Soba Spring Rolls with Peanut Dipping Sauce, 98–99, **99**
    Grilled Veggie Skewers with Cilantro-Lime Rice, Black Beans, and Avocado Chimichurri Sauce, 160, **161**, 162
    Roasted Broccoli, Bell Pepper, and Tofu Bowl with Peanut Sauce, **174**, 175–76
    Roasted Carrots with Farro, Chickpeas, and Herbed Tahini Sauce, 186–87, **187**
    Strawberry Balsamic Sauce, 200, **201**
    Tzatziki Sauce/Dip, **218**, 219
Scones
    Simple Honey Scones, 35, **36–37**
Sea salt, fine, xxvii
Seasonal foods, xiv
Seasonings, adjusting, xxv

Seeds
　Everything Spice Blend, **30**, 31
　Flax "Eggs," 221, 225
　Fresh Sesame Soba Spring Rolls with Peanut
　　Dipping Sauce, 98–99, **99**
　Green Goddess Kale Salad, **66**, 67
　pumpkin (see Pepitas)
　in salads, 48
　toasting, xxiv
Sensory cues, in recipes, xix
Serving sizes, of recipes, xix
Sesame seeds and oil
　Fresh Sesame Soba Spring Rolls with Peanut
　　Dipping Sauce, 98–99, **99**
Shakes
　Banana Pecan Shakes, **206**, 207
Side dishes, suggested recipes for, 230–31
Simple Syrup, 130, 131
　Honey Simple Syrup, 133
Slaws
　Cabbage and Black Bean Slaw, **vi**, 142, **143**
　Colorful Kale, Apple, and Fennel Slaw with Tart
　　Cherries, **xxi**, 68, **69**
　Colorful Weeknight Burrito Bowls, **vi**, 142, **143**
　Kale Slaw, for Taco Party!, **188**, 189–90
　Thai-Style Mango Slaw, **54**, 55
Smoothie bowl
　Mango Lassi Smoothie Bowl with Toasted Coconut
　　Muesli, 2, **3**
Smoothies
　Apple-Ginger Green Smoothie, **12**, 13
　Cinnamon-Almond Green Smoothie, **12**, 13
　Pineapple-Coconut Green Smoothie, **12**, 13
Snacks. See Appetizers and snacks
Soba noodles
　Fresh Sesame Soba Spring Rolls with Peanut
　　Dipping Sauce, 98–99, **99**
　where to find, 99
Sodium
　on nutrition label, x
　in processed vs. unprocessed foods, xxv
Soups. See also Stews
　Black Bean Tortilla Soup with Sweet Potatoes,
　　80–81, **81**
　Classic Tomato Soup, **92**, 93
　Creamy Roasted Cauliflower Soup, 94–95, **95**
　freezing, 79
　Hearty Lentil Minestrone, 90, **91**
　West African Peanut Soup, 84, **85**
Sour cream
　Cashew Sour Cream, 217, 225
Spaghetti
　Roasted Cauliflower and Kale Spaghetti with
　　Toasted Almonds, 151, **152**, 153
Spelt berries, cooking, 224
Spice blend
　Everything Spice Blend, **30**, 31
Spinach
　Apple-Ginger Green Smoothie, **12**, 13
　Avocado, Spinach, and Artichoke Dip with Toasted
　　Pita Wedges, 124, **125**
　Chickpea Tikka Masala with Green Rice, 157, **158**,
　　159
　Cinnamon-Almond Green Smoothie, **12**, 13
　Pineapple-Coconut Green Smoothie, **12**, 13
　Roasted Eggplant Lasagna, 163–64, **165**

Spinach-Artichoke Quiche, 38, **39**
Sun-Dried Tomato Fettuccine Alfredo with Spinach,
　154, **155**, 156
Spring rolls
　Fresh Sesame Soba Spring Rolls with Peanut
　　Dipping Sauce, 98–99, **99**
Steel-cut oats, cooking, 224
Stews. See also Soups
　Butternut Squash Chipotle Chili, **82**, 83
　Moroccan Butternut, Chickpea, and Couscous Stew,
　　88, **89**
　Tuscan White Bean, Kale, and Farro Stew, **86**, 87
St-Germain elderflower liqueur
　Elderflower Champagne Cocktail, **126**, 127
　Strawberry Rosé Sangria, **136**, 137
Storage
　of fresh herbs, xxv
　of oils and oil-containing foods, xxiii
Strawberries
　Roasted Strawberry, Basil, and Goat Cheese
　　Crostini, **114**, 115
　Strawberry Balsamic Ice Cream Sundaes, 200, **201**
　Strawberry Balsamic Sauce, 200, **201**
　Strawberry Rosé Sangria, **136**, 137
Stress
　managing, x
　overeating from, xiv
Substitutions, recipe, xix
Sugar
　brown, how to make, 225
　coconut, xxvi
　listed on nutrition label, x
　powdered, how to make, 225
Summer Grill-Out menu, 229
Sundaes
　Strawberry Balsamic Ice Cream Sundaes, 200, **201**
Sunflower seeds
　Green Goddess Kale Salad, **66**, 67
Sweet potatoes
　Black Bean Tortilla Soup with Sweet Potatoes,
　　80–81, **81**
　Kale, Sweet Potato, and Feta Scramble, 42, **43**
　Mexican Roasted Veggie Bowl with Beer Beans,
　　180–81, **181**
　Quinoa-Stuffed Sweet Potatoes, 144–45, **145**
　Southwestern Roasted Veggie Salad with Chipotle-
　　Balsamic Dressing, 64–65, **65**
　Sweet Potato, Poblano, and Black Bean Enchiladas,
　　148, **149**, 150
　Sweet Potato–Black Bean Veggie Burgers with
　　Cabbage-Pepita Slaw, 177, **178**, 179
　West African Peanut Soup, 84, **85**

Tacos
　alternative taco party menus, 191
　Taco Party!, **188**, 189–90
Taco salad
　Fresh Taco Salad with Creamy Avocado-Lime
　　Dressing, 56, **57**, 58
Tahini, xxvii
　Fresh Greek Nachos with Herbed Tahini Sauce, 116,
　　117
　Green Goddess Hummus, 120, **121**
　Roasted Carrots with Farro, Chickpeas, and Herbed
　　Tahini Sauce, 186–87, **187**

Roasted Cauliflower, Farro, and Arugula Salad with
Lemony Tahini Dressing, 76–77, **77**
Tahini Kale Caesar Salad with Whole-Grain
Croutons, 72–73, **73**
Tamari, reduced-sodium, xxvii
Tarragon
Green Goddess Hummus, 120, **121**
Tea
chai
Creamy Cashew Chai Lattes, 28–29, **29**
recommended brands of, 29
hibiscus
Hibiscus Pink Lemonade, 138, **139**
Tequila
choosing, <u>130</u>
Pitcher of Margaritas, **130**, 131
Spicy Cucumber Margarita, 128, **129**
Thanksgiving menu, 229–30
Tikka masala
Chickpea Tikka Masala with Green Rice, 157, **158**,
159
Toasting nuts and seeds, xxiv
Toasts
Burst Cherry Tomato, Basil, and Goat Cheese
Scrambled Egg Toasts, **40**, 41
Everything Avocado Toast, **30**, 31
Roasted Cherry Tomato Crostini with White Bean
Pesto, 112, **113**
Roasted Strawberry, Basil, and Goat Cheese
Crostini, **114**, 115
Tofu
Extra-Crispy Baked Tofu, 176, **176**
Roasted Broccoli, Bell Pepper, and Tofu Bowl with
Peanut Sauce, **174**, 175–76
volume of, in recipes, xxii
Tomatillos
Roasted Salsa Verde, **104**, 105
Tomatoes
Burst Cherry Tomato, Basil, and Goat Cheese
Scrambled Egg Toasts, **40**, 41
canned, xxvi
Classic Tomato Soup, **92**, 93
Creamy Arugula, Goat Cheese, and Tomato Pasta
Salad, **74**, 75
Crispy Kale Pizza with Marinara Sauce, 168–69, **169**
Everyday Red Salsa, **100**, 101
Fresh Greek Nachos with Herbed Tahini Sauce, 116,
117
Heirloom Tomato Pesto Pizza, **166**, 167
Roasted Cherry Tomato and Brown Rice Risotto,
172–73, **173**
Roasted Cherry Tomato Crostini with White Bean
Pesto, 112, **113**
Roasted Eggplant Lasagna, 163–64, **165**
Roasted Summertime Salsa, 102
Sun-Dried Tomato Fettuccine Alfredo with Spinach,
154, **155**, 156
Tortillas
Beans and Greens Quesadillas, **146**, 147
Black Bean Tortilla Soup with Sweet Potatoes,
80–81, **81**

Butternut Squash Chipotle Chili, **82**, 83
Fresh Taco Salad with Creamy Avocado-Lime
Dressing, 56, **57**, 58
Spicy Breakfast Fajitas with Fried Eggs and
Guacamole, 32, **33**, 34
Sweet Potato, Poblano, and Black Bean Enchiladas,
148, **149**, 150
Taco Party!, **188**, 189–90
Trail mix
Trail Mix Granola Bites, 14, **15**

Vegetables. *See also specific vegetables*
caramelizing, xxiv
Grilled Veggie Skewers with Cilantro-Lime Rice,
Black Beans, and Avocado Chimichurri Sauce,
160, **161**, 162
Mexican Roasted Veggie Bowl with Beer Beans,
180–81, **181**
Roasted Veggies, for Taco Party!, **188**, 189–90
in salads, <u>48</u>
Simple Roasted Veggie, Arugula, and Hummus Pita
Sandwiches, **184**, 185
Southwestern Roasted Veggie Salad with Chipotle-
Balsamic Dressing, 64–65, **65**
Sweet Potato–Black Bean Veggie Burgers with
Cabbage-Pepita Slaw, 177, **178**, 179
Vegetarianism, xviii
Vodka
Pineapple-Infused Vodka, 134
Pineapple-Tini, 134, **135**

Waffles
Best Waffles Ever, **20**, 21
Walnuts
Banana Nut Bread, 22, **23**
Carrot Cake Breakfast Cookies, 26, **27**
My Favorite Granola, **xxiv**, **4**, 5
Trail Mix Granola Bites, 14, **15**
Wheat berries, cooking, 224
Whipped cream
Coconut Whipped Cream, 220
Whiskey
Brown Derby Cocktail, 132, **133**
White whole wheat flour, xxvii
Easiest Honey Whole Wheat Pizza Dough,
170, 171
Whole foods, x, xiii–xiv
Wild rice
cooking, 224
Moroccan Roasted Carrot, Arugula, and Wild Rice
Salad, **xi**, 62, **63**
Thai-Style Mango Slaw, **54**, 55

Yogurt
Apple Crisp Breakfast Parfaits, **6**, 7
Mango Lassi Smoothie Bowl with Toasted Coconut
Muesli, 2, **3**
Tzatziki Sauce/Dip, **218**, 219